ADAMANTIUS

Dialogue on the True Faith in God

ADAMANTIUS

Dialogue on the True Faith in God
De Recta in Deum Fide

Translated with Commentary by

Robert A. PRETTY

Edited for Publication by

Garry W. TROMPF

PEETERS
1997

© 1997, Peeters, Bondgenotenlaan 153, B-3000 Leuven (Belgium)

ISBN 90-6831-893-4 (Peeters Leuven)
D. 1997/0602/2

CONTENTS

PREFACE

It gives me great pleasure to welcome the publication of Adamantius'
Dialogue On the True Faith in God, translated and annotated by the late Rev
Dr Robert A. Pretty. I am grateful to the editor of the manuscript, Professor Garry Trompf, and the publishers for making this possible. Thanks are
due also to the many people who contributed to the Robert Pretty Memorial Fund which has assisted with the costs of publication.

A short resumé of Dr Pretty's life and work has been provided by
both his daughter, Mrs Verlie Stevenson, and his fellow lecturer the Rev.
Dr Geoffrey Barnes, and there is no need to enlarge on their valuable
coverage here. It was my privilege to know Dr Pretty for some time both as
a colleague at United Theological College, Sydney, and beyond the College.
He was a wise and caring pastor, a passionate preacher and a diligent
scholar with an amazing grasp of detail. He had a good sense of humour
and as a teacher was greatly appreciated by his students.

Theological scholarship is not easily pursued in this antipodean outpost
of Western Christianity, and even when successfully undertaken, publication is a difficult problem. Dr Pretty's work on Adamantius is just one fruit
of his scholarship, which at last is being made widely available through
publication. It is regrettable that it is happening posthumously, but Dr
Pretty would have been the first to own that the reward of scholarship is
not publication, with whatever modest fame it may bring, but scholarship
itself and the wisdom and understanding it brings to those who pursue it.

Principal Gordon S. Dicker
United Theological College
Sydney, 1995

TRIBUTE

'To Robert Arthur Pretty, DD'
by his Daughter

Heraclitus*
by Callimachus (*ca.* 310-240 BC)

They told me, Heraclitus, they told me you were dead;
They brought me bitter news to hear and bitter tears to shed.
I wept, as I remember'd, how often you and I
Had tired the sun with talking and sent him down the sky.

And now that thou art lying, my dear old Carian guest,
A handful of grey ashes, long, long ago at rest,
Still are thy pleasant voices, thy nightingales, awake,
For Death, he taketh all away, but them he cannot take.

As a small child one of my secret pleasures was to wander, alone, through my father's church and admire its penetratingly beautiful stained glass windows, while at the same time planning the window which would one day be dedicated to his memory.

As time passed the impossible dream of the stained glass window memorial faded, along with the impressive grave monument in stone; perhaps the idea of my Father no longer being with us seemed an inappropriate thought — like all parents they have that quality of immortality.

However, as with all mortals he passed away; but not before murmuring that he needed no longer look "through the glass darkly" — his time of revelation had arrived.

Quietly his ashes were dispersed in a garden near the Great Hall of the University of Sydney — no plaque, no memorial marking that sad occasion. It is his family, his friends and colleagues who must be thanked for the most fitting of memorials to honour his memory, through the provision of funds to publish his beloved *Adamantius* — his doctoral thesis.

My father was born at Deeping, England, on 25th October, 1904, his background being decidedly academic — his uncle Chancellor of St John's

---

* Trans. W. Cory in T.F. Higham and C.M. Bowra (eds.) *The Oxford Book of Greek Verse in Translation*, Clarendon Press, Oxford, 1942, p. 584.

college within Cambridge University, his aunts teachers in music and literature.

Unfortunately, and yet not quite so unfortunate as it first would seem, young Robert left England, his father, grandparents, aunts and uncles, with his mother, for Australia. He was only eight years of age.

Such a loss — a real upheaval — was obviously to leave its mark; yet this loss was to a large degree compensated by the permeating nature of the Australian landscape and the stoicism and friendliness of its people. It is these influences that must be given recognition for contributing to the nurturing and development of the young man, and providing the opportunity to achieve his potential as the man and scholar so highly regarded in Australian circles and the world of philosophic and religious thought.

My father's first church, as pastor, was at Dover Congregational Church in Tasmania. It was here that he met and married his wife Laurel, who was throughout the years to provide that essential encouragement and stability which was to allow him to continue his ministerial, pastoral and scholarly activities.

Coupled with his calling to serve God was an overwhelming desire for knowledge, through formal education. With absolutely no financial means to support this dream, my father left Tasmania for Western Australia, where he was to fulfil his ambition through the University of Western Australia, whose policy of free education (the only one of its kind on the Continent) provided the opportunity.

With his wife Laurel and small daughter Verlie, he took up his ministry at Collie Congregational Church, where he was later ordained. His time in Western Australia was overall a most happy and rewarding part of his life. His son Robert John was born at Bunbury.

From Collie he became minister of the Congregational Churches in Busselton, Armadale-Kelmscott and Fremantle circuits. He was elected Chairman of the Congregational Union of Western Australia (1949-50) and lectured in Divinity for the Congregational Board of Studies (1946-50).

He served for a time as minister of Port Elliot Congregational Church in South Australia. This was followed by a period as Senior-Master in Ancient History and English at the Townsville Grammar School, Queensland.

In 1952 he was called to the Woollahra Congregational Church in Sydney, New South Wales, where he exercised a distinguished ministry for 22 years. In Sydney he became more and more academically involved. He taught in Biblical Languages for the United Faculty of Theology and in Ecclesiastical History at the University of Sydney. Having been awarded a

B.D. and M. Theol. from the Melbourne College of Divinity, his crowning academic achievement was a Doctorate in Divinity from the same institution. His doctoral dissertation, a translation from the Greek of the *Dialogue of Adamantius* together with a commentary on this hitherto little known work of the fourth century, was examined and approved by Professors W. Frend, then at Cambridge, and F.L. Cross of the University of Oxford. It is this work that follows.

My father was a man of strong convictions, a most learned and a gifted teacher. He loved his students and was regarded by them with great affection. He died on 12th November, 1985, having by then retired from the full-time ministry for over ten years.

Verlie STEVENSON M.A.

BIOGRAPHICAL REFLECTION

Robert Arthur Pretty (1904-1985)

Throughout his life Robert Arthur Pretty could never resist the call of scholarship. In the churches of the Congregational order in which he was nurtured he experienced and fulfilled his other calling as an ordained minister. Each calling complemented the other very much because Congregationalism had always upheld the value of a learned ministry.

Born at Deeping in England on 25 October, 1904, he settled in his early years in Australia and in 1930 was a resident master at The Friends School in Hobart. Then he offered for the ministry. He entered the Congregational College of Victoria in Melbourne and rapidly completed the Licentiate of Theology of the Melbourne College of Divinity, an examining body used at that time by a number of theological colleges across Australia. His studies had whetted his appetite for scholarship and after a lay ministry of three years at Dover in Tasmania (1933-36), where he married Laurel de Jersey, he made his way to Western Australia.

Robert Pretty was ordained at Trinity Congregational Church, Perth, on 19 May, 1937 and ministered to churches at Collie (1936-39), Busselton (1939-42), Armadale-Kelmscott (1942-47) and Fremantle (1947-50). The move to the West was in the interests of a scholar, for the University of Western Australia was then the only free university in the nation and Robert Pretty was one, like most clergy, whose attainments were not to be won because he possessed an abundance of this world's goods. He enrolled in the university and graduated with an honours arts degree. It was the beginning of a distinguished academic and teaching career which he successfully incorporated into an equally effective preaching and pastoral ministry. In Perth he lectured in divinity for the Congregational Board of Studies (1946-50) and was Chairman of the Congregational Union of Western Australia (1949-50).

Exercising pastoral ministry is akin to the university of hard knocks, as Robert Pretty himself once remarked. In the Port Elliott church in South Australia (1950-51) he felt removed from the academic world and his experiences were such that he accepted an appointment as senior master in History and English at the Townsville Grammar School in Queensland. His classes realized they were learning from a born teacher of the classics.

In 1952 he was called to the influential Congregational Church at Woollahra in Sydney where from 1953 he exercised a distinguished ministry for
21 years. He had now gained the B.D. degree of the Melbourne College of
Divinity and was proficient in Hebrew and Greek. The Rev. Raymond
Abba, Warden and Principal of Camden College, sought his assistance and
Dr Pretty was appointed Lecturer in Biblical Languages and Church History (1953-74). His association with Camden College not only enabled him
to fulfil his teaching and theological gifts to the full, it set him within a
milieu congenial to his academic interests and religious conviction. His
capacity for work is illustrated in his faithful attendance at classes while continuing his pastoral and denominational duties. The Congregational Union
of NSW elected him as its President (1966-67). Maintaining his research he
was the first to be awarded the newly established M.Th. degree of the Melbourne College of Divinity. Most remarkably he then found time to give to
his annotations on the *Dialogue of Adamantius*, an early fourth century anti-
gnostic writing, and its translation from the Greek. His wife remembers his
trying to decipher the fourth century Greek with a little magnifying glass.
For this work the Melbourne College of Divinity awarded him the presti-
gious degree of Doctor of Divinity in 1964, by a happy coincidence the
same year in which Camden College celebrated its centenary. As can be seen
from the following pages, it was a true expression of a scholar's meticulous
attention to detail and the doctor's knowledge of the Greek language.

Robert Pretty's teaching ministry was closely related to the preparation
of students for the ordained ministry through Camden College. He was
also to fulfil a role in the United Faculty of Theology and in Divinity studies in the University of Sydney.

Camden College had been established in 1864 as a "Congregational Col-
legiate Institution ... for the education of Young Men for the Christian
Ministry". It numbered among its founders some of the leading citizens of
Sydney, Thomas Holt, MLA, who gave his residence, Camden Villa in
Newtown, for its first home, John Fairfax, proprietor of the *Sydney Morn-
ing Herald*, and David Jones, the Welsh draper[1]. The economic crash of the
1890s and the 1914-18 War were to take their toll of the College and of the
Congregational denomination as a whole.

Nevertheless the desire to promote the ordination of young Australians
persisted and a succession of dedicated principals maintained the theological tradition of learning, albeit with limited finances and a small community of students. It proved to be a significant context for the formation of

---

[1] J. Garrett and L.W. Farr, *Camden College: A Centenary History*, Glebe, 1964, pp. 1-2.

an indigenous ministry and of several adventurous men who opted for service overseas with the London Missionary Society. This was a congenial teaching context for a convinced Congregationalist whose education had been in Australia and whose academic gifts were so evident. Dr Pretty was twice acting Principal of the College in 1960 and 1966. The church at Woollahra was happy to release their minister for some of the time to assist the principal of Camden college. Dr George Rennie, the first lay President of the College (1916-23), had been a member of the Woollahra church so that there was a continuing connection of affection between church and college[2].

Congregationalists were prominent advocates of a general university education and of studies in the humanities as a necessary component of ministerial formation. But they were proudly separatist in their attitude to the State and would not have accepted an approach from the University to establish an affiliated college thereby accepting aid from the State. K.J. Cable, later to be Professor, has written that in Melbourne an offer by the University was declined by the Congregationalists perhaps for reasons of finance rather than principle. In any case an institution such as Camden College in the suburb of Glebe was adjacent to the University, but it was not controlled by the University. An academy in the tradition of English dissent, rather than an affiliated college, seemed to be the appropriate expression of a church with scholarly interests and separatist principles[3].

After the 1914-18 War a renewed stream of candidates in the Congregational, Methodist and Presbyterian theological colleges stimulated the revival of an earlier proposal for an institution of inter-collegiate theological training. There was a commitment to ecumenical theological education; but more practically the resources of the colleges were limited. In 1918 joint classes were begun in the Theological Hall at St Andrew's college. Teachers were allotted mutually agreed responsibilities. The Principal of Camden College, Dr Thatcher, was responsible for Church History, thus beginning a tradition that was to persist. The scheme was to continue until 1974 and became known as the United Faculty of Theology. It was especially suitable for the preparation of home mission pastors who were not qualified to undertake university studies. Studies in denominational polity were done in the respective colleges. The Faculty was dependent on the goodwill and co-operation of the theological colleges: changes in the college staff were

---

[2] *Ibid.*, p. 34; see also *A Beloved Physician: Some Memories of Dr. George Rennie*, Sydney, n.d., pp. 19-20.
[3] *Ibid.*, pp. 66-67.

reflected in the Faculty. When the Rev. John Garrett resigned as Principal of Camden to take up an appointment with Pacific Theological College in Fiji and the Rev. Geoffrey Barnes from Melbourne succeeded him, the United Faculty of Theology elected Robert Pretty as Head of the Department of Church History, a position he held from 1967-74. Geoffrey Barnes taught Reformation and Modern History in the Faculty while Robert Pretty continued to concentrate on the Early Church. All the teachers in the United Faculty found Robert Pretty to be a loyal and a co-operative colleague. The writer appreciated his generous help in adjusting from a parish ministry to the tasks of teaching and administering a college.

Camden College's most erudite principal, G.W. Thatcher (1910-32), had an international reputation as a scholar of Semitic languages which linked him strongly to the University of Sydney[4]. With Canon A.H. Garnsey and Dr Samuel Angus he campaigned for the introduction of a degree in Divinity in the University. The original intention of denominational training colleges had not failed; yet it was important for the theological disciplines also to be in touch with developments in the University and for leaders in the churches, if not all the ministers, to be cognizant of advances of knowledge in other spheres. The theologians argued it was important for the University, albeit a secular institution, not to neglect the contribution of the study of Divinity to the development of Western culture. The B.D. degree was established in 1936. In 1962 Dr Pretty was appointed lecturer in Ecclesiastical History in the University of Sydney where his particular responsibility was the teaching of the history of the Early Church. He was also a member of the Fellowship of Biblical Studies which had originated among scholars connected with the University.

Students remember Dr Pretty with affection as a gifted teacher with a nice, perhaps 'bookish', sense of humour. He had a great capacity for detail. His classes discovered that a remarkable variety of heresies, of which they had never heard, plagued the early church. He hated students to fail in Greek and during examinations he would move around the room making subtle but helpful hints. No wonder they loved him. He greatly enjoyed a cartoon his students once drew showing him in a bishop's cope and mitre with students kneeling at his feet. He was patient and kind with students and loved them to seek his help at the Woollahra manse.

At heart Robert Pretty was a vigorous evangelical. He commended the Gospel with sustained passion in his preaching. Though not uncritical of

[4] See G.L. Lockley, "Griffithes Wheeler Thatcher", in E.C.B. MacLaurin (ed.), *Essays in Honour of Griffithes Wheeler Thatcher* 1863-1950, Sydney, 1967, pp. 1-18.

the tradition in which he fulfilled his ministry — his presidential address to the Congregation Union of NSW (1966) was entitled 'Is Congregationalism Dead?' — he believed implicitly in the convictions for which Congregationalists had stood. Not the least of those traditions was devotion to sound learning and in particular the witness of the New Testament to local communities each responsible to Christ alone — a polity that Congregationists believed they had restored to their churches. Quoting the *Savoy Declaration* of 1658 in his presidential address of 1966 he declared that churches are societies of Christians gathered according to the mind of Christ 'according to his word'. The sixteenth century reformers had similar recourse to the early centuries and so there was a real sense in which Dr. Pretty's Protestant ministry and his academic work were of a piece.

Robert Pretty retired from active ministry in 1974, the same year in which the United Faculty came to an end, and for a brief time taught Greek at United Theological College when it was formed in 1975, with the emergence of the Uniting Church of Australia. Always his concern was to be valiant for truth. He died in 1985.

Geoffrey BARNES
Principal of Camden College, 1967-74
Vice-Principal, United Theological College, 1990-92

SERIES EDITOR'S PREAMBLE

The Significance of the Adamantius Dialogue

G.W. TROMPF

We are fortunate to commence the monograph series *Gnostica* with the late Rev Dr Robert Pretty's edition and translation of the Dialogue *De Recta in Deum Fide* by 'Adamantius'. *Gnostica* has been instituted to serve the publication of edited Gnostic texts and various books on the history of 'the Gnostic tradition'. This tradition can no longer be said to have stopped short in Antiquity or early Mediaeval times, for there are still articulations of it in contemporary society. This means that significant works reflecting or relevant to Gnosticism(s) throughout the centuries can now be welcomed and housed under a suitable 'roof', and the series editors expect to publish monographs that demonstrate the continuation of this tradition through mediaeval into modern times. Given the prevailing view that Gnosticism was an ancient movement, however, there can be no more fitting a way of floating this new series than with a volume touching its manifestations in later Antiquity.

Robert Pretty's introduction and translation of the Adamantius Dialogue, in fact, provides access to the last important extant source about ancient Gnosticism(s) left unavailable in a modern European language. Our richest body of material, of course, comes with the Nag Hammadi 'library', unexpectedly found in Egypt in 1945, and recently translated by a team of scholars (under the editorial supervision of James Robinson). Before this discovery we were very much reliant on representations of the Gnostics in the early Church Fathers (especially Irenaeus, Hippolytus, Epiphanius) and a small collection of Gnosticizing fragments, such as those bits and pieces in pseudo-Abdias *Historiae Apostolicae*, that have been included among the New Testament apocrypha. The *Corpus Hermeticum* also informed us about an intuitive and mystical temper in Egypto-Hellenistic philosophy that was comparable (even contributing) to Gnosticism as a Christian expression. As for the separate and highly fascinating *mélange* of materials concerning the Manichaeans, the older known pieces of information, largely from Greek and Armenian Patristic sources, have now been supplemented by new accessions for scholarship — the Köln Mani codex, fragments from central Asia, Kellis, etc. Mention of Manichaeism should remind us that there were various schools of Gnosticism, and while we possess new bodies of evidence for some, we do not for others. The Nag Hammadi library, for instance, is immensely helpful for the reconstruction of Valentinian and related lines of reflection, but little or no new material has come to light concerning some other groups — the Marcionites, for example, and the followers of Bardesanes. These last-mentioned groupings, together with the later Valentinians, are the very ones involved in the Adamantius Dialogue, and thus we are very fortunate to possess the text of it, and have it now in this fine translation.

The dialogue *De Recta in Deum Fide* was composed at some point within the last decade of the third century or the first decade of the fourth century AD/CE, so that it is important as documentation of more settled Gnosticisms, rather than first or close-to-first generation outbursts of these novel heterodoxical responses to the proclamation of Christ. Because of interesting theological controversies in the third century (surrounding Origen and Paul of Samosata, for two) one tends to forget that various Gnosticisms continued, and that as late as the early 400s, to take a case in point, Prudentius was writing vigorously against the Marcionites (*Harmatigenia* I, esp. 110-125). Dr Pretty warns us, of course, that the Marcionite, Bardesonic and Valentinian positions enunciated in the dialogue are mediated by an orthodox author, who wants his hero Adamantius — as well as the pagan Eutropius whom the author constructs as a wise arbitrator — to expose the falsities of the three Gnostic positions. Anyone reading the debate *de novo*, however, will sense that the author's defence of 'the true faith' is having not a few difficulties, and the Gnostic stances, far from being poorly represented, amount to very awkward challenges for orthodoxy. In the cut and thrust of the argument Adamantius is made to set the greatest store on the correct text and interpretation of the Christian scriptures, when of course competing cosmologies or cosmogenies are really more at stake — as well as the contrasting philosophical 'assumptive worlds' behind them — than can be adequately conveyed in a dialogue involving seven persons and five different standpoints. Still, there is enough in the dialogue to help us distinguish the cosmic visions of each participant, and through the author's emphasis on differences of opinion on Biblical interpretation we learn crucial details about the nature of Gnostic groups' scriptural versions and interpretations. Despite the air of superiority over heretics, the dialogue leaves us with a genuine debate that students of Gnosticisms will ignore at their peril.

One of the more interesting implications this dialogue presents for historians of ideas generally, and of the Gnostic tradition in particular, is that the technical theological terminology employed by Adamantius against the Gnostics foreshadows the language used to oppose Arianism. The term *homoousios*, for instance, appears in this dialogue (e.g. at 836f-837c of the Greek text), along with *ousia* and *hypostasis* (cf. e.g., 865f). Ongoing debates with Gnostics, then, arguably conditioned patterns of theological discourse evident in the Arian controversy, or, to put it more provocatively, the semantico-credal response to Arius might have been different had not orthodox theological discourse developed the way it had in answering various Gnostic challenges and 'other [related] opinions' (*heterai doxai*). Essentially Gnostic outlooks are cosmogenic and cosmological in emphasis. In any case, most treatises we tag 'Gnostical' — and thus to some extent pre-constructed by scholars as being stamped by this stress — are speculative works about the aeonic constituents of the universe, about how the lower and material manifestations of the cosmos became marred, and how 'spiritual humans' can overcome cosmic alienation and return to their true divine origin and 'home'.

It is also important to see that the Gnostic challenge to orthodox Christianity is symptomatic of common Graeco-Roman intellectual responses to the new faith of Christianity on philosophical grounds, and that most of the heated high level debate between theologians and philosophers, and between theologians and theologians, was over cosmological issues — creation, ontology, the unity of the Divinity, *logos*, the ethical implications of the material world, etc.

As was typical in Hellenistic thought, however, discussion over the macrocosm always had bearing on the microcosm of the human being. Expect to find in the dialogue, then, fiery interchange over the nature of the first man and woman, over the constituents of our humanity — flesh, body, soul, spirit — and over the implications for humankind of both the original Man and the coming of Christ as new or cosmic Man. Naturally the issues as to how and by which agency humans survive death, and whether we possess a spiritual body, loom large and reflect back on Gnostic and orthodox assumptions about the Order of Things in general. Throughout the debate we sense the mounting conflict between different propositions about the world — as to whether there are one, two (or even more) deities, for instance, as to whether the Christ was in any sense a material being, as to whether any given reading of the Bible is authoritative or not — and this helps to explain how the distillation of the orthodox position came to be propositionally formulated in creeds. Indeed the Adamantius Dialogue nicely illustrates the tendencies towards credal formulae (e.g., at 804c, 833e, and 871d in the Greek texts) just before the momentous statement at

Nicaea in AD/CE 325. The accumulation of those 'statements of the true faith' found in the dialogue, however, came with reactions against Docetism, Sabellianism, Adoptionism and other doctrinal novelties over and above Gnosticism(s).

The dialogue, of course, holds more of interest than the formal presentation of competing world-views. For those working within the ambience of post-modern theory, there portends some fascination in analysing the imagined mood and temper of the interchange — the language of restraint, pre-emption, condescension, the use of irony, innuendo, sarcasm, and the like. The strength of the discourse of 'pastoral power', given by the author to the heroic Adamantius, should be noted by those familiar with the discourse theory of Michel Foucault. The literary 'act of charity', in at least allowing 'other voices to speak' (rather than engaging in open polemic), will be very much worth the attention of those concerned with dialectic (and the continuation of the Socratic mode in this respect), with inter-subjectivity, and with keeping 'the dialogue alive' (in Richard Rorty's terms). In the heat of the hermeneutical conflict it is also intriguing to discover how Gnostic arguments appear to be more literalistic in the interpretation of the Old Testament *vis-à-vis* the New, and how the orthodox case depends on a figurative or typological exegesis that will seem somewhat curious to moderns, even unconvincing to younger or inexperienced scholars used to contemporary literalisms and fundamentalisms.

And of course all ancient documents contain minor arguments and allusions that provide fascinating and unexpected links with developments and ideas in other quarters. One small case in point concerns the presumed greater likelihood of inter- rather than intra-racial tension (at 840b/IV, 2 in the Greek and Latin texts), an uncommon but significant reference to race relations in the Roman empire. A minor argument of interest, and one contextually interesting for being stated at a time when the number of Christians in the army was increasing (cf. e.g., Eusebius, *Hist. eccles.* VIII, i, 7b) and also on the eve of the 'Constantinian experiment', is Adamantius' defence of Christ's violence. Here is some reactive polemic that arises because of the strong Marcionite contrast between the violence displayed by the evil God of the Old Testament and the love of Christ (as a manifestation of the true God). Adamantius will not have it that God is all terror under the old covenant, but neither will he accept an utterly non-violent Christ. The main demonstration of a non-pacifistic Christ, mind you, is basically eschatological: Christ is coming again as a judge who will forcibly separate the righteous from the wicked (833a-c/II, 20 in the Greek and Latin texts). There is significantly no appeal to the driving of money changers out of the temple (let alone the whipping of them, although if older translations of John 2:15a apply this to both men and animals [e.g. the Revised Standard Version], a newer one [the New International Version] applies it to animals' only). And we hear nothing of the claim, found much later in John Calvin, that it was Peter who "destroyed" Ananias. Thus with the Adamantius Dialogue we find that the pacifistic temperament in the Church, just before Diocletian's great persecution, is still holding; but there is a slight hint that the physical punishment of evildoers by a Christianized polity could be legitimate, since Adamantius is shown recalling Jesus' (albeit parabolical) talk about the retributive "beating" of the unfaithful at Luke 12:47 (833a/II, 20). If in this way Adamantius salvages the sense of continuity concerning both the punitive and merciful God, in another fleeting argument of contemporary interest he is made to confirm the subordination of women — as a principle vouched for in both the Old and New Testaments (867a-b/II, 18). Thus the Dialogue yields up not a little that is crucial for understanding major streams of Gnosticism, for uncovering reasons why orthodoxy and certain expressions of Gnosis came apart, and for better informing us of various developments in ante-Nicene Christianity.

Robert Pretty's translation and editorship of *De Recta in Deum Fide* came to my attention only after I had consulted his Masters thesis on Dionysius the Great in 1979. I learnt that Pretty's work on the Dialogue was submitted for a doctoral thesis as far back as 1964 and was examined by no less a *doyen* of Patristics than Frank Leslie Cross, who also happened to be one of my old teachers at Oxford. Although prepared for publication a few years after the doctorate was awarded, Pretty's polished version suffered an unfortunate disappearance with publishers in the United States, and was not likely to made available to wider scholarly circles until I procured a copy of the thesis from the United Theological College in Sydney in 1980. Verlie Stevenson's enthusiasm for the 'first love' of her father's scholarly labours stimulated me to put his meticulous research into a more publishable form, and it was largely through her good offices and those of Principal Gordon Dicker (of the aforementioned college) that bequest money was raised from among Robert Pretty's friends and admirers to help finance the retyping of the newly edited thesis. I have to thank Lyn Leslie and Judith Lauder for the many hours they have spent at word processing, and Lucy Davey for assisting them with Greek and Hebrew orthography. Dr Garth Thomas, a member of *Gnostica's* editorial advisory committee, and Ruth Dicker, graciously helped with the final proofreading. Along with them, I should express my special appreciation to Rev. Dr Geoffrey Barnes, who has written a biographical reflection about Robert Pretty, together with Principal Dicker and Verlie Stevenson themselves, who have penned a preface and tribute respectively. The series co-editors Wouter Hanegraaff (Utrecht) and John Cooper (Sydney), have always been helpful, and I am myself extremely thankful for the initiatives taken by the former in arranging a meeting with Peeters' Kristin De Troyer on one cold autumn day in Utrecht, 1996. Before that, Groningen scholar Marc Carvallo's visit to Sydney increased my energies to go on with editing, while stimulation for me to polish everything off came with the lecturing tour of Professor Gilles Quispel (Utrecht). Professor James Tulip, as Head of the School of Studies in Religion at the University of Sydney, was always warmly supportive of the project, and I hereby acknowledge his helpful administrations. One will be able to see from the immediately preceding comments that *Gnostica* is very much the result of Australian-Dutch goodwill and cooperation!

Although I have slashed many a long Greek passage in the footnotes, I have endeavoured to preserve the integrity of Pretty's scholarship all along the way. I have found his translation very sound and changed it very marginally, except when the use of a more 'inclusive' language, truer to the Greek text, has been deemed necessary. Additions to Pretty's critical and exegetical notes have only been made when I have thought that later (but not necessarily up-to-the-minute) scholarly findings should be recognized, or when I consider readers should have their attentions drawn to something left unmentioned in the original. These additions have been bracketed within the notes and completed by the anagram 'Ed'. Pretty's thesis included in his translation the pagination of the critical edition of the Greek and Latin versions by W.H. van de Sande Bakhuyzen. I have retained these indications of that edition (almost always as pages of the Greek or the lefthand pages of his edition and placing the page numbers in round brackets), but I have also included in bold the section numbers traditionally given to both the Greek and Latin texts, so that further citation will be made easier for scholars. Dr Pretty did not live long enough to see improvements to the textual criticism of Adamantius by Vincenz Buchheit (see p. 33, n. 87), but he would be the first to acknowledge how important was ongoing Patristic research of such a high calibre.

School of Studies in Religion
The University of Sydney
St Monica's Day 1997

INTRODUCTION

The document written in Greek and generally referred to as *Adamantius*, or *De Recta in Deum Fide*[1], is one of the little-known Christian writings of the first four centuries of the Church. Apparently it had no wide circulation, and may not have been known far beyond the area in which it was composed. Rufinus of Aquileia translated it into Latin (possibly some time after A.D. 387)[2], and there are a few references to or quotations from it in Greek writers up to the end of the ninth century. The earliest extant Greek manuscript of the work comes from the eleventh or twelfth century (the Codex Venetus), but it is not until the sixteenth century that the work really began to receive any special attention. The reason for this apparent long neglect may be found in the fact that almost up to the end of the nineteenth century, the treatise was regarded as either a minor work of Origen (*ca.* 185-254) or a spurious writing foisted on him[3]. The book is written in the form of a dialogue between a member of the Catholic Church and various heretical opponents who debate with him in turn. The victory is finally adjudged to the speaker on the Catholic side.

A. TITLE AND THEME

1. THE ORIGINAL TITLE:

The name originally given to the "Dialogue of Adamantius" is completely unknown. The number of manuscripts of the Greek text known to be extant is ten. The earliest dates from the eleventh or twelfth century, and most of the manuscript versions have no particular title. Three (D E G) bear the heading, "A dialogue of Origen against the Marcionites".

---

[1] "On the Right Faith in God." Greek: Περὶ τῆς εἰς θεὸν ὀρθῆς πίστεως. For various references to the work in literature, cf. the Bibliography.

[2] Cf. J.A. Robinson, *The Philocalia of Origen*, Cambridge, 1893, p. xlviii. F.X. Murphy, *Rufinus of Aquileia (345-411): His life and works*, 1945, Washington, DC., however, favours AD 399.

[3] Cf. W.H. van de Sande Bakhuyzen, *Der Dialog des Adamantius*, in the series *Griechischen Christlichen Schriftsteller* 4 (hereafter *Griech. Christ. Schrift.*), Leipzig, 1901, pp. xiii-xiv; F.J.A. Hort, "Adamantius", in *Dict. Christ. Biog.*, vol. 1, p. 41.

The others have a prologue (no part of the author's work) that states, "A discussion of Adamantius, who is also Origen, concerning the right faith towards God, with the heretics Megethius and Marcus, Droserius, Valens and Marinus".

Preceding the translation into Latin made by Rufinus towards the end of the fourth century stands the affirmation, "The books of Adamantius, Origen, again heretics begin. Five in number, they were translated by the presbyter Rufinus, and were sent to Paul"[4]. However, we do not know whether these words come from Rufinus himself, or whether they are the work of a later copyist. In either case, there is no certainty that they give any part of an original title. What name, if any, therefore, the author gave to his book cannot be ascertained.

2. THE THEME:

This is not in doubt. The writer intended to compose a work that would be a defence of the orthodox Christian Faith as he knew it against the teachings of certain heretical sects. The statement, therefore, found in some of the Greek manuscripts, "On the Correct Faith in God", expresses this theme reasonably well. Who the heretics were that the author had in mind, or at least what the main tenets of their belief were, may be gathered from a review of the various propositions they bring forward in debate.

At the beginning of the Dialogue, a speaker named *Megethius* throws down the gage to Adamantius, and asserts:

a) *There are three governing Principles in the Universe.* They are needed to account for the existence of Good, the Creation, and Evil. These Principles can be proved to exist from the Scriptures (sects. 805a-806b, 810a [following C.V. De la Rue's divisions of the Greek]/I, 3-5; 9 [following C.P. Caspari's divisions of the Latin]).

b) *The only books that can be accepted as valid Scripture are the single Gospel and Apostolic writings acknowledged by Marcion.* From the fact that Mark and Luke were not actual apostles of Christ, it is clear that the Gospel canon of the Catholic Church is spurious. In any case, as Paul says, there is but one Gospel (sects. 806b-808a/I, 5-6).

---

[4] *Incipiunt libri Adamantii Origenis adversus haereticos numero quinque translati a Rufino presbytero et missi Paulo.* The Paul here referred to is someone whom Rufinus met when he was on a visit to Jovinus, the bishop of Pavia. Jovinus had been Rufinus' spiritual advisor.

c) *The Christ who has come is not the Son of the God of Creation (and there-fore of the Old Testament)* for:

  i. Christ abrogates the laws of the Old Testament God, and issues commands quite contrary to them (sects. 810b-814a/I, 9-16).

  ii. The God of Creation is a persecutor of Christ's followers; He cannot therefore be the Father of Christ (sects. 816d-817a/I, 21-22).

  iii. The Father of the Christ of the New Testament is quite unknown to the Old Testament writers (sects. 817a-818a/I, 21-23).

  iv. The son of the God of Creation predicted in the Old Testament has not yet come (sects. 818b-820a/I, 24-27).

  v. The fact that Christ has redeemed us shows that He does not belong to the God who created humans and the world (sects. 820a-821e/I, 27-28).

Following Megethius, a Marcionite called *Marcus* takes up the challenge with the claim that:

a) *There are only two governing Principles: Good and Evil.*

  i. They are without beginning, self-originated and infinite (sects. 822a-823b/II, 1-2).

  ii. Humanity belongs to the Evil Principle, but was rescued by the Good Principle, or God (sect. 823a/II, 2-3).

  iii. Each principle is known by its actions. Thus the Good Principle, or God is recognized by His act of redeeming all mankind who believe in Him, and also by the fact that He does not condemn the dis-obedient. On the contrary, it is the Evil One who condemns humanity (sects. 823a-824a/II, 3-4).

  iv. For it is only the spirit of the human being that is created and saved by the Good God (sects. 825e-f/II, 8).

  v. This salvation was achieved by the voluntary death of the Good God on humanity's behalf (sect. 826a/II, 8).

In part of the preceding discussion, Megethius has joined in, and now Marcus continues alone:

b) *The Christ who has come belongs to the Good God, and not to the Creator god* (sect. 826d/II, 10).

i. This can be shown properly only from the Gospel and the apostle (i.e., the epistles of Paul accepted by Marcion). All other writings are "spurious" (sects. 826d-e; 828d-829a/II, 10; 12).

ii. The Christ of the Good God was unknown and unpredicted before he came to earth. Indeed he would not be worthy of credence had he predicted His own advent! (sects. 829c-f/II, 13-14).

iii. The fact that both Christ and Paul abolished the Law and the Prophets shows that neither of them belonged to the Creator God (sects. 830a-832c/II, 14-18).

iv. The Christ we know descended from Heaven — but it was the uncreated Heaven of the Good God, not that made by the Creator God (sects. 868b-c/II, 19).

v. That we human beings belonged to the Creator God is proven by the fact that we have been *adopted* by the Good God (sects. 869c-d/II, 19).

vi. The Creator God, and all that He has created are evil (sect. 870e/II, 20).

The third speaker is *Marinus* (a follower of Bardesanes). He lays it down that:

a) *There are two separate Root-Causes in the Universe: the Good and the Evil.*

   i. both are unchangeable and uncreated; therefore the Good Root-Cause, or God, is not the author of Evil, or the Devil (sects. 834a-836a/III, 1-4).

   ii. This can be verified by the physical senses: e.g., Light and Darkness are quite separate, one belonging to the Good God and the other to the Evil One (sects. 826a-d/III, 4-5).

   At this stage, Megethius again interjects, but the argument continues:

   iii. The two Root-Causes are not equal in power, however; the Good is stronger than the Evil, and only the Good is incorruptible (sects. 836a-837d/III, 6-8).

b) *The Good Root-Cause, or God, saves but the Evil Cause destroys humanity.* The good God is also the Judge of humans, and at the same time judges the Evil One for leading them astray (sects. 838d-839a/III, 11).

c) *The Good Cause or God is almighty, and embraces all things* (sect. 839b/III, 12).

A fourth speaker, *Droserius* (apparently a follower of the Gnostic Valentinus) now intervenes to say:

a) *Matter coexists with God*:

i. But it is without qualities, and God is completely separate from it (cf. sects. 840b-841c/IV, 2).

ii. From the good elements of matter, God made the world (sect. 841d/IV, 2).

iii. From the turbid and impure elements (unfit for Good's use) comes Evil (sect. 841d-e/IV, 2).

Droserius is interrupted by *Valens*, who seeks to correct the former's views in some particulars:

b) *The qualities of Matter are eternally coexistent with it* (844e; 845d/IV, 7; 8).

i. God is the creator of the world in the sense that He changed the qualities of only the good elements of Matter (sect. 845b/IV, 8).

ii. Evil therefore comes from the turbid and impure elements of Matter through its own outflowing. So Evil consists of *qualities* of Matter, not of Matter itself (sects. 844e; 845d/IV, 7; 8).

Once more Droserius takes up the discussion to show that:

c) *Evil arises as part of the essence of being* (sect. 846b/IV, 9).

d) *But the manner of its coming is "accidental"* (sect. 846b-847a/IV, 9).

The adjudicator now invites Marinus (who had previously attempted to prove that God did not create Evil) to continue his argument. The latter then proceeds to his second thesis, dealing with the Incarnation of Christ:

a) *Christ did not assume human flesh*, but heavenly. To have done so would have brought shame upon the Godhead — but the Godhead cannot feel a sense of shame (sects. 849b-850b/IV, 12-15).

b) *The Word existed originally as "flesh"*, and so had no need to assume it when He came to earth (850d-e/IV, 16).

c) *As Christ's humanity was only docetic*, He suffered only in appearance (sects. 850f-851a/IV, 16; V, 1).

d) *Christ when on earth appeared to humans in the same way as the angels* appeared to Abraham in the book of Genesis (18:1-16) (sects. 853a-b/V, 5).

e) *Christ was born through Mary, but not from Mary.* He passes through her in the way that water passes through a pipe, taking nothing from her in the process (sect. 855e/V, 9).

Marinus then proceeds to his third thesis: that there is to be no general resurrection of the body:

a) *The human body exists as a substance in a state of flux.* Consumed by disease, or some other cause, it gradually passes away, to be made into another body by means of the absorption of food (sects. 859c-860b/V, 16).

b) *When man dies, each of the substances blended together to compose his body returns to its original state.* It is therefore impossible for the original body to arise in a future resurrection (sect. 861b/V, 18).

c) *In actual fact, the Scriptures speak of the resurrection of the soul, not the body*: for it is the soul that is immortal (sect. 861f/V, 19).

d) *The body is really a fetter to the soul,* and the cause of all evils (sects. 862c-863a/V, 20-21).

e) *At the Resurrection,* the soul obtains a spiritual body (sect. 865d/V, 25).

As a careful reading of the Dialogue will show, the orthodox speaker, **Adamantius**, combats these various theses and their exponents one by one as they appear, and at the end of each sectional debate is duly declared the victor by **Eutropius**, the heathen adjudicator. Finally, at the conclusion of the whole, the judge proclaims that Adamantius is the complete victor over all his opponents, and expresses the wish that he himself may be admitted as a member of the Catholic Church.

3. THE OPPONENTS OF ADAMANTIUS:

Of the various heretical speakers, Marcus is definitely stated in the Greek text to be a Marcionite, while Marinus is called a follower of Bardesanes. Inasmuch as Megethius says that Marcion is his bishop, we are presumably expected to regard him also as a Marcionite. Adamantius, indeed, so designates him. With respect to the others, Droserius claims to adhere to the teaching of Valentinus, the famous Gnostic of the second century A.D[5].

[5] 822a/II, 1 (Marcus), 834a/II, 1 (Marinus), esp. 809b/I, 8 (Megethius), 840a/IV, 1 (Droserius). As Droserius quotes from Methodius' *On Free Will*, a book written to oppose the

Valens seems to hold much the same views as Droserius, except that he believes Evil to have originated from 'qualities' of Matter, and not from Matter itself, as Droserius stated. Apart then from Marinus the Bardesanian, the different opponents of Adamantius appear before us in the Dialogue as representing various forms of Gnosticism. With this their teaching as presented in the debates fairly well agrees — both from what can glean from the Fathers and newly available materials, such as the Hag Hammadi library[6].

What then of Marinus? We know all too little of the teaching of Bardesanes, unfortunately, but what Marinus advances in our Dialogue is not inconsistent with that little. Bardesanes, or Bar Daisan (the true Syrian form of his name), lived *ca.* AD 154-222, and was apparently born in Edessa, Syria. He seems to have taught the phantom or docetic appearance of Christ when on earth, and he denied the resurrection of the body and the Divine creation of the world[7]. What we know of him and his doctrine is largely taken from Epiphanius, from a book called *Dialogue on Fate,* from Moses bar Kepha (died 903), and from Eusebius of Caesaea (*ca.* 260-340). Eusebius respected Bardesanes, and appears to have considered him in his later years almost, if not quite, orthodox[8].

It is not certain that any extant work should be attributed to Bardesanes' pen. However, one of his lost treatises is a dialogue against Marcion (see Eusebius, *Hist. eccles.*, 2, 30), and this fact, along with all the other evidence, suggests that the teaching of Bardesanes was of a Gnostic type[9] but opposed to Marcion's view that the world was created by the Demiurge, or Inferior God. Bardesanes asserted that the elements from which the world came into existence were as eternal as God Himself (in this respect he is nearer to Marinus, Droserius, and Valens, than to Megethius and Marcus).

---

dualism and determinism of the Valentinian Gnostics, he presumably means by "Valentinus" the outstanding Gnostic teacher of that name.

[6] [For an update survey of Gnostic studies and different ancient Gnosticisms, in R. van den Broek, "The Present State of Gnostic Studies", in *Vigiliae Christianae* 37 (1983), pp. 41-71. Ed.]

[7] Bardesanes apparently also believed that it is only man's immortal soul that is saved by Christ, for by nature man is a mortal being. For fuller references cf. esp. Hans Lietzmann, *History of the Early Church* (trans. B.L. Woolf), London, 1953 edn., vol. 2, pp. 260-264.

[8] Epiphanius, *Adversus lxxx haereses* (*Griech. Christ. Schrift.*, pt. 1, p. 169 to 3, p. 496); Anon., *Dialog. Fat.*, using the edition of W. Cureton, *Spicilegium Syriacum*, London, 1855, pp. 1-21 (Syriac) and English trans., pp. 1-34; and for Eusebius on Bardesanes, *Hist. eccl.*, 4, 30.

[9] There is some difference of opinion about this, but the truth seems to be that, although Bardesanes claimed to uphold the orthodox Christian faith, he nevertheless had a strong interest in several other forms of religious thought, among which Gnosticism held a prominent place; cf. H.E.W. Turner, *The Pattern of Christian Truth*, London, 1954, pp. 90-94.

Evil, which is hostility towards God, was the result of causes within the nature of the world itself, and so beyond the Divine will. Thus God organized the world without actually being its creator, or responsible for evil.

In this way, Bardesanes also avoided Marcion's ditheism, with its Good God and its inferior Creator God, for unlike Marcion, he "affirmed the world, with its light and splendour", and also "discovered in the human soul ethical powers which freed it from the might of darkness"[10]. Also unlike Marcion, he was not ascetic, and did not abhor marriage. To him the process of conception and birth is the means whereby something is brought into existence which can escape from the present contaminated world to the region of clear light[11]. God was master, after all, of the elements, though He did not create them, and He showed humankind "the way to liberation from evil by means of a virtuous will obedient to the Logos"[12]. Bardesanes believed himself to be in the mainstream of the Christian Faith, and wrote against Marcion in that spirit; yet we can see that his view that God did not create the world, but was merely the organizer of it, could not go unchallenged by the Church.

Applying all this to the material placed under the name of Marinus in the Adamantian Dialogue, we must conclude then that even his speaker was, as a disciple of Bardesanes, of a Gnostic way of thought, though not of the school of Marcion, and the result is to show that "the Dialogue of Adamantius" as a whole has as its theme the refutation of Marcionism and various forms of Gnosticism as the author understood them at the close of the third century[13].

[10] Lietzmann, *op.cit.*, p. 263.

[11] See Moses bar Kepha, in F.C. Burkitt, *The Religion of the Manichees* (Donnellen Lectures), Cambridge, 1925, pp. 76-77.

[12] Cf. Lietzmann, *op. cit.*

[13] It is of interest to note that in Rufinus' translation Megethius is called a Manichaean and Marcus a "schismatic of Marcion, as Manichaeans are." Marinus is named a Bardesanian (as also in the Greek text), while Droserius and Valens are left without any title (again as in the Greek text). In the *Philocalia of Origen*, compiled by SS Gregory (Nazianzus) and Basil, the Dialogue is said to be "with the Marcionites and other heretics" (Robinson, *op.cit.*, pp. 225-26). The designation of the first two speakers as in some way connected with Manichaeism may be due to the fact that by the close of the third century A.D. the majority of the Marcionite groups had been absorbed in Manichaeism. Cf. G. Widengren, *Mani and Manichaeism* (trans. C. Kessler, rev. Widengren), London, 1965, esp. pp. 105-06.

B. AUTHOR: TIME AND PLACE OF WRITING

1. THE AUTHOR:

Practically all writers of ancient and mediaeval times refer to the author of the Dialogue under the name of Origen. The earliest mention of the work is in the *Philocalia of Origen*, which is a selection of passages from Origen's writings made by St. Basil of Caesarea (*ca.* 330-379) and St. Gregory of Nazianzus (*ca.* 329-389). At the end of chapter 24 stands the following:

> The preceding has been drawn from the *Preparation for the Gospel* of Eusebius of Palestine, Book 7. He says it is from Maximus, a writer of some importance among Christians. But exactly the same words have been found in the Dialogue of Origen against Marcionites and other heretics in which Eutropius is adjudicator, and Megethius the opposing speaker[14].

Assuming that Basil and Gregory are responsible for this statement, it can hardly have been written later than 379 (the death of Basil) and therefore our Dialogue must have been composed earlier than this. The *Philocalia* declaration also makes it clear that towards the latter part of the fourth century, the work was attributed by some to Origen.

The next witness is Rufinus (*ca.* 345-410), who probably made his translation of the Dialogue soon after 387[15]. If one accepts his was the initial inscription (see *supra*), he definitely claims Origen as the author[16]. However, the next writer to refer to the book, Theodoret, Bishop of Cyrrhus (*ca.* 393-458), makes an important distinction. In the preface to his *Compendium of Heretical Fables* he says, that he had "collected these fables of the ancient heresies from the ancient teachers of the Church — Justin,... Origen, and Adamantius". Again in chapter 25 of this work he states, "Most, however, wrote against the impiety (of the Marcionites) — Justin, Origen

---

[14] Cf. Robinson, *op.cit.*, pp. 225-6.

[15] This is the suggestion of Robinson (*ibid.*, p. xlviii). As already indicated in *supra* n. 2, Murphy thinks it to be around about 399, the time when the anti-Origenistic movement received new impetus under Theophilus of Alexandria and Jerome.

[16] In the accompanying letter to Paul, Rufinus says, "After examining in these [debates?] the assertions by means of which he [Adamantius] converted either heretics to the true teaching, or heathen to the faith, and then observing how irreproachably he stood out as an orthodox defender of the Church's doctrines, I think you will shudder with horror at the swinish and foul crime of trampling words of pearl underfoot, and tearing teachers apart". From this it is clear that Rufinus' main purpose in translating the Dialogue was to rehabilitate Origen by showing that the errors appearing in his other works were actually interpolations (cf. also Murphy, *op.cit.*, pp. 124-25).

and Adamantius". Here Adamantius is given a place separate from Origen. Another certain reference is found in the *Guide* of Anastasius Sinaita (d. *ca.* 700). Among other material, this book contains 154 Questions and Answers. Although Anastasius is thought not to be responsible for their present form, their main substance no doubt goes back to him. The answer to Question 48 is "Of Origen, from the Dialogue against Megethius the Marcionite". There follows a somewhat free translation of a passage from the First Part of the Dialogue (from sect. 818c). The only other mention of our work in ancient times comes from Photius (*ca.* 810-895), Patriarch of Constantinople. In his *Bibliotheca* (cod. 231) we read, "Sophronius informs us 'that another is Origen the Ancient, and another after him, named Adamantius'"[17]. Of these five references to the Dialogue in ancient times, therefore, three (the note in the *Philocalia*, Rufinus and the *Guide* of Anastasius) attribute it to Origen, while two (Theodoret and Photius) state it was written by someone distinct from Origen[18].

To complete the external evidence, it needs merely to be said that, until comparatively recent times, only a few scholars questioned authorship by Origen. Rivetus, Andreas Gerhard and Labbeus[19] appear to have doubted, on internal grounds, whether the Alexandrian scholar could be held responsible for the work. P-D. Huet (1685) was also uncertain[20], while De la Rue, although he included the Dialogue in his great edition of Origen's works in 1733, disputed its genuineness. Nevertheless, J.R. Wettstein, in his edition of the Greek Text issued in 1674, maintained authorship by Origen, as did the sixteenth century translators of the Dialogue into Latin.

The fact is that the question of Origenic authorship can be answered only on internal grounds. A careful examination of the work will indicate three main reasons for rejecting Origen as the composer:

---

[17] Cf. the Greek in Bakhuyzen, *op.cit.*, pp. xi, xii, and xl:

a) Theodoret: τοὺς μέντοι τῶν παλαιῶν αἱρέσεων μύθους ἐκ τῶν παλαιῶν τῆς ἐκκλησίας διδασκάλων συνέλεξα. Ἰουστίνου... καὶ Ὠριγένους καὶ Ἀδαμαντίου.

Πλεῖστοι μέντοι κατὰ τῆσδε τῆς ἀσεβείας συνέγραψαν καὶ γὰρ Ἰουστῖνος... καὶ Ὠριγένης καὶ Ἀδαμάντιος.

b) Anastasius: Ὠριγένους ἐκ τοῦ πρὸς Μεγέθιον τὸν Μαρκιωνιστὴν διαλόγου.

c) Photius: ὡς ἄλλος μέν ἐστιν Ὠριγένης ὁ παλαιός, ἕτερος δὲ ὁ μετ' ἐκεῖνον ὁ ἐπικληθεὶς Ἀδαμάντιος.

[18] Another treatise, *Praedestinatus*, probably written in Rome between 432 and 440 has been thought to refer to our Dialogue, but more credibly speaks of a work of Origen.

[19] A. Rivetus, *Critici sacri specimen*, Geneva, 1642, 2.13; J. Gerhard, *Patrologia* (ed. J.E. Gerhard), [Jena], 1668, pp. 141-42; P. Labbeus, *De Script. Eccles.*, Paris, 1660, vol. 2., p. 144; cf. J.R. Wettstein (ed.), Origines, *Opera*, Leipzig, 1674, introd.

[20] In his *Origeniana*, Cologne, 1685, p. 276.

a) *The style of writing is different* from Origen's. This is difficult to bring out in an English translation, and it should not be unduly emphasized, but to anyone conversant with Patristic Greek, a glance at almost any page of Origen's undisputed works will reveal a more complex and rhetorical use of the Greek language than that of the author of Adamantius.

b) *The doctrinal teaching of the Dialogue is different at some points from that of Origen*:

   i. Origen interprets the "garments of skins" made for Adam and Eve after the Fall (Gen. 3:21) allegorically as meaning humanity's liability to die[21], and seems to have asserted that "this body which we wear is the cause of our sins; wherefore also he called it a fetter, as it can hinder the soul from good works"[22]. This teaching is denied in Adamantius (see sect. 862c-e/V, 21).

   ii. Against Origen's view that the blood of Christ was the price paid to the Devil for the redemption of our souls[23], the Dialogue claims that we had become slaves of sin, not of the Devil, and that Christ redeemed us from the slavery of sin, not of the Devil (sect. 820c/I, 27).

   iii. Adamantius questions the immortality of the soul (sects. 862b-d/V, 20-21) which Origen upheld[24].

   iv. He also stands firmly for a resurrection of the very bodies we now have. The resurrection body is indeed a changed one outwardly (transfigured), but the earthly body keeps its identity, and does not become a different one (859c; 865d-g/V, 16; 25-26). Origen, how-

---

[21] For further references to Origen's view of the "coats of skin", see Methodius, *Aglaophon*, or *De Resurrectione*, 1, 2; 2; 8 (hereafter using G.N. Bonwetsch edn., *Griech. Christ. Schrift.*, vol. 27, Berlin, 1917); and here = in Eng. trans. by W.R. Clark, under *Discourse on the Resurrection*, in *Ante-Nicene Christian Library* (hereafter *Ant.-Nic. Lib.*), Edinburgh, 1869, vol. 14, pp. 139, 154-55; Dionysius of Alexandria, *Anal. Sol.* (using C.L. Feltoe (ed). *The Letters of Dionysius of Alexandria* [*Cambridge Patristics Texts* Series], Cambridge, 1904). See also *infra*, note to the text at pt. 5, n. 162.

[22] Cf. Methodius, *apud* Photius, *Bibliot.*, 1 (*Ant.-Nic. Fathers* edn.), p. 153.

[23] See his comments on Matt. 23:9; and Rom. 2:13, cf. also Gregory of Nyssa: "Hence it was that God, in order to make Himself easily accessible to him who sought the ransom for us, veiled Himself in our nature. In that way, as it is with greedy fish, he [the opposing power] might swallow the Godhead like a fishhook along with the flesh, which was the bait" (*Logos Katech.*, 24).

[24] *The Philocalia*, 18, 7 (Robinson edn., p. 102); *De Principiis*, 4, 1, 36. Cf. also J. Quasten, *Patrology*, Utrecht-Antwerp and Westminster, 1962, vol. 2, p. 64 on the *Discourse with Heraclides*.

ever, though believing that the present body will rise in incorruption, does not hold that it will resume its original nature, but that
"a certain power is implanted in the body, which is not destroyed,
and from which the body is raised up in incorruption"[25]. "Origen
therefore thinks that the same flesh will not be restored to the soul,
but that the form of each, according to the appearance by which
the flesh is now distinguished shall arise stamped upon another
spiritual body; so that every one will again appear the same in
form; and that this is the resurrection which is promised ... it is
necessary that the resurrection should be only that of the form"[26].

c) *Large use is made in this Dialogue of the writings of Methodius of Olympus*
(d. *ca.* 311), Bishop is Lycia, one of the first to oppose Origen[27]. This
third point is perhaps the most important for the rejection of the Origenic authorship of the Adamantian dialogue. The argument from style
would not be strong enough in itself, and from doctrine not conclusive,
for as Tixeront says, the teaching contained in the Dialogue "does not
aim precisely at opposing the teaching of the Alexandrian master"[28].
Indeed, it has many points of contact with the doctrine of Origen, and
there is no "sign of any controversial intention"[29]. Yet the fact of the use
of Methodius would appear to clinch the argument against Origen's
composition of our work:

[25] *Contra Celsum*, 5, 23. It is to be noted that Origen in the same passage will not grant
the applicability of Luke 18:27 ("with God, all things are possible") to a consideration of the
doctrine of the Resurrection. To him it is "a most absurd refuge", but 'Adamantius' freely uses
the verse (cf. 861b-c/V, 18).
[26] Methodius is the authority: *De Resurr.*, 12 (Photius' summary), trans. Clark, *Ant.-Nic.
Lib.*, vol. 14, p. 168. As Murphy rightly says (*op. cit.* p. 125), the extracts from Methodius
used by 'Adamantius' are in direct contradiction of Origen's teaching on the Resurrection. Cf.
also Quasten, *op. cit.*, vol. 2, pp. 2, 65, 87; J.N.D. Kelly, *Early Christian Doctrines*, London,
1960 edn. pp. 475ff.
[27] Robinson (*op.cit.*, pp.xl-xlvi) has shown fairly conclusively that Methodius (and not Maximus) wrote the extract from Eusebius contained in the *Philocalia* and found in the *Dialogue
of Adamantius*. For the life and writings of Methodius, see esp. Quasten, *op. cit.*, pp. 129-137;
Lietzmann, *op. cit.*, vol. 3, pp. 171f. Murphy, *op. cit.*, p. 124 well observes that the Dialogue is
often anti-Origenistic in its tendencies and doctrine, and leans heavily on Methodius.
[28] L.J. Tixeront, *History of Dogmas* (trans. H.L.B.), St. Louis and Freiburg, 1921 edn.,
vol. 1, p. 397.
[29] G. Cayré, in *A Manual of Patrology* (trans. H. Howitt), Paris, 1935, vol. 1, p. 287. The
situation is well explained by Lietzmann: "Methodius swore to the witch of Endor, in oppo-
sitions to Origen's interpretation, and so prepared the way for Eustathios. Nevertheless he
lived on the feast of good things Origen had provided, even when attacking him. His purpose
was only to help the tradition of the Church to obtain its due, and according to this view to
fit the theology traditional to Alexandria to the average faith, a feat which could not be
accomplished without mutilation" (*op. cit.*, p. 172).

i. Methodius lived at the end of the third and the beginning of the fourth centuries, but Origen died *ca.* 254[30].

ii. Methodius was frankly anti-Origenistic. Not only is his *Discourse on the Resurrection*, from which our writer quotes freely, quite obviously directed against Origen's teaching on the Resurrection[31], but Methodius wrote, in addition, another book against Origen, the *Pythonissa*, besides an extensive treatise against Porphyry (d. *ca.* 232-303), the Neo-Platonist philosopher, and the treatise *On Free Will* (also extensively quoted by the author of the *Dialogue of Adamantius*).

iii. Even if we were to suppose that it was chronologically possible for the two writers to be contemporaneous, it is highly unlikely that so great a master as Origen would have been willing to copy almost verbatim from someone else. "It is quite inconceivable that Origen, who was certainly accustomed to think for himself, should have taken down from another, and even more, an opponent, whose intention was to attack the Origenistic teaching. No one today believes any more in the Origenistic source of the writing"[32].

How does it come about, then, that the name of Origen became attached to the work of another writer? The answer may lie in the use of the name "Adamantius". Eusebius the Church historian (*ca.* 260-340) states that this was also another name for Origen[33]. Since our author chose this name for the orthodox debater in his Dialogue, and as the word stands at the very beginning of the book, it may well be that in time the Dialogue came to be known as "The Dialogue of Adamantius on the Correct Faith in God". From here it would be but an easy step to the supposition that 'Adamantius'

[30] The precise dates of the various compositions of Methodius are uncertain, but they must all have been written by AD 311 (the date of their author's death). Robinson (*op. cit.*, p. xlv) thinks that the *Dialogue on Free Will* may be placed as far back as 270. So far as the *Symposium* is concerned, H. Musurillo, introducing *St. Methodius, The Symposium* (*Ancient Christian Writers* Ser., vol. 27), Westminster and London, 1958, p. 5 states that its date cannot be fixed more certainly than in the latter half of the third century.

[31] Note particularly the Photian sections of the *Discourse* as given in the *Ant.-Nic. Lib.* edn., vol. 14, pp. 153f, 163, 167f, 170f. Cf. also Quasten, *op. cit.*, pp. 134-136.

[32] Bakhyyzen, *op.cit.*, p. xiv.

[33] *Hist. eccles.*, 6, 14, 10. Rufinus, Basil and Gregory made the mistake of thinking that the name "Adamantius", given to the orthodox debater in our Dialogue, was intended to refer to Origen, because this had been a favourite homonym of the great Alexandrian, even during his own lifetime. The mistake was clearly well fixed in tradition by the time of Rufinus (*ca.* 345-410). Cf. Murphy (*op.cit.*, pp. 123f.) and O. Bardenhewer, *Geschichte der altkirchlichen Literatur*, Freiburg im Bregau, 1914-32, vol. 2, p. 77.

was none other than the great Origen — especially as the name is not met
with very frequently in ancient literature[34]. But what would make the identification still more plausible is the fact that Origen himself did actually
write extensively against the Marcionities[35], and the first part of the Dialogue has to do specifically with Marcionite views.

But if the great Alexandrian scholar was not the author of our Dialogue,
it is impossible to say with any degree of certainty who was. The best we
can do is to examine the work itself to discover what the internal evidence
may suggest. From this the following become clear:

a) the author is an opponent of the heresies of Marcion, Bardesanes and
   Valentinus, and intends his champion Adamantius to represent the
   orthodox faith of the Church (esp. sects. 804b; 871a/I, 2; V, 28).

b) as he makes use of Methodius' treatises *On Free Will* and *On the Resurrection*, he cannot have written much earlier than the latter part of the
   third century;

c) comparison with Irenaeus, Tertullian and Origen shows that the writer
   of the Dialogue has used older controversial works against the heretics[36].
   Which ones these were we cannot know, but "he has brought forward
   good material in abundance"[37]. This, along with his knowledge of
   Methodius, shows him to be a man well read in the Christian and semi-
   Christian literature of his own and earlier times;

d) his Greek is the ordinary kind of the Patristic period[38], but without the
   finer adornments of the new Attic and the rhetorical schools seen, for

[34] St. Basil of Caesarea (*ca.* 330-379) speaks of an Adamantius in his day ("Adamantius
comes again to us, carrying a third letter." *Epist.* 58); Photius also refers to an Adamantius,
one of the twelve disciples of Manes (I, 14). The name occurs again later, given to a Greek
writer on physiognomy, see *Scriptores Physiognomonici Graeci et Latini* (ed. R. Foerster),
Leipzig, 1893, vol. 1, pp. 297-426). It is instructive to observe that in W. Smith and
H. Wace's *Dictionary of Christian Biography*, London, 1877 (a work containing very full
entries), the only Adamantius given any special mention — other than Origen — is the
author of our Dialogue (vol. 1, pp. 39-41, the article being by F.J.A. Hort).

[35] Adolf von Harnack speaks of "the polemics of Origen, which were much more thor-
ough and full of matter than the remains preserved to us" (*Marcion: das Evangelium vom
fremden Gott*, Leipzig, 1921, Beilage 3, p. 58).

[36] T. Zahn has gone into the matter very thoroughly in his *Geschichte des Neutestamentlichen Kanons*, Erlangen, 1888-1892, vol. 2, pp. 419ff., and in his earlier essay "Die
Dialoge des 'Adamantius' mit den Gnostikern", in *Zeitschrift für Kirchengeschichte*, 9 (1887),
pp. 193ff). Bakhuyzen says 'Adamantius' "utilised older anti-Marcionite writings, and it is
this that makes the Dialogue interesting for us" (*op.cit.*, p. xv).

[37] Harnack, *op.cit.*, p. 58

[38] In the more restricted sense: i.e., of writers between the end of the first century and the
close of the eighth. "The Christian authors, judged by the kind of Greek that they wrote, do

example, in Chrysostom (*ca.* 347-407) and Gregory of Nazianzus (*ca.* 329-389); it does not even reach the standard of Methodius whom the writer quotes so freely (as notes to the text will show). In style and arrangement, the Dialogue of Adamantius is loose and sometimes lacking in coherence[39]. Nevertheless, it has a literary power of its own, and

not form a single homogeneous group. The 'classical' language of the Cappadocian Fathers is very different from the vocabulary and style of Malalas or the popular Greek of much of the monastic literature. There is too great a difference between the *Didache* or Clement of Rome, with their strongly 'Biblical' language, and such an author as Cyril of Alexandria, to warrant their classification under a single literary label" (Migne, *Patrol. Graec. Lat.*, Pref., p. viii).

It is impossible in an English translation to indicate at all satisfactorily the peculiarities of Greek grammar revealed by the Greek original of our Dialogue, but which are characteristic of Patristic Greek. What can be said, however, is that there is a form of the language being used which is an adaptation of the classical pattern to meet the needs of a later age and of a Christian community. In particular, the language and style of the Greek Bible, the new concepts and ideas of Christianity, and the personal impact of Christ on the Patristic writers were three ever potent factors in the moulding of the Greek tongue to become at last the universal language of the early Christian writings throughout the Empire. Cf. also F. van der Meer and C. Mohrmann, *Atlas of the Early Christian World* (trans. M.F. Hedlund and H.H. Rowley), London and Edinburgh, 1958, p. 173.

A careful examination of the Greek text of 'Adamantius' shows the following peculiarities which this document shares with other Patristic writings:-

a) The tendency for μή to displace οὐ in constructions where οὐ would be expected in Attic.

b) The modification of conditional clauses; e.g., the use of past unfulfilled conditions without ἄν.

c) the levelling of comparative and superlative degrees.

d) The interchange of the prepositions ἐν and εἰς.

e) The use of the dative case growing less frequent.

f) The tendency to confuse the aorist and perfect tenses in narrative, a process which ulimately led to the disappearance of the latter.

g) Modifications in the use of the optative mood.

h) The general loosening of the syntax of the language as compared with the more elaborate structure of Attic.

Examples of some of these deviations from classical models will be found discussed in the notes to the text.

[39] Examples are found on sects. 806b-c/I, 5; 821a/I, 28; 828b-c/II, 11 of the text. Bakhuyzen is too severe, however, when he says, "The art of making a suitable transition from one argument to another the author did not understand at all... The deficiencies in his composition are to be reduced to this, that he did not offer the results of his own investigation and thought, but merely compiled" (*op.cit.*, p. xv). That the connection between one topic and another, or between one speaker and another is not always smooth does not admit of contradiction, as a merely casual reading of the Dialogue will show, but that this is entirely due to the lack of care or skill on the part of the author is less well-founded. We have, for instance, to take account of the possibility that in some cases the composer may have deliberately intended this — to suggest the straits to which the heretics were reduced in facing the arguments of Adamantius: they jump from one line of reasoning to another when they are cornered to avoid admitting defeat. Moreover, a work that incorporates (as this Dialogue does) so much from other writers almost *verbatim* is bound to show an unevenness of style, but this is inevitable unless the incorporated passages are to be rewritten. Generally Eutropius

as a debater the author knows how to defend his faith with clarity and sometimes real vigour[40]. If his language seems at times 'bald and unattractive' this may to some extent be due to the fact that the writer's sources were so varied in style as to make a smoothly flowing dialogue almost impossible;

e) the composer stands revealed as one who possesses considerable exegetical ability with regard to Holy Scripture; he is also a good theologian, and not without some genuine knowledge of current philosophy. He may have had some elementary understanding of the medical science of his day, in addition[41]. Although the orthodox character in the Dialogue (Adamantius) adopts a certain air of intellectual superiority, and the adjudicator (Eutropius) is often but an echo of the Catholic speaker, there is an obvious attempt to be fair to the Opposition[42]. Moreover, the author has provided us with much important material from sources now lost, and this may more then compensate for a certain lack of originality. We are indebted to *Adamantius* for some worthwhile additions to our knowledge of certain semi-Christian and heterodox forms of teaching as they existed at the end of the third century.

2. The Date of Writing:

The time when the Dialogue was composed can be determined to within a period of perhaps three decades. The extracts from Methodius set the lower limit. The *On Free Will* may have been written as early as 270[43], but it is better to follow Zahn who says that both this and *On The*

---

the adjudicator makes a pronouncement before a new aspect of the subject is considered, and his summing up at the end of the whole Dialogue comes in quite smoothly and naturally. The interruptions that occur from time to time, as when Megethius or some other speaker joins in unexpectedly, give a certain naturalness to a debate that would otherwise be over-formal. It may be that our author desired the reader to feel that the various speakers were not so much formal enemies as friendly opponents.

[40] In early times the *Dialogue of Adamantius* was evidently highly esteemed for its literary worth. The author of the longer prologue appended to the Paris codex F (cf. the note to the text at pt. 5, n. 254) speaks of it as "learned and elegant".

[41] Note the use made of the ancient practice of phlebotomy to illustrate an argument in the Dialogue (860d-e/V, 16), and the reference to medical science at 860b-c/V, 16 (along with notes to the text).

[42] In this respect the Adamantian Dialogue does much better than a number of other Christian writings of that Age. In the heat of controversy, then as now, the concept of moderation in the use of language tended to be forgotten, even by some of the greater Fathers [as in Gregory Nazianzus' invectives against Julian the Apostate, or in the Jerome-Rufinus correspondence. Ed.].

[43] So Robinson, *op.cit.*, p. xlv.

Resurrection could have been composed "just was well *ca.* 280-290 as after 300."[44] The upper time limit for the Dialogue cannot be later than 313, the date of the legal recognition of Christianity by Constantine and Licinius at Milan, for the situation presupposed in 'Adamantius' is one of the persecution of Christians by the State (816e-817a/I, 21). Within his period of some 33 years, then, the Dialogue was written. The date cannot be determined with any greater degree of exactitude, although if we suppose about ten years to have elapsed between the publication of Methodius' works and the composition of 'Adamantius' (to allow of our author's access to them), we may think of the dialogue as being composed somewhere between AD 290-300[45].

3. THE PLACE OF COMPOSITION:

Because of the references to persecution, the author may be presumed to have been resident within the Empire, and may even have suffered in persecution[46]. Again, the teachings of the particular heretics dealt with in the Dialogue (Marcion, Valentinus and Bardesanes) flourished especially in the eastern half of the Empire around the end of the third century[47]. Further, Methodius, whose writings the author of 'Adamantius' knew so well, was certainly bishop of Olympus, in Lycia, southern Asian Minor, while Bardesanes himself lived and wrote in and around Edessa in Syria[48]. It is also a

---

[44] Zahn, *loc.cit.*, pp. 236ff; Bakhuyzen, *op.cit.*, p. xvi.

[45] Approximate as this date must be, most authorities have reached a somewhat similar, if not identical, position. Thus, e.g., Bakhuyzen, *op.cit.*, p. xvi; Harnack, *Marcion, op. cit.*, p. 266, n. 2); Quasten, op. cit., vol. 2, p.146f.; B. Altaner, *Patrology* (trans. H.C. Graef), Freiburg and Edinburgh, 1960, p. 244; G. Cayré, *op. cit.*, vol. 1, p. 287; P. Brandhuber, "Die sekundären Lesarton bei I Kor. 15, 21; Ihr Verbreitung und ihr Entstehung", in *Biblica*, 18, (1937), pp. 303ff., cf. also Bardenhewer, *Patrology*, (trans. T.J. Shahan), St. Louis and Freiburg, 1908, pp. 167f; G. Bareille, in *Dict. Théol. Cath.*, vol. l, s.v., "Adamantius", p. 391; E. Stommel, in *Lexic. für Theol. und Kirche*, vol. 1, s.v., article "Adamantius", p. 133. The fact that nowhere in the Dialogue of Adamantius do we meet any strong invective against the State or a persecuting power may suggest that the book was written before the outbreak of the persecution of Diocletian in 303 (see also notes to the text).

[46] If we are right in thinking that the Dialogue was composed just before the persecution of Diocletian, the author can hardly have shared in any widespread outbreak — unless as a youth he was involved in that of Decius and Valerian (250-260). But local outbursts of persecution were liable to occur at any time in any part of the Empire. Our author may well have had experience of one of these. Does his statement "we have been frequently persecuted and are hated", put into the mouth of Megethius, look back to this?

[47] Cf. Lietzmann, *op. cit.*, vol. 1, pp. 249f, 261, 287, 29s, cf. van der Meer and Mohrmann, *op. cit.*, maps 5, 6, 42b.

[48] Cf. Lietzmann, *op. cit.*, vol. 2, pp. 260-264, vol. 3, pp. 171-72, cf. van der Meer and C. Mohrmann, *op. cit.*, maps 6, 8, 42b.

fact that at the end of the third century and the beginning of the fourth, the Marcionites were particularly firmly established in the area where Syriac was the chief language spoken[49]. The converging lines of evidence therefore tend to suggest that our author lived and wrote in the region of southern Asia Minor or Syria[50]. This is also supported by the note in the *Philocalia* (see *supra*), for it is easy to understand how Basil of Caesarea and Gregory of Nazianus, who both lived in the eastern part of Asia Minor, came to know of the Dialogue and its use of Methodius, if its writer had lived in their area.

4. CONCLUSION:

It has already been stated that we cannot identify the author of the Dialogue with any certainty. In such circumstances, perhaps we may be permitted to guess: the author may himself have borne the name Adamantius, and so is actually the speaker on the orthodox side in the Dialogue. Alternatively, he may been the Maximus to whom Eusebius erroneously attributes the dialogue of Methodius *On Free Will* in his *Preparation for the Gospel*. This Church historian does sometimes confuse his dates and characters[51]; he may therefore have heard that a certain Maximus had written on the subject of free will (whom we may suppose to be the composer of our Dialogue), and so had assumed that the treatise on free will from which he was taking his extract for insertion in his *Preparation* was none other than the writing of Maximus of which he had heard, although in actual fact it was the work of Methodius. The error would be all the more understandable if the Adamantian Dialogue had been written *ca.* 290, some twenty years before Eusebius composed his *Preparation for the Gospel*[52].

---

[49] Lietzmann, *op.cit.*, vol. 1, p. 261.

[50] With this most of the authorities already mentioned in n. 45 are in general agreement, but the emphasis is mostly on Syria.

[51] There is an example of this kind of confusion in *Hist. eccl.*, 2, 16:
"they may say that it was this Mark [i.e., the one referred to in 1 Peter 5:13] who was the first to be sent to preach the Gospel in Egypt — he had also composed this Gospel as a written work — and that he was the first to set up churches in Alexandria itself. Indeed, so large a body of Christians of both sexes was established there as a result of his first effort, and their austere life was so deeply in earnest and so philosophic, that Philo thought it worthwhile to give an account of their conduct and assemblies; their meals and other customs".
Apart from the fact that tradition generally associates Mark with Rome rather than Alexandria (see Turner, *op. cit.*, pp. 46, 77f.), Philo's reference is not to Christians at all, but to the *therapeutae*, a monastic community of Egyptian-Jewish origin in pre-Christian times.

[52] Eusebius' *Praeparatio Evangelica* seems to have been commenced during the persecution of Diocletian (303-311), but it was not concluded until some time afterwards, judging

If we wish to carry our 'guess' further, we can surmise that Maximus, in addition to being the writer of the Dialogue of Adamantius, was also a disciple or follower of Methodius who felt that his master had gone a little too far in his treatment of Origen's views in his writings. He therefore wrote the Adamantian Dialogue, giving the orthodox speaker a name of Origen

from the references in it to contemporary events (and absence of reference to the Constantinian victories).

The name "Maximus" constitutes a problem quite apart from the Adamantian Dialogue. As we have already seen, Eusebius states that the extract from another writer incorporated in his *Praep. Evang.*, 21 was from a work by Maximus. His actual words are: "However, as a book singularly appropriate to the subject, 'Concerning Matter,' has also been written by Maximus, a distinguished member of the Christian faith, I have resolved to adduce from this work material pretty relevant to the proper discussion of the question before us" (*Praep. Evang.*, 2, 7, 21). However, Robinson has shown reasonably satisfactorily, through a careful analysis of this 'material' (or extract), that it was really taken from a book by Methodius, not Maximus (of whom we know pratically nothing); cf. Robinson's *Philocalia*, pp. xl-xlvi.

We are thus left with the question, How did Eusebius get the name of Maximus mixed up with the work of Methodius? The matter is further complicated, as previously indicated, by the fact that his very same extract is found in the Dialogue of Adamantius. This problem is also faced by Robinson (*ibid.*, pp. xlvi-xlviii). His conclusion is that there were *two* writers who borrowed from Methodius, each independently of the other: Eusebius, and the author of the Dialogue of Adamantius. The extracts, however, are not exactly parallel, for the author of our Dialogue began his borrowing at a point in the Methodian dialogue *prior* to that at which Eusebius' excerpt commences, and continued to use Methodius' work for some time *after* the Eusebian borrowing has concluded. This result has one important fact relative to the Dialogue of Adamantius: obviously the Adamantian author made his extract directly from Methodius, and not indirectly through Eusebius. We are not, therefore obliged to postulate a date for the composition of the Dialogue of Adamantius subsequent to Eusebius.

There still remains the question of Eusebius' association of the name of Maximus with the Dialogue of Methodius. Apart from the passage in the *Praep. Evang.* already given, there is only one other place where Eusebius mentions Maximus at all: *Hist. eccl.*, 5, 27:

"Moreover, there are still preserved by many large numbers of writings composed with commendable zeal by men of the early Church living at the time [i.e., the period of the emperors Commodus to Septimius Severus, 180-211]. From those of which we ourselves do indeed have certain knowledge might be mentioned the treatise of Heracleitus, 'On the Apostle': that also of Maximus, on the question much debated among the heretics, 'The Origin of Evil,' and 'Concerning the Origin of Matter'...." (τοῦ πόθεν ἡ κακία, καὶ περὶ τοῦ γενητὴν ὑπαρχειν τὴν ὕλην).

From this passage, it appears that Eusebius thought of Maximus as living somewhere about the beginning of the third century, but the extract he quotes comes from a book of Methodius who died *ca.* 311. Therefore it seems clear that a) Eusebius did not know the true author of the passage he was extracting from Methodius' dialogue *On Free Will*; b) he assumed that the author was Maximus because he had heard that a certain person of that name had written on a similar subject. This Maximus he placed at the end of the second century because the question of the origin of evil and free will was much discussed at the time. If, however, the theory advanced in this thesis be correct, Maximus was none other than a disciple of Methodius, and the author of the Dialogue of Adamantius. But until more information is forthcoming, such theories can be little more than guesses.

(Adamantius) as an attempt to correct the balance[53]. In support of this, there is the statement of the Church historian Socrates (*ca.* 380-450) that Methodius, after writing against Origen, retracted his previous objections, and composed a dialogue called *Xeno* in which he expressed admiration of Origen[54]. In this case, the *Dialogue of Adamantius* would go far towards showing that Origen and Methodius had more in common than many supposed.

C. THE DIALOGUE

1. LITERARY FORM:

That the work is cast in the style of a dialogue need not occasion surprise, for this kind of literature was sufficiently common in the Ancient world. Methodius wrote his *Symposium* and his *On Free Will* in that style, and the Syrian Bardesanes also used this literary device. Moreover, an Age that was striving to recover Plato and his teaching would be familiar with the Socratic method of discourse. Further, if (as has been suggested) the creator of the Adamantius document was a disciple of Methodius, it would be natural for him to adopt his master's style of composition, since he was to deal with much of the master's subject-matter.

The characters all appear to be fictitious. There was a Marcus, a disciple of Valentinus, representing a decadent form of Gnosticism, about the middle of the second century[55]. Our author may be thinking of him in his choice of names for his debaters, although the Marcus of the dialogue is made a finer character than the historical person, who was alleged to have been something of a charlatan. A Droserius is mentioned by the Christian apologist Marcarius Magnes (fourth or fifth century)[56], but he can hardly be equated with the Droserius of the Dialogue, for the latter seems to be purely a literary figure. Of Megethius we know nothing more than what the Adamantius dialogue tells us. The same can be said of Marinus[57] and

---

[53] Rufinus, in any case, as an admirer of Origen, doubtless felt that the Adamantian Dialogue was a worthy testimony to the orthodoxy of his hero, and therefore accepted the Origenic authorship the more readily.

[54] Socrates, *Hist. eccl.*, 6, 13.

[55] Cf. Irenaeus, *Adversus haereses*, I, 7, 14.

[56] *Apocriticus*, 4, 15.

[57] A Marinus is mentioned by Augustine (*Contra Cresconium*, 3, 30) who was a bishop of Numidia, *ca.* 305; while Eusebius, *Hist. eccl.*, 10, 5, 18, gives a letter of Constantine to Miltiades, bishop of Rome, in which Marinus, bishop of Arles (*ca.* 313) is referred to in passing.

Valens, except that perhaps the name of Valentinus (whose teaching he seems to have followed) may have suggested the latter.

This leaves the orthodox speaker Adamantius. We may add to what has already been said in regard to this name that some modern writers feel that the author really did intend to refer to Origen under this head. Among these are Zahn, Harnack, and others[58]. On the dissenting side are F.J.A. Hort and van de Sande Bakhuyzen[59], on the grounds that the use of Methodius precludes this. However, as Tixeront remarks[60] the doctrine of Adamantius, though often differing from Origen's, need not be supposed to be directly aimed at that of the great Alexandrian. Bardenhewer's view is to the effect that the author really did mean Origen by the designation 'Adamantius', but only as the sponsor of the teaching of the Dialogue, not as the writer of the book[61]. If, however, we can believe that a follower of Methodius composed the Adamantian work, then it is possible to accept the idea that he chose a name of Origen deliberately, either to show what he believed the Alexandrian Father ought to have taught, or (which is more likely) to demonstrate that Origen was actually more 'orthodox' than had been supposed.

2. Sources and Importance of the Dialogue:

It can be said without fear of contradiction that it is his source-material that makes our author's work so valuable[62]. It may be felt that the writer has offered little that is the fruit of his own research, but to compensate for this he has brought forward considerable matter from older authors. Apart from the large use made of Methodius, the Dialogue provides information that makes it one of our main sources for Marcion's *Antitheses*[63]. Harnack has also made good use of it in his reconstruction of Marcion's Bible Text[64]. At

---

Neither these, nor the several others mentioned in early Church history (cf. *Dict. Christ. Biog.*, vol. 3, s.v., 'Marinus'), would be suitable as the prototype of the Marinus of our Dialogue.

[58] Zahn, *loc. cit.*, pp. 209ff.; von Harnack, *Marcion, op. cit.*, p. 57.

[59] Hort in *Dict. Christ. Biog.*, vol. 1, p. 39; Bakhuyzen, *op. cit.*, pp. xvii, xviii.

[60] *History of Dogmas*, 2nd edition (5th French), 1921, *op. cit.*, vol. 1, p. 397.

[61] *Patrology, op. cit.*, pp. 167, 168.

[62] Bakhuyzen, *op. cit.*, xv; Harnack, *Marcion, op. cit.*, (1921 edn.), Beilage 3, pp. 57f., 62; Beilage 5, p. 266, n. 2.

[63] *Ibid.*, Beilage 5, p. 266, n. 3; Beilage 3, p. 58, n. 1. This is the more important since no manuscript of the *Antitheses* has come down to us. Apart from the use made by the author of 'Adamantius,' some of the main references are found in Tertullian's five volumes against Marcion, written from 207 onwards. Harnack has gathered up the chief of these in his *Marcion*.

[64] Von Harnack has made an attempt to reconstruct Marcion's Bible text, and therefore often has recourse to the Adamantian Dialogue. His conclusion is that the author of our

the time when the writer of the Dialogue was alive, there already existed a dozen or more treatises against Marcion or Gnosticism. To these we may add the books of Origen, which were much larger than the surviving fragments suggest. From any one (or several) of these our author could have drawn, although we cannot now determine which ones. Even Bardesanes' dialogues against Marcion[65] had been translated into Greek, and may have been available to the composer of the 'Adamantius' document. A comparison with the works of Irenaeus, Tertullian and Origen suggests that yet another anti-Marcionite book, older than those already referred to, whose author had read Marcion's treatise, was among the sources relied on by the writer of our Dialogue. Such a book may have been written before Tertullian[66].

It can therefore be confidently affirmed that even if our author did not himself have personal knowledge of either Marcion's Bible or his *Antitheses* (as both van de Sande Bakhuyzen and Harnack seem to think), he has nevertheless given us much valuable material from both, culled from other sources no longer open for investigation. Add to this what is said in the Dialogue, either directly or indirectly, about Valentinus and Bardesanes (possibly even Manichaeism), and it will be recognised that in the 'Case of Adamantius' we have new material (and sometimes old material presented in a new way) for a clearer understanding of several of the most threatening heresies that ever confronted the Christian Church. We shall also gain an added appreciation of some of the arguments and methods used by the Catholic Church in the late third century in combatting them.

Dialogue had no personal knowledge of the Marcionite Bible text, and is supported here by Bakhuyzen. For both Marcion's *Antitheses* and Bible our author was indebted to older anti-Marcionite writings — one or other of the several works against Marcion written before the end of the third century (cf. Bakhuyzen, *op. cit.*, p. xv; Harnack, *Marcion, op. cit.*, Beilage 3, pp. 56-59). At the same time, this does not detract from the value of what is said in the Dialogue regarding either Marcion's Bible or *Antitheses*, for the sources upon which our author draws have all been lost, and we are indebted to him for preserving them.

[65] Apparently Bardesanes caused quite a controversy by means of these writings, for Hippolytus (*Refutatio*, 7, 31), claims that an Assyrian by the name of Prepon composed a treatise against 'Bardaisan' in Marcion's defence (see H.J. Lawlor and J.E.L. Oulton, *Eusebius: The Ecclesiastical History and The Martyrs of Palestine*, London, 1927, vol. 2, p. 152).

[66] Zahn, *loc. cit.* Cf. Harnack (*Marcion, op. cit.*, p. 55 n. 1), who thinks this work may have been the *Against Marcion* written by Theophilus of Antioch in the late second century, and referred to by Eusebius of Caesarea (*Hist. eccl.*, 4. 24): "That Theophilus, along with others, contended against these [heretics] is clear from a book he took pains to compose, *Against Marcion* — a work that is by no means unworthy of him. This, with others I have mentioned, is still extant". Cf. also Quasten, *op. cit.*, vol. 2, p. 275.

3. RECIPIENTS AND PURPOSE:

For whom was the book intended? Probably first of all for teachers and leaders in the Catholic Church, to be used as a Manual of Instruction when they were contending with various heresies. It may also have been meant to sustain the faith of some among the laity of the Church who, through lack of proper knowledge of their faith, were being severely tempted by these heretical teachings. It is even possible (though less likely) that the writer had in mind pagan society as well, seeing he chose a pagan (Eutropius) to be the adjudicator in his Dialogue. The Christian apologists before him had been in the habit of addressing their treatises in defence of the faith to pagan emperors, and our author would therefore have a certain precedent for his choice of a judge.

In any case, the readers, whoever they were, would have in the Dialogue most valuable material for refuting heresy and building up their Christian faith, presented in a clear and vigorous manner (if not with any great literary skill). They would also find a Biblical exegesis and a theological reasoning to compare very favourably with most of the Church Fathers of the first three Christian centuries[67]. In a work such as this, the readers could not expect to find the depth of learning nor the adventurous speculations of an Origen, but at least they would be spared Origen's sometimes excessive allegorism, and, above all, the invective to which some of the Fathers resorted in writing against their opponents (as in the volleys between Jerome and Rufinus).

4. THE INTEGRITY OF THE TEXT:

The Dialogue of Adamantius did not escape the hand of the reviser. This was not properly appreciated until the Latin translation of Rufinus had been published by Caspari in 1883, when it was seen that certain references in the accepted Greek Text to the position of the Church in the Empire had no parallel in the Latin. In addition, there were revealed some displaced pages[68] and other minor divergencies. Although at times Rufinus' renderings

---

[67] Hort recognizes this (*loc. cit.*, vol 1. p. 41).

[68] In the English translation of the Dialogue, this misplaced section extends from page 98 to 107, which was apparently its original position. In the course of copying or transmission these particular pages of the Greek manuscript became detached, and found themselves eventually inserted at a place in the Dialogue corresponding to page 188 of the English translation. In the editions of the Greek text published prior to Bakhuyzen they can be seen in this erroneous position (cf., e.g., Migne, *Patrol. Graec.*, vol. 11, cols. 1869-1881). The dislocation was first clearly revealed by the discovery and publication of the Latin translation of Rufinus by C.P. Caspari. Cf. also the notes to the text, *infra*, esp. pt. 2 ns. 88, 136 and pt. 5, n. 242.

of his Greek originals are mere paraphrases, or at best, rather free translations, in the case of the Adamantius Dialogue there is greater accuracy[69]. In
the view of the fact therefore that the Latin rendering of the Dialogue
(ca. 399) was made probably within a hundred years of the time of its composition in Greek (ca. 290-300), it seems reasonable to suppose that Rufinus had access to a much earlier and better manuscript that any of those
which lie behind the Textus Receptus of the Dialogue today, and that his
translation consequently reflects a truer Greek original[70].

At first it was thought that the revision of the Greek Text had been thor-
ough and drastic, but van de Sande Bakhuyzen has shown conclusively that
it is much slighter than supposed, and he is supported here by Harnack[71].
Bakhuyzen believes that revision has been made "only in a few places". He
sums up: "Revision because of a changed chronological situation has happened in two places [at 816e-817a, and in the Epilogue]; the original text
has been abbreviated in two or three passages and expanded in perhaps one;
while a new Epilogue was made and has intruded into the old one."[72] There
is also the matter of the misplaced pages to which we have already referred.

Yet we must not suppose that, because these alterations of the original text
of the Dialogue have been discovered largely through Rufinus' translation,
that the Latin is therefore always to be preferred to the Greek MSS. Even
with 'Adamantius', Rufinus has taken considerable liberties, and very often
his divergencies from the Greek are the result of this freedom. As the critical
editor Bakhuyzen has warned, only a careful weighing of all the evidence in
each given case can hope to yield a satisfactory text (and in any case new critical editions of both the Greek and Latin texts need to be made).

---

[69] See esp. Robinson, op. cit., pp. xxxi-xxxix; Bakhuyzen, op. cit., pp. xli, xlii.

[70] At the same time, caution is still needed in the case of Rufinus, not only because of the
liberties he takes as a translator, but also because more closeness in time to the original does
not necessarily mean closeness in fidelity to the text. Apart from the fact that in the course of
90-100 years errors can creep into any hand-written document, it is just possible that our earliest Greek manuscript of the Dialogue of Adamantius (the Codex Venetus, eleventh or
twelfth century) may be copied from an earlier transcript of the original than the one which
lay before Rufinus. [Cf. the weight given by New Testament textual critics to Codex Koride-
thi (eighth or nineth century) and Families 1 and 13 (eleventh to fifteenth centuries), because
it is felt that these manuscripts have been transcribed from copies very much earlier]. As Harnack observed (Marcion, op. cit, p. 56), the signficance of Rufinus' rendering of the Greek text
of 'Adamantius' has been overrated — even by Zahn — and we must guard against over-hasty
conclusions. In the case of the misplaced pages, however, as also in that of the chronological
alterations, the Dialogue gains in intelligibility and clarity if we accept the guidance of the
Latin. [Buchheit's recent recension of Rufinus' Latin was unavailable to Dr Pretty, cf. infra,
p. 33, Ed.].

[71] Thus ibid., against Zahn, loc. cit., and Bardenhewer, op. cit, pp. 167f.

[72] Op. cit., p. xxii, sect. 5.

What date should be put on of the revision on the original Greek Text? In spite of Zahn and Bardenhewer who both place it between 330 and 337, it is safer to be less precise, and agree with Harnack that it took place 324 to 337[73].

5. THE HISTORY OF THE TEXT:

The Dialogue of Adamantius was seldom mentioned in the early Christian centuries or in the Middle Ages[74]. Then, quite suddenly, the Greek manuscripts begin to appear with greater frequency. Seven of our ten extant Greek MSS were available from the sixteenth century[75] and in addition, four Latin translations come from the same period[76]. Nothing can be gathered from either the Greek or Latin MSS as to the reason for this sudden rise of interest in the Dialogue. The most we can glean is from the Preface to the printed Latin translation of Lawrence Humphrey (1557), who claims that his aim in making the version is to provide the reading public of his time with good Christian literature in place of the profane authors so widely current:

> If you ask for eloquence; if you are looking for literary adornment and rhetorical grace, why do you run to Demosthenes, Homer and Cicero, rather than to Chrysostom, Gregory Nazianzus, the Sibylline Oracles[77], Lactantius or Jerome[78]?

---

[73] In his *Marcion*, Beilage 5, p. 266, n. 2.

[74] Our oldest Greek manuscript (the Codex Venetus) dates from the eleventh or twelfth century; Codex Vaticanus is probably from the fourteenth century, while the codex used by Wettstein (E) is dated in either the thirteenth or fourteenth century.

[75] See section V of the Introduction for the list of MSS used by Bakhuyzen.

[76] These are: J. Picus, 1556, from a Greek MS similar to H, and possibly related to it, the translator accepting Origen as the author of the Adamantian Dialogue; J. Perionius, 1556, from the Paris codex F, who also believes Origen composed our Dialogue; L. Humphrey (an Englishman), 1557, who may have used manuscript D, but this is not certain. Then there is work that is not so much a translation as a paraphrase by A. Ferrarius, dedicated to Pope Julius II (1550-1555). Cf. Bakhuyzen, *op. cit.*, pp. xlix-liii.

[77] The Sibylline Oracles consisted originally of fifteen books, 3 to 5 being probably mostly Jewish, the rest chiefly Christian. They appear to have been written intermittently between 160 B.C. and the 5th century A.D., and were probably modelled on the pagan Sibylline Books. Many of the Church Fathers believed that they contained the utterances of the Greek Sibyls of various periods. The aim seems to have been to commend the Jewish or Christian faith to the pagan world. The Fathers frequently used them (e.g., Theophilus of Antioch, who died after 181, and Clement of Alexandria, who died before 215) to provide arguments in defence of Christianity. Lactantius and Augustine also knew of the Oracles. Cf. R.H. Charles, *Religious Development between the Old and New Testaments*, Oxford, 1914, pp. 226f.

[78] Quoted by Bakhuyzen, *op. cit.*, p. xii, sect. 2.

Humphrey's words may offer the clue to the puzzle: the Renaissance had already stimulated interest in classical learning as more and more Greek and Latin writings became available. This concern may have been extended to specifically Christian literature in the century that witnessed the beginnings of the Reformation. When we think of the immense amount of learning and labour spent on the great Polyglott Bibles in this period[79], it is surely not to be wondered at that there should be a revival of interest in early Christian writings generally.

The first printed edition of the Greek text of 'Adamantius' was that published by J.R. Wettstein in 1674. This became the basis of subsequent editions, for the text of De la Rue (1733) is fundamentally that of Wettstein, while those of Lommatzsch and Migne (the latter published in 1857) are, apart from some unimportant details, simply the repetition of De la Rue's text[80]. Superseding these earlier editions was the work of W.H. van de Sande Bakhuyzen, *Der Dialog des Adamantius*, published in the *Griechischen Christlichen Schriftsteller* series in 1901. This includes the Rufinus translation as well as the Greek text. It is from the critical Greek text of Bakhuyzen that the English translation here offered arises, although constant reference has been made to the Latin rendering of Rufinus. Of Bakhuyzen's work little need be said except to emphasise its thoroughly scholarly character, and its general accuracy. The text is not perfect, as the editor himself freely confesses[81], and Harnack considers that not sufficient use has been made of the Codex Venetus[82].

[79] The most important of these are the Complutensian of Cardinal Ximenes (1522); the Antwerp (1569-1572), the Paris (1629-1645), and the London or Walton's (1657) Bibles.

[80] Migne's work is in *Patrol. Graec.*, vol. 11, cols. 1711-1884, included among the works of Origen, but placed as an appendix immediately after the *Contra Celsum*. The editor provides a Latin translation which sometimes proves useful in elucidating the Greek text, particularly by contrast with the rather free Latin of Rufinus.

[81] P. lvii, sect. 13: "The intention that guided me in the new edition was to give the Greek text, if possible, as it ran originally, before all revision. But it was no easy task to sift out the genuine text from such corrupt manuscripts. There was very little previous work — actually, only the work of Th. Zahn, but this has great value, and I have much for which to thank his suggestive book". The material referred to is not only to Zahn's article (*loc. cit*), but his *Geschichte, op. cit.*, vol. 1, sect. 2; vol. 2, sect. 2. Bakhuyzen goes on, "Where Methodius and Rufinus rendered help, it was not difficult to uncover the mistakes, but where these sources dried up — Rufinus translates, as has been noted, often all too freely — I was dependent on the faulty manuscripts. I dared not aim at anything from conjectures; unfortunately, too often I had to close my investigation with a 'not certain'. Perhaps others will be more fortunate than I". "That my work (since the doubtful cases are so many) is not free from error, I myself realize best. I hope, however, to have done something regarding the Dialogue for Patristic studies, especially to have made it serviceable for the investigation of the questions relating to Marcion". [Fortunately others are now following in Bakhuyzen's footsteps. Ed].

[82] *Marcion, op. cit.*, Beilage 3, p. 54, n. 2 (cf also his 1924 edn., pp. 56-67,181). However, Koetschau's criticism of Bakhuyzen's method of collating his manuscripts is considered invalid

Nevertheless, the Bakhuyzen text is the best valuable to me, and if it is carefully collated with the Latin of Rufinus, it may be regarded as adequate for all practical purposes. Publication of finer textual work on the Greek and Latin MSS has not yet been forthcoming in my time.

D. THE TEACHING OF THE DIALOGUE

An outline of the various arguments brought forward by the opponents of Adamantius has already been given. It remains to indicate the main doctrines enunciated by the Catholic speaker in the course of the debate:

a. *There is One God, Creator and Maker* of all things — even of Matter itself. He is altogether kind and just, and is the author of the Two Covenants (sects. 804b; 869b; 844c; 871d/I, 2; II, 19; IV, 6; V, 28).

b. *The Origin of Evil*: Moral evil is not a positive thing in itself, but is the absence of Good. It is the result of the human being's exercise of God's gift of Free Will — something that has come in afterwards (i.e., it is an 'accidental'), and is in no sense the product of the Essentially Good (sects. 837d; 839c; 846a; 848d-e/III, 9; 13; IV, 8; 11).

c. *The Nature of the Human*: Humans were created free to choose either good or evil, but is intended to progress continually towards higher things.

d. *God the World*. The divine Word was born of the One God of the same essence[83] and is eternally existent. He is Son of God by nature (in contrast with us, who are sons and daughters of God only by adoption). He became incarnate through the Virgin Mary, thus taking on human flesh, but not thereby changing or destroying His own personality, nor losing His identity (sects. 804b; 855b; 869c; 871e-f/I, 2; II, 19; V, 7; 28). In His Divine nature, since He is part of the Godhead, He is impassible, but in His human nature passible (sects. 849d; 855b/IV, 14; V, 7). In Christ, therefore, the Divine and the human exist as distinct elements in His nature (sects. 855d-e/V,8). He also rose from the dead, and took up our humanity into heaven (sects. 804b; 855a/I, 2; V, 7).

---

by O. Bardenhewer (*op. cit.*, vol. 2, p. 254) for the reason that Bakhuyzen leans heavily on the Latin of Rufinus and Methodius' *Free Will*. On this see Murphy, *op. cit.*, p. 123, n. 43.

[83] ὁμοούσιος. G. L. Prestige thinks that probably Adamantius is here using ὁμοούσιος with the meaning it had in ordinary secular literature of the time, in order to emphasize his conviction that "what the Father is, that also the Son is," and that therefore there is not reference made to the problem of ther unity (thus *God in Patristic Thought*, London, 1959, p. 200).

e. *The Holy Spirit.* An eternally existing member of the Godhead (sect. 804b/I, 2).

f. *The Salvation of Man.* Jesus Christ, the Son of god, was crucified for us, and is thus redeemed us from the slavery of sin (sects. 804b; 820b/I, 2; 27). Both body and soul are capable of redemption, since God has created them both (sects. 862b; 871f/V, 20; 28).

g. *The Catholic Church holds by the Truth.* Therefore those who reject her teaching actually reject the Truth (sects. 809a; 872a/I, 8; V, 28).

h. *Eschatology.* There are two Advents of Christ spoken of in Holy Scripture: one in humility (past); the other in glory (future) (sects. 818e-f/I, 25). At the Second Advent, God will reward every person according to his works (sects. 814d-e; 824b/I, 16; II, 4). There will be a General Resurrection at the consummation of all things, when we shall rise with the same bodies as we now have, only transfigured. We thus shall not lose our identity (sects. 860a-b; 865d/V, 16; 24).

In addition to these major themes, the Dialogue has much to say about other matters. Among these are:-

i. *Christ* while on earth *possessed Divine foreknowledge* (sects. 858b-d/V, 13).

j. *Christian Baptism* is a sign that the body as well as the soul can be redeemed and inherit the Kingdom of God (sect. 864a/V, 22).

k. *The Four Gospels are all authentic,* and are indeed the work of the men whose names they bear in our New Testament. This of course, rules out Marcion's 'Gospel' and his 'Apostolicon' (sects. 806d-808b/I, 5-6).

l. *The Eucharist* is a sign that the one Good God is not only the Father of Jesus Christ, but also the Creator of the World (sect. 870d/V, 20).

m. *The Office of Bishop* is a recognized Order of the Ministry within the Christian Church (sect. 870a/V, 28) but the Marcionite Order of Bishops is repudiated (sect. 810a/I, 8).

n. *Statements of Belief,* resembling Creeds, summarise the main Christian doctrines (sects. 804b; 833e; 839e; 871d/I, 2; II, 21; III, 3; V, 28).

o. *The Teaching of Megethius and Marcus.* Although both these speakers are called followers of Marcion in the Dialogue, neither *fully* represents the real position of their master. This we know by reference to other sources giving Marcion's beliefs[84] (sects. 804b-810c; 822a-824d/I, 2-9; II, 1-5).

---

[84] "Two Marcionites are brought before us, but already both no longer represent the genuine teaching of the master; for Megethius is an adherent of the three-principles doctrine, but

p. *The use of Holy Scripture.* This is generally in line with the practice of the Early Church Fathers. With regard to:

Marcus of a gloomy two-principle teaching" (so, Harnack, *Marcion*, Beilage 5, p. 266). Cf. also Eusebius: "Some, like the sailor Marcion himself, bring forward two Principles... while others of them again run into worse difficulties by presupposing not merely two but three natures" (*Hist. eccles.*, 5, 13).

It may be as well, at this point, to recall that the main facts about Marcion, so far as they are known, come from the writings of his enemies; e.g., Irenaeus, Tertullian, Clement of Alexandria, Origen, Eusebius and (by no means least) the Dialogue of Adamantius. Marcion was born in Sinope in Pontus, on the Black Sea, and was the son of a bishop. His family was wealthy, and he himself has been described as a shipowner. He went to Rome (*ca.* 138-140), joined the Church there, and became influential in it. However, he developed unorthodox views about some aspects of the Christian faith, and was excommunicated in 144. He continued on in Rome, where he established his own church, with its own order of bishops. He believed himself to be proclaiming a purer form of Christianity than that of the Catholic *communio* from which he had separated. The teaching of Marcion and his church spread very rapidly, and proved to be one of the greatest dangers the Church ever had to face. The Marcionite leader died *ca.* 160, but his movement grew strong, spreading over large parts of the Roman Empire. By the close of the third century, Manichaeism had absorbed the majority of the Marcionite groups, but Marcion's Church was still a grave threat in the East right into the fifth century (cf. Turner, *op. cit.*, pp. 81-83, 119f.)

In spite of his Gnostic leanings, Marcion can hardly be called a full-blooded Gnostic, for the reason that he was not really interested in the typical Gnostic cosmological speculations, and did not regard the salvation of man as dependent so much on initiation into an esoteric knowledge (γνῶσις) as on simple faith in what he conceived to be the Gospel. Harnack seems to have regarded Marcion as a forerunner of Protestantism. After admitting the limitations of his teaching, he exclaims, "Dennoch kann man nur wünschen, dass in dem Chor der Gottsuchenden sich auch heute wieder Marcioniten fänden!" (*Marcion*, p. 265, cf. esp. chs. 9 and 10).

Marcion set his views down in a single book — the *Antithesis* — the contents of which we must gather from the writings of his opponents, since the work itself has not been preserved. From these sources it may be deduced that:-

  a) There are two Gods: one is the God of the Old Testament, the Demiurge or Creator. He is a "just" but inferior God. The other is the good God who sent His Son His Son Jesus Christ to redeem mankind.
  b) The just God caused the death of Jesus, but Christ was delivered from his power by the good God, who, in recompense, gave Him all the souls believing in Him.
  c) This Gospel was revealed to the Apostle Paul by Christ Himself.
  d) Matter is evil, therefore Christ's body and physical resurrection were unreal.
  e) the true canon of Scripture is the Gospel (a doctored version of St Luke) and the Apostolicon (ten epistles of St Paul, omitting the Pastorals. Hebrews was also absent).
  f) Marriage after baptism is not to be permitted.
  g) Believers are of two classes: i. the baptized; ii. the unbaptized.

The chief sources for the Marcionite theology and movement are: Irenaeus, *Adversus haereses*; Tertullian, *Adversus Marcionem* and *De praescriptione haereticorum*; Justin Martyr, *Apologia*; Eusebius, *Hist. eccles.*, 5, 13, 2-7, and the *Dialogue of Adamantius*. There are also scattered references in Clement of Alexandria and Origen (who actually wrote much more than has been handed down to us). The best modern treatments are: Harnack, *Marcion, op. cit.* (1921 and 1924 edns.); E.C. Blackman, *Marcion and His Influence*, London, 1948; Lietzmann, *op. cit.*, vol. 1, ch. 14; J. Knox, *Marcion and the New Testament; an essay in the early history of the Canon*, Chicago, 1942 [New York, 1980 new edn. Ed.].

i) *The Text and Canon*: Altogether, the author of the Adamantian dialogue quotes from or refers to some 38 books (OT, 19; NT, 17; Apocrypha, 2). The quotations from the OT appear to be made generally from the Septuagint version of the Hebrew Bible, although there are some significant variations from the modern editions of the Septuagint. The more important of these are referred to in our notes to the text. The books of the Apocrypha seem to be accepted by the author of the Dialogue as on the same level of inspiration or authority as those of the Hebrew canon. Tobit 11:9-11 is used to support an argument in much the same way as books from the canonical Scriptures are. This is true also of the story from one of the books of the Maccabees (cf. sect. 816e/I, 21). Here again we meet the regular practice of the Fathers before Jerome. The New Testament quotations are mainly from a Greek text similar to, but by no means identical with, the modern recensions. The deviations are more noticable where the author of 'Adamantius' claims to be using the Bible of Marcion. The main variations are dealt with in my notes to the text. The only NT books from which our writer does not quote are Philippians, Titus, Philemon, James, 1 Peter, 1, 2, 3 John, Jude and the Revelation. It would appear therefore that, at the time when the Dialogue of Adamantius was being written, the canon of the New Testament books was very similar to that of today — at least in the area where the writer lived.

ii) *The Dialogue as a source for the recovery of Marcion's Bible (Main recensions)*. A careful study of 'Adamantius' makes it clear that the author intends to quote Scripture from the canon of Marcion (cf. sects. 807a; 809b; 824a; 868d-f; 858c; 864a/I, 5; 8; II, 4; 19; V, 14; 22). He is also well aware of Marcion's editorial methods: "The wretched Marcion, although he corrupted the statements of the Apostle, did not completely erase them, but these people [his followers], right up to the present, remove anything that does not agree with their opinion." (cf. 867a/II, 18). This is an important passage, for it shows that Marcion's Bible underwent changes long after his death, and that these changes were the result of his own disciples' work.

iii) *The Dialogue of Adamantius is our only authority for certain readings of the author's Greek Biblical Text*. Most of these variations from the main recensions may be presumed to be readings of the Bible of Marcion, but if so, 'Adamantius' is our *only* source for them. Such readings are:-

Matt. 5:17: I did not come to fulfil the Law, but to abolish it (sect. 830d). οὐκ ἦλθον πληρῶσαι τὸν νόμον ἀλλὰ καταλῦσαι.

Main recensions: οὐκ ἦλθον καταλῦσαι [τὸν νόμον] ἀλλὰ πληρῶσαι.

Lk. 24:25: Foolish men. Slow in mind to believe all that I said to you! (sect. 857d). ὦ ἀνόητοι καὶ βρασεῖς τῇ καρδίᾳ τοῦ πιστεύειν ἐπὶ πᾶσιν οἷς λάλησα πρὸς ὑμᾶς.

Main recensions: ὦ ἀνόητοι καὶ βρασεῖς τῇ καρδίᾳ τοῦ πιστεύειν ἐπὶ πᾶσιν οἷς ἐλάλησαν οἱ προφῆται.

The evidence here is divided. Epiphanius (*Schol.* 77) claims that Marcion wrote ἐλάλησα ὑμῖν, but Tertullian (*Adversus Marcionem*, IV, 43) says he put ἐλάλησεν πρὸς ὑμᾶς (*locutus est ad vos*). Rufinus sides with Epiphanius (*locutus sum vobis*). Harnack[85] thinks ἐλάλησα is "probably a Marcionite disciple's reading close to Marcion's ἐλάλησεν". Whichever reading is accepted, it is plain that the alteration was made for the purpose of avoiding reference to the Old Testament, which both Marcion and his followers rejected.

1 Cor. 10:11: These things happened to them without a type (cf. 832c). ταῦτ' ἀτύπως συνέβαινεν ἐκείνοις,

Main recensions: ταῦτα δὲ τυπικῶς συνέβαινεν ἐκείνοις,

Gal. 6:17: Let no man trouble me without cause (cf. 864a). εἰκῇ κόπους μοι μηδεὶς παρεχέσθω.

Main recensions: κόπους μοι μηδεὶς παρεχέτω.

Col. 1:22: But now He has exchanged (you) in the body of His flesh (cf. 852a). νῦν δὲ ἀντικατήλλαξεν ἐν τῷ σώματι τῆς σαρκὸς αὐτοῦ.

Main recensions: νυνὶ δὲ ἀποκατήλλαξεν ἐν τῷ σώματι τῆς σαρκὸς αὐτοῦ.

E. THE GREEK TEXT

Generally speaking, the translation has followed the critical text of Dr W.H. van de Sande Bakhuyzen (*Griech. Christ. Schrift.*, vol. 4, 1901). This is the best obtainable, for in addition to being based on a scholarly collation of the earliest known MSS, it makes use of the Latin rendering of Rufinus, first published in 1883. Bakhuyzen has also offered copious notes

[85] *Marcion*, *op. cit.*, Beilage IV, p. 220.

and variant readings in his critical apparatus which have not infrequently been of great value in determining the text.

Occasionally the English translation is based on a reading distinct from that of Bakhuyzen. Where this is so, it is indicated in the notes to the text. Migne's edition of the Greek text has also been referred to at certain points of extreme difficulty.

Other Translations:

There is no known previous translation of the Dialogue into English, or indeed into any language other than Latin. In the case of the extracts from Methodius, however, it has been possible to consult, at specific points, the English renderings of W.R. Clark (*Ante-Nicene Fathers*, 1869), and George Lewis in the *Philocalia of Origen* (T. and T. Clark, 1911). These have sometimes proved suggestive. In the main, however, the English translation breaks new ground, and one may therefore be pardoned, perhaps, for expressing the hope that the reader will "be indulgent in cases where, despite our diligent labour in translation, we may seem to have rendered some phrases imperfectly."[86]

Chief Authorities used for the Critical Greek Text

Dr. Bakhuyzen has listed these as follows:-

A.	Codex	Vaticanus 1089 — probably 14th century.
B.	"	Venetus 496 — 11th or 12th century.
C.	"	Bodleianus E. 4 16 — 15th or 16th century.
D.	"	Bodleianus E. 1. 11 — 16th century.
E.	"	Wetstenius — 13th or 14th century.
F.	"	Parisiensis Bibl. Nat. 461 — 16th century.
G.	"	Parisiensis Bibl. Nat. 817 — 16th century.
H.	"	Parisiensis Bibl. Nat. 460 — 16th century.

Two other (Codices Cantabrigiensis I and K) are virtually copies of Codices D and G respectively.

For the extracts from Methodius, the edition of Bonwetsch, 1891, was used in most cases.

For the Latin translation of Rufinus, the edition of C.P. Caspari, *Kirchen-historische Anecdota* (Christiana, 1883) was the source.

---

[86] From the Prologue of Jesus ben Sirach to the Book of Ecclesiasticus.

In addition, the Latin translation of Picus (1556), Perionius (1556) and Humphrey (1557) were consulted, along with the editions of the Greek text put out by J.R. Wettstein (1674) and C.F. de la Rue (1733). [We are now fortunate to have modern critical editing and annotating done for the Latin version by V. Buchheit,[87] though we await an up-to-date critical edition of the Greek by German scholars. Ed.].

---

[87] Vinzenz Buchheit, *Tyranni Rufini librorum Adamantii Origenis Adversus haereticos interpretatio* (*Studia et Testimonia antiqua*, I), Munich: Wilhelm Fink, 1966, lii + 156 pp.

THE DIALOGUE OF ADAMANTIUS

FIRST PART

[De la Rue 803/Caspari I, 1]*

803 1 ADAMANTIUS[1]. People who are sincere, and have a genuine (2) concern for others, desire to live as worthy a life as possible in the world. They therefore cherish[2] a high and noble faith in God[3], and so gain for themselves something perfectly and gloriously good[4]. **804a** It is the opposite, however, with those who insult, rather than honour, God with their dubious opinions, futile "knowledge"[5] and foolish reasoning. I believe that it is extremely dangerous to hold an uncertain and mediocre faith in God. To me, a right conception of God and a faith befitting it are the basis and support of all the virtues. Therefore, sir, with your permission let us begin the debate.

MEGETHIUS. Brother[6] Adamantius has taken the words out of my mouth. We also realize that faith in God and a right understanding of

---

* On sectioning, see Series Editor's Preamble, p. xxi.

[1] The names of those engaged in the dialogue evidently are fictitious, with the possible exception of Adamantius. See full discussion in the Introduction, sect. A, 3.

[2] τὴν... πίστιν τὴν εἰς θεὸν ἀφορῶντες. Literally, "fix their eyes on faith in God;" ἀφοράω is the word used by the writer to the Hebrews at 12:2; ἀφορῶντες εἰς τὸν τῆς πίστεως ἀρχηγὸν καὶ τελειωτὴν Ἰησοῦν, "looking away to Jesus the originator and perfector of faith". Its essential meaning is "look away, fix one's eyes on" someone trustingly.

[3] τὴν ἀξιέραστον καὶ ἀξιάγαστον πίστίν τὴν εἰς θεόν. This could also mean "the faith in God that is worthy of love and admiration," i.e., the orthodox Christian faith.

[4] ἐγκρατεῖς τῆς ἀμείνονος καὶ τελειοτάτης δόξης γίνονται. Literally, "become possessors of the better and most perfect glory". Δόξα, in this context, means either "glory" or "honour". Migne renders, *praestantiorem perfectissimamque gloriam consequuntur* ("attain to a more distinguished and most perfect glory"). Rufinus is at this point little more than a paraphrase.

[5] Γνῶσις is the famous Gnostic catchword. It is in the view of the Gnostics that special knowledge revealed by God without which the spiritual in humanity cannot be redeemed. Within Gnosticism, it came to mean something like a secret science, or the Gnostic doctrine. The adherents of the system claim to have τελεία γνῶσις in contrast to ordinary Christians. [For a useful, if older, introduction, H. Jonas, *The Gnostic Religion*, Boston, 1963 edn., pt. 1. Ed.]

[6] Christians Gnostics always considered themselves to be a part of the genuine Christian Church, hence the use of the term "brother" by Megethius. Thus, later on, he exclaims, "But surely I *am* a Christian!" (sect. 808e/I, 8). Adamantius is apparently and immediately

Him are of supreme importance.   **b** The adjudicator then must listen to both sides, and determine which one holds the true and correct faith. [I think the learned and experienced Eutropius[7] eminently suited for this position[8].]

On my side I will show, Adamantius, that you and your party defame rather than honour God, and that you are not concerned to make the really good God known[9]. You intend to honour another God instead of the true One. But Christ says, "No one is good, except One — The Father"[10].

EUTROPIUS.   Do you both choose me as a adjudicator?

AD.   We do.

EUTR.   Will You accept my verdict?

MEG.   I will accept it and submit to your judgements.

AD.   A distinguished audience is present, not casual (4) onlookers. **c** If therefore your verdict is just and acceptable to them, I also will abide by it as the truth.

2   MEG.   Do you wish to debate with me first from the evidence of Scripture?

disposed to question this. Not all Gnostics, however, were as friendly as Megethius towards the orthodox Christians. A difference can be seen, e.g., in the attitude of the second speaker for the Gnostics in this very Dialogue. Marcus refrains from calling Adamantius "brother" (see sect. 822aff./II, 1ff). There is also a difference in tone observable. Most Gnostics felt themselves superior to the Catholics, on the grounds that they possessed a higher form of Christianity.

[7] The choice of a heathen to be adjudicator may have been intended by the author to assist in commending his work to the pagan world (see Introd. C3). It would be an evidence to non-Christians that the orthodox Church was prepared to have its beliefs come to the full light of day for impartial examination and judgement. In actual fact, however, Eutropius is far from meeting the requirements of impartiality. We may endorse the opinion of F.J.A. Hort (in *Dict. Christ. Biog.*, vol. 1, pp. 40, 41) that the language of the heathen umpire for the most part whimsically resembles that of the orthodox champion. Harnack takes much the same view: "He is from the first biassed and in truth, no judge, but a sponsor of the Catholic disputants" (*Marcion*, Leipzig, 1921 edn., Beilage 3, p. 57, n. 1).

[8] The words enclosed in double brackets are taken from the Latin of Rufinus. There is a lacuna in the Greek text which obviously calls for some such statement as the Latin provides; otherwise the question of Eutropius following seems rather pointless.

[9] Here is the typical Gnostics and Marcionite separation of the Supreme Good God from all other Powers — mundane and supra-mundane. However much Marcion may have differed from the main stream of Gnosticism, he had this in common with them all, that the Good God was parted from the world as evil. He was therefore separated from mankind, since the human has a material body, and material things are evil. It followed from this that the Godhead could have no real contact with a human body, and so there was no true Incarnation of the Son of God. Our Lord's human form while on earth was Docetic only. In the end, the maker of Matter — the Demiurge, the Creater-God — brought about the death of Christ.

[10] Mk 10:18; Lk. 18:19. In the Lukan passage, Marcion and Origen have "God the Father." The main recensions have εἷς ὁ θεός ("God alone").

AD.   Let Megethius explain first what his opinions are, so that (as he says) the debate and the reasoning in support of his opinions may be guided by the evidence of Scripture.

MEG.   Let Adamantius express *his* views first, for it was he who initiated the debate.

EUTR.   It is correct that the initiator of the debate should state his beliefs.

AD.   I believe[11] in One God, Creator and Maker of all things; and in God the Word, Who was born of Him, of the same Essence[12], and exists eternally. In the last times[13] He assumed human form through Mary, was crucified and rose from the dead. I also believe in the Holy Spirit, existing eternally. Now let Megethius state *his* beliefs, please.

805a   MEG.   I say[14] that there are Three Principles[15]: the Good God,

[11] It is interesting to compare this confession of faith with some of the fuller creeds; e.g., the Apostles' Creed, the Creed of Nicaea, and the Constantinopolitan Creed of 381. In common with the two latter, the 'creed' of Adamantius contains the famous and crucial word ὁμοούσιος. The confession stresses on the one hand the only God as Creator over against the Gnostic and Marcionite belief in an inferior Creator-God or Demiurge. On the other, by using the word ὁμοούσιος and expressing that Christ "exists externally" (ἀεὶ ὄντα), it anticipates the Arian controversy.

[12] We need not, by the way, suppose that the appearance of the term ὁμοούσιος in the Dialogue indicates a post-Nicaean date for authorship, for it was in use in the third century. It is found in Origen (*ca.* 185-253); in Plotinus (*ca.* 205-270), and was used by other Plotinians as well as by the Gnostics and Paul of Samosata, bishop of Antioch (*ca.* 260). Nevertheless, the writer of the Dialogue would seem to be the first to use ὁμοούσιος in a Christian credal context. That the word is not an interpolation in the confession of Adamantius appears to be proven by the fact that the translation of Rufinus has its Latin counterpart (*consubstantiuum*). We might, of course, assume that the interpolation is earlier than Rufinus (*ca.* 400), in which case the introduction of ὁμοούσιος could have been the work of a reviser living in the last days of Constantine; but this is unlikely. Cf. *infra*, n. 134.

[13] Ἐπ' ἐσχάτων καιρῶν. Καιρός is eschatological in sense in this context. In the New Testament (henceforth NT) it often means "the time of crisis." Used along with ἔσχατος (rendered "last" in the translation), it referred to the Last Days, which were sometimes thought of as beginning with the birth of Christ (as here), and sometimes with the Second Advent.

[14] This "creed" of Megethius can hardly represent the faith of Marcion himself. The Master held to *two* Gods — the God of Love to whom Christ belongs and who is supremely good; and the Demiurge who created the world and who, though just, is fickle, ignorant, cruel and despotic. He is the God of the Old Testament (henceforth OT), while the Good God is the God of the New. See also Harnack, *Marcion, op. cit.*, Beilage V, p. 266; Lietzmann, *History of the Early Church* (trans. B.L. Woolf), London, 1953 edn., vol. 1, pp. 251-253; H.E.W. Turner, *The Pattern of Christian Truth*, London, 1954, p. 123.)

[15] ἀρχάς. Ἀρχή originally meant "beginning," "origin," but at a later stage the idea of "first cause" or "first principle" emerged, and the word then was often used as a philosophical term. Ἀρχή also stood, in certain contexts, for angelic and demonic powers, and for ruling

Who is the Father of Christ; another, the Demiurge[16]; another, the Evil One. The Good God is not the creator of evil, nor was this world made by Him. He is alien to all evil, and to every created thing. I am prepared to prove my statment.

3   AD.   You said that there are Three Principles. You must now make good your promise to prove it. I suppose that a Principle is so called because it exercises the authority of a prince over someone, just as a lord is so named because he exercises the authority of a lord[17] over certain persons. Now, do the three Principles exercise authority over someone? Please answer!

MEG.   The Good Principle exercises authority over the Christians; the Creative Principle over the Jews, and the Evil Principle over the heathen.

b   AD.   Are the three like-minded and partners, or do they have nothing in common with one another?

MEG.   They have nothing in common with one another.

AD.   Did the three as a group form or create (6) humankind, or did each create a human being for himself, and exercise authority over him?

MEG.   The Three did not create humankind — only the One.

AD.   Which of the Three?

MEG.   The One that exercises authority over the Jews.

AD.   Since the God of the Jews has created humanity, how and why do the Good God and the Evil One exercise authority over them? Whatever way we look at it, the Demiurge appears to be good: if he will-

authorities generally. For the "Three Principles" teaching of Valentinus, see Irenaeus: *Advers. Haereses*, 1, 8, 5.

[16] The Greek term δημιουργός is used only once in the NT (Heb. 11:10, but it is found in 2 Mac. 4:1; Philo (*fl.* AD 20) and Josephus (*ca.* AD 37-100). It is met with not infrequently in Classical Greek in the sense of "craftsman," "maker," "creator," referring to mankind, and in many Greek States it meant "magistrate." In later philosophy, however, it indicated particularly the Creator of the visible world, and this is its signification in the NT and early Christian literature generally. Δημιουργός was also a favourite term with the Gnostics.

[17] Principle = ἀρχή, here meaning "authoritative power" or "ruler"; rule as prince, hence ἄρχω, to rule over something or someone; lord = Κύριος, Lord, lord, master; and having authority or rule of a Lord = κυριεύω.

ingly yields to the two others the rulership over those who belong to him, the Demiurge will of necessity be good, for he has freely given up those who are his own [i.e., humans] to strangers. c On the other hand, if, because the Demiurge is powerless to stop it, the Good God and the Evil One snatch them [i.e., humans] away, these two [Principles] will both be evil, for they will have coveted what belongs to someone else.

EUTR. If He who seized what belongs to the Demiurge and exercises authority over other people's possessions is good (as you state), how can the stealer of another's property be called "good"?

MEG. He did not steal, but out of mercy, because, He *is* the Good God, He sent His Good Son and rescued us[18].

AD. To have mercy on someone means that there is a certain affection for what is one's own. Did the Good God, then, show affection for His own, or for what belonged to someone else?

MEG. For what belonged to someone else.

d AD. When He showed affection for them, were they good or bad people?

MEG. They were sinful people.

AD. Before humans sinned, were they created good by the Demiurge, or bad? Did he desire them to be good or bad? If he desired them to be bad, that is a desire for bad people. But one who is good does not desire bad people. On the other hand, if he desired them to be good, the Demiurge will be a maker of good people. [Therefore he is good. For a person is named from what he does. If he shows mercy, he is called "merciful"; and so with the other qualities][19].

MEG. He did not desire them as either good or bad, but He[20] was compassionate, and had mercy on them.

[18] The first "good" in this sentence (ἀγαθός), referring to God, is not found the Greek text, but is represented in Rufinus. Bakhuyzen therefore accepts it as in all probability original. The statement of Megethius purports to give Marcion's soteriology: there is no question of the Good God's stealing from the Demiurge. As the Good God He is superior to the Creator, and therefore out of his great mercy has the right to deliver Man from an inferior and cruel under-lord. This He achieved by means of His good Son, Christ. In placing emphasis on the salvation of Man through Christ, Megethius is in line with what we know of Marcion's teaching from other sources.

[19] The bracketed passage is not found in the Latin of Rufinus, but the context seems to require some such further remark to complete the thought. Bakhuyzen is not certain, however, as to its genuineness.

[20] What is the antecedent of the second "He" in this statement? Presumably the Good God, but if so, it does not logically follow from what has preceded.

EUTR.   Megethius intends to say that there is neither day nor night — only something in between. Let him explain what he means. If he says that humankind has been created neither good nor bad, what is there in between the good and the bad?[21]

4   MEG.   This is quibbling. I will prove from the Scriptures that there are Three Principles.

AD.   Are the Three Principles equal in power or does (8) one surpass the others?

MEG.   By no means! They are not equal.

AD.   Which one, then, is supreme?

MEG.   The Good Principle is the strongest.

AD.   Are the weaker Principles subject to the stronger one?

MEG.   They are.

806a   AD.   Then the weaker Principles do everything at the wish of the stronger one?

MEG.   It is not in accordance with His will that they do evil. [He is at once stronger than they][22]. Christ, indeed, by His coming, has conquered the Devil, and overthrown the decrees of the Demiurge.

AD.   That they exist is by the will of the Good God?

MEG.   No.

AD.   He is ignorant, then, that they exist?

MEG.   No, He is not ignorant.

EUTR.   You said that the Good God is the strongest, and further, that He does not desire them to exist. How can this be possible? If He is Himself the strongest, and does not desire them to exist yet they do exist

---

[21] This may be regarded as the first partial summing-up of Megethius' argument by the adjudicator. Throughout the Dialogue Eutropius acts in this way, and then passes final decision at the conclusion of each debate. There is sometimes, however, a certain looseness in the action of one argument with another which detracts from the literary smoothness of the composition as a whole. See *infra*, n. 24.

[22] The genuineness of the bracketed sentence is uncertain. It is found in the Greek MSS, but not in the Latin of Rufinus.

(as you claim), either He desires them to exist, or He cannot destroy them, or He is ignorant of their existence[23].

b 5   MEG.   I can prove that the Gospels are spurious[24].

AD.   What proofs have you to offer that this is so?

MEG.   I will show from the Gospels themselves that they are spurious.

AD.   Will you agree if I show from the Gospels that they are *not* fabrications?

MEG.   I will agree if you prove it. First state the names of the Gospel writers.

AD.   The disciples of Christ wrote them: John and Matthew; Mark and Luke[25].

MEG.   Christ did not have Mark and Luke as disciples, so you and your party are convicted of producing spurious writings. Why is it that the disciples whose names are recorded in the Gospel did not write, while men who were not disciples did? Who is Luke? Who is Mark? You are therefore convicted of (10) bringing forward names not recorded in the Scriptures.

EUTR.   If Christ had disciples, would He not have committed the work to them rather than to men who were not disciples? **c** Something seems wrong here. The disciples themselves ought rather to have been entrusted with the task.

AD.   These men are also disciples of Christ.

[23] This is covering Megethius' first thesis: that there are Three Principles, etc., and it is adjudged invalid.

[24] At this point Megethius introduces his next argument: that there are not four Gospels, but one. The transition is somewhat abrupt. The Latin translator must have felt this, for he makes Megethius say, "This conclusion (i.e., the judgement of Eutropius) is reached by argumentation, but I want to prove what I say from the Gospel writings. But I will first show that the Gospels which you people read are false". As the above passage down to the words "Gospel writings" is absent from the Greek MSS, Bakhuyzen rightly deletes it as unoriginal. Nevertheless it serves to highlight what was already been said, that the writer of the Dialogue has produced a work which, though valuable as it is in other ways, sometimes suffers from a lack of cohesion as one argument ends and another begins.

[25] The writer of 'Adamantius' accepts the traditional view that the four Gospels were all written by apostles or disciples of Christ, but at the same time he places Mark and Luke among the wider group of our Lord's followers — the Seventy. See sect. 806d.

MEG.   Let the Gospel[26] be read, and you will find that their names are not recorded.

EUTR.   Let it be read.

AD.   The names of the twelve apostles were read, but not those of the seventy-two as well.

d   EUTR.   How many apostles did Christ have?

AD.   He first sent twelve to preach the Gospel; then, after this, seventy-two[27]. So Mark and Luke, who were among the seventy-two, preached the Gospel along with the apostle Paul.

MEG.   It is impossible that these men ever saw Paul.

AD.   I will show that the Apostle himself bears witness to Mark and Luke.

MEG.   I do not accept your spurious Apostolicon[28].

AD.   Produce *your* Apostolicon — even though it is much muti-lated[29] — **807a** and I will prove that Mark and Luke worked with Paul.

MEG.   Prove it.

AD.   I read at the end of Paul's letter to the Colossians: "Aristarchus, my fellow-prisoners," he says "sends you greetings; also Mark, the cousin of Barnabas, concerning whom you have received instructions that he may come to you; receive him, therefore; and Jesus who is called Justus. These are from the circumcision. They alone are my fellow-workers for the Kingdom of God — men who have been a comfort to me." And

---

[26] "The Gospel" presumably means, on the lips of Megethius, the mutilated edition of Luke produced by Marcion. In the canonical Luke, at 6:14-16, we have the names of the twelve apostles recorded.

[27] The account of the appointment of the Seventy is found in Lk. 10:1, but in no other Gospel, nor is it referred to in the rest of the NT. The main textual evidence for the number is: for "seventy two," B D P45 Marcion, Adamantius, the Vulgate, the Peshitta and Epiphanius. Most of the other MSS and authorities omit "two".

[28] Τὸ ἀποστολικόν. This is a technical term given to the whole body of the Epistles collected into one volume.

[29] Again τὸ ἀποστολικόν. The term came to be used especially of the Marcionite collection of Paul's epistles. This consisted of ten epistles of Paul, with the Pastorals excluded. It is interesting to note that the Muratorian Fragment (from the latter part of the second century) speaks of a Marcionite epistle of Paul to the Laodiceans, and another to the Alexandrians. Some had also "composed a new book of Psalms for Marcion." (See H.M. Gwatkin, *Selections from Early Christian Writers*, London, 1958 edn., pp. 83-88).

following this, "Luke sends you greetings; also Demas."[30] I have offered proofs from the Epistle. You see that even the   b Apostle himself witnesses to them.

EUTR.   The proof is clear from these statements.

6   MEG.   I will demonstrate from elsewhere that the gospels are spurious. The Apostle says that there is one Gospel, but you people say that there are four.

AD.   There are four who preached the Gospel, but one (12) Gospel[31]. They proclaimed one Christ, and are in agreement. Now, if each of them had proclaimed or preached a different Christ, you would be right, but if the four speak of one Christ there are no longer four Gospels but one.

MEG.   The Apostle did not say, "according to my Gospels," but "according to my Gospel."[32] Note how he says that there is *one*. He also says, "If anyone should preach a gospel to you contrary to what we have preached to you, c let him be accursed."[33] When he states that there is one, how can you people say that there are four?

AD.   We also say that there is one Gospel, but there are four who preached the Gospel.

MEG.   Nor are there four who preached the Gospel, but one, for he says, "[I am amazed that you should so soon be changing over to another gospel][34]; there is not another according to my gospel — but there are some who are troubling you, and want to pervert the Gospel of Christ into another."

AD.   When Paul says there are more who preach the Gospel, how can you say that there is one?

---

[30] Col. 4:10, 11, 14. Instead of Adamantius' "in order that he may come," the main recensions have "if he should come."

[31] Note the play on words: εὐαγγέλιον, "good news, the Gospel".

[32] Rom. 2:16; 16:25. The phrase is found again in the Pastorals, which Marcion rejected: 2 Tim. 2:8.

[33] Gal. 1:9, 8. ἀνάθεμα, meaning "a votive offering" set up in the Temple, when used in the Septuagint (LXX), generally translates the Hebrew word חֵרֶם, "what is devoted to the divinity". This could be either consecrated or accursed. In most of the New Testament passages the latter meaning is intended, as in this case.

[34] The section of the passage in square brackets corresponds to Gal. 1:6 (Vulgate). It is in Rufinus, but absent from the Greek MSS of 'Adamantius'. We cannot be certain of its genuineness. The whole quotation is from Gal. 1:6-7.

MEG. He did not say that there are many preachers of the Gospel.

808a AD. I hold the apostle in my hands, and I point out that he says in the letter to the Galatians, "But even if we, or an angel from heaven, should preach a gospel to you contrary to that which we preached." He said, *We preached*. Now, if there had been one, he would have said, "besides that which I have preached." The *we preached* indicates many.

EUTR. The expression *we preached* indicates many not one.

MEG. He does not refer to these, but Sylvanus and Timothy.

EUTR. At first you said that only Paul was a preacher of the Gospel; now you admit that there were others. It is possible, then, that the rest of them — the rest of the disciples — preached the Gospel. If Sylvanus, Timothy and Paul preached the Gospel, **b** and Paul says *according to my Gospel*, it is reasonable that, though there are many preachers of the Gospel, the Gospel should be called one.

7   MEG. The gospels disagree, and say first one thing and then another, from which it is apparent that they are spurious (14).

AD. Do they preach first one Christ and then another? Do you think that they disagree in this respect?

MEG. No, but they are contradictory.

AD. Explain what you mean: do you hold that the Scriptures are to be understood in the spiritual or in the literal[35] sense? Make your position clear, please, so that the debate may proceed.

MEG. They are to be understood in the literal sense. As they have been written, so they are to be taken, and not otherwise.

AD. Well then, Christ says, "*I am the Son of Man.*"[36] Is He, in your view, Son of Man, and not Son of God?

MEG. Christ is Son of God.

[35] νοητάς: "falling within the sphere of the mental or intellectual (νοῦς)" (Rufinus has *spiritalem*, "belonging to spirit, spiritual", while Migne renders *spirituales*. And here 'literal' translates ψιλάς, "bare, simple," (Rufinus having *purum et historicum* and Migne *nudas*).
[36] Matt. 16:13; Mk. 8:27; Lk. 9:18. Adamantius conflates, for Matthew has: "the Son of Man is" while Mark and Luke have "I am". Or else the reference here may be to Lk. 5:24 (on the healing of the man sick of the palsy).

EUTR.   You said that what has been written must be taken as it stands. How is it, then, that He is Son of God when **c** He calls Himself Son of Man?

MEG.   He spoke figuratively[37] when He called Himself Son of Man.

EUTR.   Is a figure to be understood in a spiritual sense, or in its natural meaning?

MEG.   In a spiritual sense.

EUTR.   How is it then, that you said the Scriptures are to be understood in the literal sense? They are, thus, to be taken in the spritual, and not in the literal sense, [and where the words seems to be contradictory, the same meaning is found][38].

MEG.   Some passages are to be taken in the spiritual sense, and some in the literal.

EUTR.   You seem to me to be guided by a fickle opinion.

MEG.   Where figurative language has been used, the passages are to be taken in the spiritual sense; but the literal sense is to be accepted in the other ones.

AD.   You maintain, then, that figurative language has been used in regard to the term "Son of Man"? Do grasp the fact that figurative language has not been used here. [How then do you show that He is Son of God? — for you will admit one of the two terms!][39]   **d** By your theory, either Christ is found to be a liar because He calls Himself "Son of Man", although He is not man; or all the Holy Scriptures are to be understood in the spritual sense, even if figurative language has not been used. Their agreement is found to be in the meaning, and what was written literally is not the real and true content[40].

---

[37] παραβολῇ. The Greek word παραβολή means a likeness or similitude; a figure or type; figurative language. In the Synoptics the word denotes a characteristic form of the teaching of Jesus (in Matthew 17 times, in Mark 13 times, in Luke 18 times) by way of parables and illustrations. The LXX also used the term for various words and expressions that involve comparisons or even riddles.

[38] The words in angle brackets are not given by Rufinus, but are probably original, for they help to complete the thought in the mind of Eutropius. Bakhuyzen thinks that Rufinus may have abbreviated here.

[39] The Latin of Rufinus does not contain the enclosed passage, but in this case it is not easy to determine whether the words were in the original text or not.

[40] What Adamantius says here may seem to suggest that he endorses the allegorical method especially favoured by the Alexandrian School. The fact is, however, that very little evidence of its use is found in the Dialogue. The author would probably admit that some

8   MEG.   I will prove that the Gospel is one. (16)

AD.   Who is the writer of this Gospel which you said is one?

MEG.   Christ.

AD.   Did the Lord Himself write that He was crucified, and rose on the third day? Does He write in this way?

e   MEG.   The Apostle Paul added that.

AD.   Was Paul present at the crucifixion of Christ?

MEG.   He himself plainly wrote the Gospel.

AD.   If now I should show that he was not present, but even persecuted the members of the Church after this, would you become a Christian?[41]

MEG.   But surely I *am* a Christian?

809a   AD.   How can you be a Christian when you did not condescend to bear the name of Christian? You do not call yourself a Christian, but a Marcionite[42].

Scriptural passages are best interpreted in an allegorical manner, but it is doubtful (judging by the method of exegesis seen in the Dialogue) whether he would have permitted himself to allegorize to the extent of an Origen or a Clement. See also *infra*, n. 54).

[41] Apparently for Adamantius and his companions the only true Christians were those who accepted the 'orthodox' teaching. Megethius on the other hand is equally certain that he is deserving of the name, and refers to the use of sub-titles.

[42] There can be no doubt that the Marcionite movement was one of the greatest dangers the Church had to face; indeed, in the latter half of the second century, it was the main threat in the sphere of doctrine. The ordinary Gnostic sects, in spite of their appeal to the speculative-philosophical mood of the age, could be more readily combatted because of their characteristic systems of aeons or emanations (quite foreign to Christian teaching), the very subordinate place they gave to Christ, and their over-emphasis on mere knowledge ($\gamma\nu\tilde{\omega}\sigma\iota\varsigma$), as the means of Man's salvation. Marcion, on the other hand, though he shared some of the typically Gnostic views — matter as evil; God as separated from the world; the Docetic nature of Christ's human body, etc., — nevertheless did put a strong emphasis on salvation, and on the Gospel of Love. True, he could not conceive of the Good God of Jesus Christ as being the Creator of he world, nor could he think of Him as in any way related to the God of the Old Testament, yet it must be realized that apart from a proper sense of the historical and progressive nature of the Divine Revelation as contained in the OT, there seems no adequate way to relate the OT to the NT with its teaching and message, unless resort is had to the allegorical method of Philo and the Alexandrian Christian Fathers. As Marcion could not adopt this, he took the one logical step open to him: the rejection of the entire Old Testament and its teaching. The extent of the threat of Marcion to the Church may be gauged by the number and importance of the Christian writers who opposed him. Among these were Justin Martyr, Irenaeus, Theophilus of Antioch, Hippolytus, Tertullian, Origen, and others. It is a tribute to the Christian Faith, and to the ability of the Fathers who defended it, that by the

MEG.   And you people say you belong to the Catholic[43] Church, so *you* are not Christians, either!

AD.   If we possessed the surname of some human being, then you would be right. But if we are called "Catholic" because we have a truly catholic existence[44] is this wrong? You must show, therefore, that it is proper to carry the name of a human being. I will show that it is not only improper to bear the name of a bishop, but also that of an apostle. Who was the greater — Marcion or Paul?

MEG.   Paul.

AD.   Then listen, if you will, to the more distinguished Paul, when he demands, "It has come to my hearing", he says "through Chloe's folk, that there is wrangling among you: one of you says,   **b** 'I belong to Paul,' or 'I belong to Apollos,' or 'I belong to Cephas'. Has Christ been divided up? [Surely Paul was not crucified for you? Surely you were not baptized into the name of Paul?]"[45]

MEG.   *You* gave me a name, but actually I am called a follower of Christ, and there are some here who are called followers of Socrates[46].

AD.   I refuse the name of Socrates, for I do not acknowledge him[47].

end of the third century the danger had been largely passed, and most of the Marcionite bodies merged in Manichaeism. The Dialogue of 'Adamantius' is a witness, however, to the fact that, in the East at least, Marcionite teaching was still a force to be reckoned with by the Church at that time.

[43] The use of this word in the Early Church is interesting. It is derived from the Greek καθολικός, which has the meaning, "general, universal, catholic." So ἡ καθολικὴ ἐκκλησία is the universal church, as distinct from a single, local church. In the early and mediaeval Church, there are, therefore, three main senses in which it was used: (1) The Universal Church. This is the meaning in the first instance of its used in Christian literature, i.e., by Ignatius of Antioch (*ca.* AD 35 to *ca.* 107) in Smyrn. 8. By the latter part of the second century the full term "Catholic Church" was being thus used. (2) The "Orthodox" or "Undivided" Church, to distinguish it from heretical or schismatical bodies. (3) The Whole Church before the final split between East and West in 1054. After this date, the West referred to itself as "Catholic", while the Eastern Church used the word "Orthodox".

[44] Καθ ' ὅλου is an adverbial phrase used here meaning "entirely, completely". There is therefore a play on the word καθολικός, "Catholic", in Adamantius' reply.

[45] 1 Cor. 1:11-13. The section in angle brackets is omitted by Rufinus. Its use by Adamantius is doubtful. The quotation varies in some details from the text of the modern Greek recension of the NT.

[46] Presumably a reference to the famous Greek philosopher of the fifth century BC. In an age when the Neo-Platonists were seeking to revive the teaching and philosophy of Plato, it is to be expected that groups of these would be proud to bear the label "followers of Socrates" (Σωκρατιανοί). Compare with this the term used for followers of Christ (Χριστιανοί).

[47] Literally: "I do not know who he is" (οὐκ εἰδὼς τίς ἐστιν). This remark may mean no more than that Adamantius does not wish to be identified with the party of the "Followers of

EUTR. If you are giving one another names, you must both refuse them.

AD. I do not acknowlege Socrates. Does Megethius also refuse Marcion?

MEG. Marcion was my bishop[48].

810a AD. Since the death of Marcion, there have been so many succes-sor-bishops among you, or rather, pseudo-bishops: why, (18) then, have you not been named after the successors, instead of after the schismatic Marcion[49]?

Socrates", nor with the Neo-Platonists. From the use of the present tense, however, it is just possible that Adamantius thinks Megethius is referring to a Socrates alive in his own day of whom he has not heard. On the attitude of Christian scholars generally in the early centuries to Greek philosophy it may be said that from the time of Justin Martyr (*ca.* AD 100-*ca.*165), and especially in the East under the influence of the School of Alexandria, attempts were made by some of the Fathers to give it a place in the preparation of the world for Christian-ity. "Christians like Justin Martyr after their conversion continued to wear the philosopher's robe, which Tertullian considered to be the dress most becoming to a Christian teacher" (F.J. Foakes-Jackson, *History of the Christian Church to 461*, Cambridge, 1914, p. 189). Clement of Alexandria (*ca.*150-*ca.*215) regarded Greek philosophy as a gift of God to Man. He went on to say, however, "wherefore, since the Word himself has come to us from heaven, we need not, I reckon, go any more in search of human learning to Athens and the rest of Greece, and to Ionia. For if we have as our teacher him that filled the universe with his holy energies in creation, salvation, beneficence, legislation, prophecy, teaching, we have the Teacher from whom all instruction comes; and the whole world, with Athens and Greece, has already become the domain of the Word" (*Exort. ad Pag.*, 11). Thus Greek philosophers like Socrates and Plato would be regarded as "schoolmasters leading to Christ".

[48] This is an important statement. Along with the following remark of Adamantius, it shows that the Marcionites had established an Order of Bishops. Whether Marcion himself was called "Bishop" (ἐπίσκοπος) in his lifetime is, however, uncertain. E.C. Blackman (*Marcion and His Influence*, London, 1948, p.5) thinks it probable that Marcion himself instituted the order of bishops, as well as those of presbyters and deacons, since these are mentioned by Paul — Marcion's teacher and guide.

[49] Rufinus translates: *qui et schisma ab ecclesia primus fecit?* ("who was the *first* to make a separation from the Church"). This may actually be the force of the Greek σχισματοποιός. Marcion began to form his own communities before 144, when he was formally excommu-nicted from the Church of Rome; he was therefore the first we know of to secede from the Church and form his own group. Montanus (if we regard his movement as schismatic) did not begin to prophesy until 156-7, at the earliest. The making of a division in the Christian ranks was from the first regarded most seriously. Marcion therefore did not receive the Church's disapproval merely on the score of erroneous teaching, bad as that was. He also split the Body of Christ. In a later age, Dionysius of Alexandria spoke most strongly of the evil of schism, brought about by Novatian's allowance for himself, sometime after 251, to be conse-crated bishop of Rome in opposition to the properly elected Cornelius. Dionysius says in a letter to the Presbyter Dionysius, "It is indeed with very good reason that we dislike Novat-ian, seeing that he has cut the Church in two, and has drawn some of the brethren into impi-eties and slanders" (*apud* Eusebius, *Hist. eccles.*, 7, 8). To Novatian himself, Dionysius wrote, "It was right to endure anything for the sake of not cutting the Church of God in two. And

EUTR.   Since the Apostle Paul blames the Corinthians because some were taking his name, or that of Apollos or Cephas, it is clear that the name of a bishop should not be used. The superior rather than the inferior name should be taken.

9   MEG.   If you will permit me to speak, I will prove that there are three Principles[50]: one, the God of the Law, and another the Evil God[51] and I will show that it is so from *your* Scriptures.

EUTR.   First let it be shown whether there *are* three Principles or Natures, and   b then the governing function of each will be evident.

AD.   Prove that there are three Principles, and then proceed as you wish.

MEG.   I maintain that the Demiurge framed one set of laws, and that Christ made another set opposed to him.

AD.   Because you suppose that there are different and opposing laws, you therefore conclude that there is first one and then another God?

MEG.   Most certainly! No one ever contradicted or opposed himself in the way that the Gospel opposes the Law.

AD.   You said that the Demiurge is the God of the Jews. Does He exist by Himself, and as a Unity, or as Many?

MEG.   The God of the Jews is a Unity.

c   AD.   It is indeed not unseemly to quote an example borrowed from earthly life[52] in order to make what is said in the Scriptures clearer:

---

martyrdom for the sake of avoiding idolatry — it is even more glorious, as I see it." (*Ibid.*, 6, 45). Such were views bent on preserving the unity of the Church just before the production of the Adamantius dialogue.

[50] Bakhuyzen points out that it is extraordinary that, after mentioning *three* principles, Megethius refers only to *two* Gods — the God of the Law and the Evil God. Evidently Rufinus felt the difficulty, for he substitutes "good" (*bonus*) for "evil" (*malus*). However, rather than suppose a mistake on the part of the Greek copyist in writing πονηρός for ἀγαθός, it is better to suppose that between "the God of the Law" and "and another, the Evil God," words have fallen out, such as καὶ ἄλλος ὁ ἀγαθὸς θεός. We may then render, "one, the God of the Law; another, the Good God, and another, the Evil God."

[51] In postulating the Evil God (ὁ πονηρὸς θεός), Megethius would appear to depart from his master's teaching. Marcion spoke of *two* Gods — the "Just" God, the God of the OT and its Law, and the Good God, the God of the NT, the God of Love, whom Christ came to reveal.

[52] The Greek MSS have "To take a not likely small example" (οὐδενός εἰκὸς μικροῦ παραδείγματος ἄψασθαι). But this can hardly be the correct reading. Bakhuyzen emends so as to read, "It is indeed not unseemly to quote an example which is borrowed from earthly life" (οὐδὲν ἀπεικὸς κοσμικοῦ παραδείγματος ἄψασθαι).

the position resembles that of a woman who has just given birth to a child. She does not at first give him adult food, but nourishes him with milk, and afterwards uses richer and stronger food. The Apostle Paul, too, recognizes (20) that the human beings' codes of law are provided according to their advancement. Thus he says, "I gave you milk to drink, not solid food, for you could not yet take it — nor indeed can you now, for you still have the fleshly nature"[53]. God acted in the same way; He made codes of law for humankind in harmony with their development; some for Adam, as a babe; d some for Noah; some for Abraham. Others were given through Moses, and yet others through the Gospel, according as the world progressed from its beginning through the middle period to its perfected state[54]. In this way He reserved what is mature for the time of the world's maturity. However, lest you should think that I am guilty of confused reasoning, I will prove that the same God has framed laws of both kinds: He commanded Abraham to kill his son; after this He gave a law through Moses that men must not kill, but that he who has committed murder shall be killed in return[55]. Because now the same God upholds killing and its opposite, do you claim that there are two Gods, opposed to one another?

EUTR.   Does the same God give a command to kill, and then not to kill?

AD.   The very same. Moreover, He will be found to have done so not only in this instance, but also in very many instances. For example, He gave laws for sacrifices and whole burnt-offerings to be made to Him, and then for them not to be made[56]. Let Megethius answer this: is He who commanded Isaac to be slaughtered and Who required sacrifices to be made one God, while He who forbad killing and the offering of sacrifices, another God?

EUTR.   If Scripture does say this, that God did sometimes allow sacrifices to be offered, and on other occasions did not permit it, what do you say, Megethius? Does the same God alter the laws, or are there two? 811a [Which one of these have you decided is the Demiurge? Add to this

---

[53] 1 Cor. 3:2-3.

[54] Here is an insistence on the historical, progressive character of the Divine Revelation far removed from the excessive allegorising of some of the Alexandrian exegetes. Adamantius' statement is a worthy fore-gleam of the scholarly Biblical exegesis of modern times! [For notions of progress in early Christianity, see A. Funkenstein, *Heilsplan und natürliche Entwicklung*, Munich, 1965, ch. 3. Ed.]

[55] See Gen. 22 on Abraham. Exod. 20:13; 21:12 on killing.

[56] Cf. Amos 5:25; Hos. 6:6; Jer. 7:22.

that there are now not three Principles, but *four*, and the teaching of your party can no longer stand!][57]

10   MEG.   The God of the Jews and the Demiurge are one and the same, but *our* God is not His son.

AD.   What proof do you offer that Christ is not the son of the Demiurge?

MEG.   Christ destroyed the works of the Demiurge, and I will prove that He destroyed them.

AD.   Show that He destroyed them.

MEG.   The Creator God[58] commanded Moses when he was (22) leaving the land of Egypt. "Be ready; gird your loins; put shoes on your feet; have your staffs in your hands and your knapsacks on you; carry away gold, silver and all the other things from the Egyptians."[59]   **b** But our good Lord, when He was sending His disciples in to the world, said, "Neither shoes on your feet, nor knapsack, not two tunics, nor gold in your belts"[60]. See how clearly the good Lord is opposed to the teachings of the Creator God!

EUTR.   The God who gives orders to kill, and then not to kill; to offer sacrifices and then not to offer sacrifices seems one and the same to me. So also with the order to take silver and scrip, and then not to take them. I *do* want to be clear about this: **c** Since the Demiurge commanded Abraham to kill his son, was there one God who made laws against killing, and another who ordered Abraham to kill?

[AD.   If it is a single God who has framed these contrary laws, and He has approved them as good — even though they seem to us to be contradictory — why do you say, because some of the injunctions in the Gospel seem to oppose the commands of the Law, that there are two Gods issuing orders? You have not yet shown how it happens that the same God — of the Law — although He is a unity, gave command both to kill and

---

[57] Rufinus does not have the enclosed words. Although we cannot be sure of their genuineness, they fit in well with what has preceded, and add the point (made by the adjudicator) that since the OT speaks of a God who commands sacrifice, and again of a God who forbids it, there must logically be *two* Gods of the OT, and so Megethius evidently holds a belief in *four* Gods, not *three*, as he had claimed!

[58] ὁ θεὸς τῆς γενέσεως, cf. Rufinus: "The God who is proclaimed in Genesis".

[59] Scripture allusions to this are found in LXX Exod. 12:11; 3:22; 11:2; 12:35.

[60] Matt. 10:9; Lk. 9:3; 10:4.

not to kill. If it is permissible for Him as God from time to time to make such laws as He desires — or rather, considers useful, then He is revealed as the same God who gave orders for provisions to be taken for the journey, and also forbad them to be taken.   d The cause of this I am not able to state, nevertheless such are the facts.][61]

EUTR.   What do you say, Megethius? Is it one and the same God, or are there two Gods commanding opposites in the Law?

MEG.   He is the same, but Christ is not His son.

EUTR.   If, because the laws seem to be contradictory, you claim that Christ is the Son of another God, you are making it up, Megethius, for it has been shown that God Himself reversed His own enactments. Even *you* have admitted that.

AD.   Even if the matter he brought forward were contrary to the precept of the Gospels, it would be shown to emanate from one and the same God[62].   e However, I maintain that it is not (24) contrary, but that the circumstances are different: in the one instance, some were sent from Jerusalem by Christ, commissioned to preach peace[63]; in the other certain people were driven out of Egypt in war by their own servants[64]. These servants, since they had chosen war, had necessarily to be destroyed by war; even the Gospel recognizes the right of retaliation and the slaying of evil men. Thus it says, "The lord of that evil servant will come on a day when he knows not, and in an hour when he is not expecting, and will cut him in two and will assign him a place among the unbelieving."[65]   f Hence it is right to wage a just war against those who go to war unjustly[66]. In the

---

[61] This speech of Adamantius is absent in Rufinus. It may be that the latter has, as often, abbreviated. But we cannot be sure. However, as Bakhuyzen says, the conclusion put by Adamantius here that "the cause of this I am not able to state, etc." reads a little strangely when we remember that the author knew the cause quite well when writing these passages.

[62] For this speech of Adamantius, the translation follows Bakhuyzen's emendation of the text, based on Rufinus. The actual Greek is καὶ εἰ ἦν ὃ προέτεινε κεφάλαιον, ἐδείκνυετο ἑνὸς καὶ τοῦ αὐτοῦ θεοῦ, which makes difficult reading. Rufinus has *Etiam siesset contrarium caput istud quod protulit legis evangeliorum praecepto, unus tamen esse deus posset ostendi*. It is possible that a word has fallen out in the Greek text, but even when emendations are made, the thought of the passage is by no means clear, and we are in places reduced to conjecture.

[63] Acts 10:36.

[64] Gen. 9:25-26.

[65] Lk. 12:46. διχοτομέω may also in this place carry the meaning, "punish with the utmost severity" (following W. Bauer [rev. W.F. Arndt and F.W. Gingrich], *A Greek English Lexicon of the New Testament and other Early Christian Literature*, Cambridge and Chicago, 1957, s.v.).

[66] The problem of the Christian attitude to war had to be faced very early in the Church's history. Under the pagan Roman Empire, and in the days of persecution, few Christians felt

same way it was right that those who preached peace should preach it without arms. Moreover, Isaiah the prophet said, "How pleasant are the feet of those who preach peace!"[67]   **812a** There had also been a time designated in the prophet when arms would have to be broken up. He said, "A law shall come out of Sion, and a word of the Lord from Jerusalem, and He shall judge between nations, and convict many people, and they shall break up their swords for ploughs, and their spears for sickles; and nation shall never take sword against nation, and they shall never again learn to make war"[68].

EUTR.   This is not a discrepancy, since it has been shown that even Christ retaliated against evil men, when He said that the evil slave was to be separated[69].

b 11   MEG.   The prophet of the God of creation, when war came upon the people, went up to the top of the mountain and stretched out his hands to God so that he might destroy many in the battle[70]. Yet our Lord, because He is good, stretched out *His* hands, not to destroy, but to save men. So where is the similarity? One, by stretching out his hands, destroys, the Other saves.

AD.   It may, perhaps, be necessary to make close examination of the stretching out of the hands of both Moses (26) and Christ. If there be a resemblance, all should be well; if however, there be no resemblance, this must be demonstrated, for Moses, by stretching out his hands, saved the people faithful to God, but destroyed their opponents, and Christ's action did the same.   **c** If indeed Christ's outstretched hands had saved everybody

---

able to enter the army. Yet as time went on, especially during the two Long Peaces (211-250, and 260-303) more and more Christians were found in the Army. When the last great persecution began, one of the first things Galerius did was to remove from his forces all soldiers who refused to offer sacrifice, and he encouraged Diocletian to do the same. With the coming of the Christian Empire, however, it was a different matter. The Emperor was Christian; therefore, his wars were "just", and for the advancement of the Christian Faith. The principle laid down in this Dialogue, written probably just prior to Diocletian's persecution, "It is right to wage a just war against those who go to war unjustly" was accepted without question. Only schismatics like the Donatists raised any objection: *Quid Imperatori cum Ecclesia?* (What has the Emperor to do with the Church?) But even they did not hesistate to seek the help of the state when it suited their purpose. Unfortunately, in the heat of the controversy, the other principle, laid down in Adamantius' following remark, was often forgotten: "In the same way, it was right that those who preached peace should preach it without arms".

[67] Isa. 52:7. The wording is similar to but not identical with that of LXX.

[68] Isa. 2:3-4. Practically the wording of LXX.

[69] Presumably a reference to the fate of unworthy servant in the parable of the talents (Matt. 25:28-30).

[70] Exod. 17:8ff.

— believers and unbelievers; murderers and adulterers — then you would seem to have made a point, but if those who believed in Him were saved, while those who disbelieved perished (like Amalek), where is the contradiction? Christ stretched out His hands[71], and afterwards the temple and city of the unbelievers were destroyed, while the people were scattered and perished. So the stretching out of the hands of both Moses and Christ has the same effect — Moses' action becoming a prefiguration of Christ's. Both saved the believers, and both destroyed the unbelievers.

MEG.   The case is neither equal nor similar.

d   EUTR.   You do not seem to me to grasp what is being said: if one had saved believers and the other unbelievers, then it would appear discordant. But both are found doing the same thing, so there is no contradiction. What else have you to say?

12   MEG.   The Lord brought to view in the Law says, "*You shall love him who loves you and you shall hate your enemy*"[72]. But *our* Lord, because He is good, says "Love your enemies, and pray for those who persecute you"[73].

AD.   If it lay only in the Gospel, you spoke well; but suppose we find it commanded in the Law also? Thus: "If you should see", it says, "your enemy's ox roaming, you shall not let it be lost.   e You shall bring it back, and restore his ox to him."[74] And again it says, "If you should see your enemy's ass fallen on the road you shall in no circumstances pass it by on the other side until you have lifted and loaded the ass."[75] But take the

[71] This may refer to the lament of our Lord over Jerusalem as recorded in Lk. 19:41-44. More likely, however, Adamantius is thinking of Christ's hands stretched out on the Cross. The destruction came with Fall of Jerusalem in AD 70.
[72] Lev. 19:18; Matt. 5:43. The first passage resembles LXX, but has τὸν ἀγαπῶντα σε for LXX τὸν πλησίον σου. The second statement, "and thou shalt hate thy enemy" is not found in any part of the OT. Even in Leviticus itself we have, "If a stranger (גֵּר) abide among you let him be among you as one of the same country. And you shall love him as yourselves" (19:33-34), and "the duty of loving the stranger is stressed thirty-six times in Scripture and is placed on the same level as the duty of kindness to, and protection of, the widow and the orphan" (trans. J.H. Hertz, *The Pentateuch and Haftorahs*, London, 1952, p. 504) [Certainly the Torah contained prescriptions to eliminate enemies in the Land (Deut. 20:16-18) Ed.]
[73] Matt. 5:44. Jesus emphasizes the need for active goodwill (ἀγαπᾶτε), not only to one's "neighbour", but also to τοὺς ἐχθρούς — those who are at enmity with us. It is certainly more than absence of hate: it is active, loving concern for their welfare, and challenges accepted codes of the day.
[74] Exod. 23:4; Deut. 22:1. The wording differs from the LXX, but the sense is the same.
[75] Exod. 23:5. Differing from LXX, which has, "If you should see your enemy's beast of burden fallen under its load, you shall not pass it by, but shall raise it with him". Bakhuyzen suggests for "load" (γομώσης) the emendation "unload" (ἀπογομώσης). The Masoretic Text

case of Moses, when the people advanced to kill him, and the glory of the Lord overshadowed him. It was Divine justice that those who had advanced should be destroyed like enemies. According to the record, the destruction fell, and the people would have perished had not Moses, ignoring their hatred, besought God on behalf of his enemies. He said, "Aaron, take the censer in your hand, and go to meet the destroyer"[76]. Hearing this, (28) Aaron met him, and the destruction abated.   f Again, there was David, who, when he was pursued by Saul, found an opportunity to destroy him, but did not do so. On the contrary, he offered a prayer for him[77]. Once more there is Jeremiah, who, though he was cast into a pit by his enemies, bore no malice, but actually prayed for them[78]. Now, it says in the Gospel writing, "Depart from Me, you who work lawlessness [into the outer darkness! there it will be weeping and gnashing of teeth"[79], so you see that the Gospel 813a agrees with the Law.

MEG.   In what respect does it agree?

EUTR.   Surely this must be so! What Christ stretched out His hands to achieve had already been achieved in the Law. He gave orders to love one's enemies, while the Law commanded not to retaliate against enemies; on the contrary, it demanded that not even an ox or ass should be overlooked. And most certainly Christ will hate as enemies those who practise evil! Does He not say, "Depart from Me?" This is not love — to repel[80] [and drive out] enemies [into the outer darkness]![81]

13   MEG.   The prophet of the God of Creation, so that he might destroy more of the enemy, stopped the sun from setting until he should finish slaying those who were fighting against the people[82]. But the Lord, because He is good, says, "Let not the sun   b go down upon your anger"[83].

has וְחָדַלְתָּ מֵעֲזֹב לוֹ עָזֹב תַּעֲזֹב עִמּוֹ (literally, "Thou shalt cease from leaving it to him: thou shalt certainly loosen (it) with him").

[76] See Num. 16:46 for the allusion.

[77] Two incidents may be in the mind of Adamantius: 1 Sam. 24 and 26.

[78] Jer. 38:6ff., 18, 20.

[79] Matt. 7:23; Lk. 13:27-28. For the portion of the quotation in brackets from Rufinus, see Matt. 8:12; 22:13; 25:30. Whether Adamantius included this latter part is uncertain.

[80] Thus ἀπώσασθαι (From ἀπωθέω, to push aside, reject, repudiate); Rufinus: abicere. [It might be supposed that the pagan adjudicator is deliberately made to draw a distinction that does not square with Christian Orthodoxy here, for in normative Christian views God's love and just chastisement are not mutually exclusive, cf. Augustine, De Civit. Dei, I. But in 813e-314a/I, 14 Adamantius makes a similar point of logic — even if he then goes on to show that goodness and the meting of punishment are not contradictory (814d/I, 16). Ed.]

[81] Both enclosed passages are of doubtful authenticity in Adamantius.

[82] An allusion to Jos. 10:12-14.

[83] Ephes. 4:26.

AD.   So far as those are concerned who wrongly brought war upon their masters, it has been shown that their destruction was just; consequently Christ also gave orders that one who had lived a bad life should be cast "into the outer darkness! there it will be weeping and gnashing of teeth."[84] With respect to the statement, "Let not the sun go down upon your anger", this teaching is found operating in the Law, not only in command but also action. There it stands written that Aaron and his sister Miriam angered Moses by their deeds[85]. The result was that Miriam contracted leprosy through the anger.   c When asked by Aaron, Moses did not await the setting of the sun, but immediately besought God to heal his sister. You see, then, that provision was made even in the Law to prevent the sun from going down (30) upon anger. However, the Prophet, as well, openly declares "Do not bear resentment in your hearts, each against his neighbour"[86]. It has become clear, then, that the teaching "Let not the sun go down upon your anger", is found in both the Law and the Gospel.

MEG.   The command about the sun's not setting is not found written in the Law.   d Why do you make contradictory statements?

EUTR.   You would debate unfairly, Megethius. The teaching has been found both in precept and practice in the Law. Surely the Prophet's instruction not to be resentful must seem to you to meet the case perfectly? Christ actually allowed a period of one day for the anger to subside, but the Prophet forbad resentment altogether!

MEG.   It would appear that you are not an adjudicator, but an opponent![87]

AD.   Eutropius is not your opponent, but the Truth is. It is her nature to oppose those who speak falsely. Truth is unconquerable and immortal, for she is the offspring of the Good God[88].

---

[84] Matt. 8:12; 13:42, 50; 22:13; 24:51; 25:30. [Adamantius does not stop to explain that the verses he uses refer to Christ's role in eschatological judgement, and not to any violent actions in Jesus' life. He could have used John 2:15a, on the (possible) *whipping* of the moneychangers (yet cf. New Internat. Version trans.; also *om.* Mk. 11:15; Matt. 21:12; Lk. 19:45), an allusion later important in popular reactions to pacifism, but he does not take such a line. Ed.]

[85] See Num. 12:1ff.

[86] Zech. 7:10; 8:17 which resembles, but is not identical with, the wording of LXX.

[87] This remark of Megethius is not altogether without foundation. Time and time again the adjudicator seems to be partial to the Catholic debater. Hort even goes so far as to say, "the language of the heathen umpire for the most part whimsically resembles that of the orthodox champion". (Hort, in *Dict. Christ. Biog.*, vol. 1, pp. 40, 41.)

[88] καὶ γὰρ ἀήττητος καὶ ἀθάνατος ὑπάρχει ἡ ἀλήθεια: a noble sentiment, evoking fine thought in the Greek philosophers. Clement of Alexandria uses ἀήττητος, "unconquerable", of Christ (*Strom.*, 4, 7).

e   EUTR.   Let the audience here present determine whether I have represented the matter unfairly. Indeed, though I am myself a man of non-Christian upbringing[89] I would become a Christian [were its truth made clear to me]. Therefore I must [investigate what is being said more closely] so that I may choose that which is best[90].

14   MEG.   I will prove that the Gospel is opposed to the Law.

EUTR.   The fact of being opposed does not at once prove that there are two Gods. Even you have admitted that it was a single person who said, "Kill", and "Do not kill".

MEG.   This very fact shows that the Creator God is not good; For he opposes Himself![91]

AD.   If you claim that He is not good because he has instituted divergent laws, observe that even Christ does not differ from Him in any way, for like the Creator God, He enacts divergent laws. He says, "Love your enemies", and afterwards tells the enemies of the Faith, "Depart into the outer   814a darkness!"[92] How could He love the enemies whom He sent into the outer darkness? What sort of love would this be? (32)

15   MEG.   It says in the Law, "Eye for eye and tooth for tooth"[93], but the Lord, because He is good, says in the Gospel, "If anyone should slap you on the cheek, turn the other one to him"[94].

AD.   The legal requirements have been laid down in a most satisfactory and convenient manner. The first injunction, found in the Law, was

---

[89] Ἕλλην. Lit. "a man of Greek language and culture"; or more generally, a non-Christian, pagan.

[90] The two places where the words of Eutropius are put in single brackets are, in the Greek text, lacunae. They have been filled from Rufinus, where they seem to represent the original. However, it is felt that Eutropius had added more words at the end which are not now recoverable. Although Bakhuyzen agrees that the insertions from Rufinus are probably right, he thinks that "the unconditional demand of Eutropius to become a Christian does not suit here. It comes much too early". He would rather insert it at the end of the First Part of the Dialogue, where the debate with the two Marcionites, Megethius and Marcus, is concluded.

[91] It was the essence of the teaching of Marcion that the Demiurge, or Creator-God, contradicted Himself over and over again, and involved Himself in opposing courses of action. It was the purpose of the Good God to overcome Him. Inasmuch therefore as the Demiurge is the very heart and centre of the OT and its Law, the Christian must abandon the OT; which, of course, Marcion did.

[92] Matt. 5:44; Lk. 6:27; Matt. 8:12; 22:13; 25:30, 41.

[93] Exod. 21:24; Lev. 24:20; Deut. 19:21 (LXX).

[94] Matt. 5:39; Lk. 6:29.

a precautionary measure, given to prevent someone from attempting to deprive another of his eye, and to put a stop to the spirit of revenge. Now, as in the Law, fear prevented strife,   b so also in the Gospel, in the same manner, retaliation and resentment, brought about by a paltry blow, were checked by means of submission and persuasion. So both fear and gentleness are fitted to bring peace. One man stopped fighting because of fear, while the other clung to peace through gentleness. If you claim that reprisals have been spoken of only in the Law, take note of what the Gospel says, "The measure you give will be the measure you get"[95]. Perceive[96] still more clearly from the same Gospel how every one is rewarded in the measure that he has done this — as it were, *eye for eye* — c when He says, "Whoever shall deny Me before men — him I also will deny before My Father in heaven"[97]. It has been shown, then, through both the Law and the Gospel, that what each one has done to his brother — this he will receive back.

16   MEG.   The prophet of the God of Creation told a bear to come out of a thicket and devour the children who met him[98], but the good Lord says, "Let the children come to Me, for of such is the kingdom of heaven"[99].

AD.   We must examine the manner of approach of all the children. If this were the same in both cases, you would have a point —   d for both parties had a genuine reason for their coming. Those who approached Christ did so with a view to receiving a blessing, while it was those who came forward in mockery and insolence who drew on themselves savage destruction. It has been demonstrated that as each one acts, so he is rewarded; it was right, then, that those who had come to receive blessing should obtain their request, and conversely, that those who had (34) insulted the prophet of God should be torn by wild beasts. It was in just such a way that Judas was punished when he had acted wickedly towards the Lord. Christ Himself declared, "Alas to the man through whom the Son of Man is betrayed! It   e would be better for him if he had not been born, or if, when he was born, he had been tied to a great millstone and drowned

---

[95] Matt. 7:2; Mk. 4:24. (θ, the Vulgate, and a number of other authorities have ἀντιμετρηθήσεται with Adamantius, instead of μετρηθήσεται of the modern recensions [v. Mark and BS2.])
[96] μάθετε. Plural, indicating Megethius and his party.
[97] Matt. 10:33.
[98] An allusion to the story of Elisha and the bears as found in 4 Kgs. 2:24 (LXX).
[99] Matt. 19:14; Mk. 10:14; Lk. 18:16.

in the depth of the sea"[100]. You will also find that the prophets often had mercy on many people — even to the extent of raising the dead! For example, the Shunammite, when she besought the prophet, received back her dead son alive[101]. It has been clearly demonstrated, then, that the prophets and Christ own one and the same God. If He is one, and, as you say, He is known to be good only, without being just, why does He[102] command Judas, wickedly unjust, to be justly cast into the sea? **f** I think that the punishment of sinners belongs to the nature of a just God[103], and not to One who is 'good' after your fashion. A God who is merely good, and not at the same time just, ought not to punish anyone, but if He *does* punish, He will at the same time be just. This must also be pointed out: it is obvious that the just God, the Creator, had no occasion to punish Judas, for he had received no injury from Him. No more could the Devil, **815a** for Judas had not hurt him, but rather the opposite — he had assisted him. Instead, the Devil sees Someone brought to death by Judas — One whom he feared and to whom he called out: "Leave me alone! Have you come to torment me before the time?"[104] Nor is it likely that Judas was punished by the Good Christ, for "a good God never punishes"[105]. Which, then, of the three do you consider, punished Judas? It has been established that the just God did not punish, for He was not wronged nor suffered any harm. If He did punish, He must have been appointed to carry out justice by Him who had been injured. If the Devil punished Judas, he will be just, and not evil, for he who condemned the wicked betrayer would be just. So he will be just and not wicked. **b** But if Christ punished, it would be contrary to your argument: "A good God never punishes". So if He punished, He will be just

[100] Matt. 26:24; 18:6. The words "if he had been tied ... depth of the sea" are not found in the context of the Eucharist meal in any of the Gospels, but are part of an earlier address of our Lord on offences. Matt. 18:6 is parallelled in Mk. 9:42 and Lk. 17:1-2.

[101] 4 Kgs 4:17-37 (LXX).

[102] He presumably refers to the good God in this context. However, the actual words are spoken by Christ, and seemingly not in connection with the statement regarding the betrayal by Judas. Cf. *supra*, n. 100.

[103] Here is a clear expression of the Christian view of God — One who is both just and good. Christianity demands that the God shall be perfectly just and at the same time perfectly good. Only so can humanity's sins be adequately dealt with.

[104] Matt. 8:29; Mk. 5:7; Lk. 8:28.

[105] ἀγαθὸς γὰρ οὐδέποτε κολάζει; which could also be rendered "a good Christ" or "a good person, never punishes.". The context, however, seems to require the translation given in the English text. Adamantius is quoting an argument already offered by Megethius, that the good God could never by His very nature punish anyone, so that where the OT speaks of divine punishment the reference must be to the Demiurge, and not to the good God.

— but not good![106] What is more, (36) listen to the Apostle when he says, "Every one receives from Christ either good or evil"[107].

MEG. Where is there similarity? The prophet killed, but Christ saved.

[AD. On the contrary, He destroyed the unbelievers. He would say to each supplicant, "Your faith has saved you"[108]. If then each one's faith — the result of deliberate choice — sprang up to save, on the other hand want of faith destroyed][109].

EUTR. Did those who came to the Prophet come to receive blessing?

c   AD. No. With mockery and insult, they actually called him bald-headed.

EUTR. It was right that the reward should fit the purpose of their approach, especially when the Apostle says that good and evil are received from Christ.

17   MEG. The Creator God did not know where Adam was, when He asked, "Where are you"?[110] Christ, however, knew even men's thoughts[111].

AD. How is it then that Christ said concerning Lazarus, "Where have you laid him?"[112] Perhaps[113] He was ignorant where he lay!

MEG. This is not written in our Gospel.

AD. You know that you undertook to make your proof from our Gospel. d But since you do not want this, what is meant when Christ inquired from the chief of the demons, "What is your name?" and he

---

[106] A good example of an *argumentum ad hominem* — a method of debate much favoured by the ancients.

[107] 2 Cor. 5:10. Instead of Adamantius' ἕκαστος παρὰ χριστοῦ κομίζεται εἴτε ἀγαθὸν εἴτε κακόν, the main recensions have ἵνα κομίσηται ἕκαστος τὰ διὰ τοῦ σώματος πρὸς ἃ ἔπραξεν, εἴτε ἀγαθὸν εἴτε φαῦλον.

[108] Matt. 9:22.

[109] This speech of Adamantius is lacking in Rufinus, but it seems to follow on logically from the preceding statement of Megethius, and is therefore probably genuine. [Note the important stress here on the role of free will in salvation. Ed.]

[110] Gen. 3:9.

[111] See Lk. 6:8 and 9:47.

[112] Jn. 11:34.

[113] ἴσως, "equally" or "probably, in a similar manner." Adamantius here takes Megethius on his own ground: "By your view, Christ probably said this because He was ignorant!"

replied, "Legion"?[114] So according to *your* Gospel He was ignorant, and therefore asked the question.

MEG.   This is not a similar case.

EUTR.   Both cases seem to me to be instances of ignorance: "Where are you?" and "What is your name?"

AD.   God did not ask Adam, "Where are you?" because he wanted to make enquiry, but rather to recall something to his mind. By asking "Where are you?" He reminded him who at first had lived in happiness, but soon afterwards had disobeyed the command and was now naked: Behold in what condition you once lived, and note your present state, deprived of the pleasures of Paradise!

e 18   MEG.   What then does it mean in the Law when it (38) says, "Cloak for cloak"[115], while the good Lord says, "If anyone should take your cloak, give him your tunic also"?[116].

AD.   This particular statement is similar to that which says, "Tooth for tooth"[117]. But so that you may not think that we are answering your arguments ineffectively — although you have been very quick to assume the position of judge in   **816a** propounding the matters to be investigated from the Scriptures (he who propounds, mark you, is more important than he who expounds) — this expression, "If anyone take away from you your cloak", is written in the Gospel, but the act itself happened among the patriarchs. After he had been deprived of his cloak by this brothers, Joseph not only parted with his tunic (in harmony with what is written in the Gospel), but also provided corn, and, in time of famine, food and a very large sum of money[118]. Even in the Law it was directed: "If your brother receive money, in the seventh month you shall remit both the interest   **b** and the sum loaned"[119].

19   MEG.   The Prophet of the god of Creation records, "My bow is bent, and my arrows are sharpened"[120]. But the Apostle says, "Put on the

[114] Lk. 8:30.
[115] This particular command does not seem to be found in any book of the OT [Cf. Lev. 6:11; 16:23-24. Ed.].
[116] Lk. 6:29; cf. Matt. 5:40. Not an exact quotation, however.
[117] Exod. 21:24; Lev. 24:20.
[118] Gen. 37:23; 42:25-27.
[119] Deut. 15:1-3; Exod. 22:25, 26. A rather "free" rendering. The Masoretic Text and LXX have "year", not "month". Rufinus has: "in the seventh year".
[120] A free combination of Isa. 5:28 and Deut. 32:23 (LXX).

armour of God, that you may be able to extinguish the fiery darts of the Wicked one"[121].

AD   Good is not opposed to good, nor evil to evil nor light to light. White is not the opposite of white, but of black. So you can hardly claim that what the Prophet says is the opposite of what the Apostle states. You realize, of course, that bow and sword; shield and arrows; armour — all have to do with war?

EUTR.   To whom did the Prophet belong — the Just god or the Evil One?

MEG.   To the Just god.

c   AD.   What, then, does the Apostle mean by referring to the Just God as evil in his statement, "the darts of the Wicked One"?

EUTR.   It is not the same case[122].

20   MEG.   After Isaac had become partially blind[123], the (40) God of Creation did not restore his sight, but our Lord, because he is good, opened the eyes of many blind.

AD.   You are ignorant of What God's purpose was here. The God who gave sons to Abraham in old age, contrary to expectation[124], and who granted Tobit the power of sight[125] — not to prolong the

---

[121] Ephes. 6:13, 16 (small variations from main recensions).

[122] Οὐ ταὐτόν ἐστιν. Bakhuyzen's note is opposite here, when he writes: "The complete demonstration of proof is not really clear. What οὐ ταὐτόν ἐστιν at the end is intended to mean I do not understand. Rufinus' *eadem sunt omnia* signifies, it seems, 'Prophet and Apostle say the same.' Should a question mark stand after ἐστιν? Should οὐ be struck out? has a clause fallen out? I would not attempt a decision".

[123] ὑποχυθέντα. (ὑποχύνω is "cause a cataract"). The Masoretic Text has the verb פָּהָה "be dim", while the LXX uses ἀμβλύνω, "make dim", in Gen. 27:1.

[124] Gen. 21:2.

[125] Tobit 11:8-16. Note the reference to a book of the Jewish Apocrypha as on the same basis as the canonical Scriptures. This is in keeping with the practice of the pre-Nicene Church and many Fathers after Nicaea. It was Jerome (*ca.* 342-420) who introduced the term "apocrypha" for those books which, though in the LXX, were not in the Hebrew Canon. In the West, however, most writers still regarded all the books as equally canonical (cf. J.N.D. Kelly, *Early Christian Doctrines*, London, 1960 edn., pp. 53ff.) At the Reformation, Protestant leaders refused to regard as canonical any books not in the Hebrew Canon. Luther added the Apocryphal books (except 1 and 2 Esdras) to his translation of the Bible in 1534 as "useful and good to be read". The Geneva Bible includes them as valuable for "knowledge of history and instruction of godly manners". The Thirty-nine Articles of the Church of England say that "the Church doth read (them) for example of life and instruction of manners; but yet

discussion by enumerating in detail all His might acts — could have prevented Isaac from becoming partially blind. However, Isaac was about to give Esau his blessing at a time when Rebecca had been told: "The elder shall serve the younger"[126]. **d** In harmony with God's secret purpose for the two peoples, he was partially blinded in order that he might inadvertently bless the younger Jacob — that is, the people of the Catholic[127] Church, who came into being a later period than the Jews[128].

21   MEG.   From the fact that we[129] have been frequently persecuted and are hated, surely it is clear that we belong to another God, and are alien to the God of Creation? It says, "The heart of the King is in the hand of God"[130]. From the circumstance that He holds the hearts of kings in His hands, it is evident that it was the God of Creation Himself who persecuted us.

     AD.   [True, if you could advance this argument with respect to some particular time, it might, perhaps, seem to have a measure of probability — even though there would be a simple explanation. But as matters are, I think you have raised your objection most inappropriately. **e** By your line of reasoning, all rulers whose heart are in the hands of the god who opposes the Good God, and who favour those servants, ought to have persecuted the Christians; it would not be feasible that a later ruler should act in any way differently from an earlier one. However, what we actually do find is a ruler of a former time hating certain people, and a ruler of later period esteeming certain others. Cyrus, for instance, built God's Temple in Jerusalem, which nevertheless other

---

it doth not apply them to establish any doctrine". The Council of Trent (sess. IV, 8 April 1548) confirmed the full canonicity of all these books (except 1 and 2 [i.e., 2 and 4] Esdras and the Prayer of Manasses). The decision of Trent was confirmed by the Vatican Council of 1870 (see A. Wikenhauser, *New Testament Introduction* [trans. J. Cunningham], London, 1958, pp. 18-19). For non-Catholics, the value of the "apocryphal" books came to be increasingly recognized in the nineteenth century and onwards. They help to bridge the gap between the narrative of Ezra-Nehemiah and the opening of the NT, and throw light on customs and beliefs referred to in the NT but which do not appear in the books of the Hebrew canon.

[126] Gen. 25:23.

[127] τῆς καθολικῆς ἐκκλησίας; Rufinus: *ecclesiae populus*.

[128] One of the few instances of figurative or 'allegorical' interpretation found in 'Adamantius'.

[129] ἡμᾶς. Presumably Megethius is seen here referring to Christians generally, rather than merely his own Marcionite party.

[130] Prov. 21:1 (LXX, which is a correct rendering of the Masoretic Text).

kings afterwards destroyed. What are we to conclude then? That one god was with the former king, while the other was with the later ones? That *would* indeed be foolish! Nor is it we Christians alone who suffer persecution. The prophets suffered in the same way, and many of them were slain as martyrs; The Three Children[131] endured martyrdom — although they were wonderfully delivered by the power of God. However, the Maccabees entered fully into martyrdom, with much bloodshed.   817a The prophet also cries, "For Thy sake we are put to death all the day long"[132]. On this account, Paul, too, in the same prophetic voice, said, "For Thy sake we are put to death all the day long"[133]. Similarly, Christ's disciples, following the example of the prophets, bear severe persecution. So the reason for persecution is the same in our case as in that of the prophets][134]. Surely you must be a stranger to the roll[135] of (42) the per-

[131] Dan. 3:13-23.
[132] Ps. 43(44):22. (Heb. better translating "it is for you that we face death all the day long").
[133] Rom. 8:36.
[134] The passage enclosed in angle brackets very largely follows the translation of Rufinus. This is one of the two places where revision has, with reasonable certainty, been made in the interests of an altered chronological situation. Bakhuyzen's comment (*op. cit.*, p. 40, n. 7) runs, "We find the oldest original text in Rufinus. A Greek reviser has altered the Greek text in order to adapt it to the changed conditions of the time (the reign of a Christian emperor)". For purposes of comparison the fuller text of the reply of Adamantius should be noted. In the Greek the words are altered or added by a reviser (in the opinion of Bakhuyzen). The whole passage should be compared with the Latin rendering of Rufinus and translated from the Greek reads:

But now, since the King worships God, why do you say that it is one God who holds the hearts of those kings in earlier days and persecutes, and another God who holds the heart of the present King? This king rules better than and the opposite of those earlier ones. He rebuilt what they destroyed; he loved the people whom they hated, and he destroyed the shrines and idols that they revered.

It will be seen that, besides differences, the reviser made several smaller, but very significant, alterations: πρὸ τούτων τῶν χρόνων ("prior to these days") has been added, along with τοῦ καιροῦ. He also formed from the present tenses διωκόμεθα, διώκονται the past forms ἐδιώχθημεν, ἐδιώκότο, putting persecution into the past].
    The section, with its textual discrepancies as a whole, is obviously very important for the purpose of determining the date of composition of the Dialogue of Adamantius. The Latin of Rufinus at this point makes it clear that the author lived *prior* to the time of Constantine and the cessation of the long days of persecution. It is therefore of great assistance in narrowing down the *ad quem* limit to not later than just before 313 (the time of the legal recognition of Christianity). Cf. *infra*, pt. 5, n. 249.
[135] τοῦ κανόνος. Migne: *regula*. The Greek κανών originally meant a straight rule or measure; then, metaphorically, the rules of a trade, etc. So there developed the idea of a list or catalogue. The Church used the term to denote the list of religious books regarded as inspired Scripture, and so authoritative for faith and doctrine. Cf. Wikenhauser, *op. cit.*, pp. 19f.

secuted prophets and just persons — unaware of apostles, and of the disciples persecuted for Christ![136]

22 EUTR. Now, how does the Apostle use the Prophets? If the Prophets and he speak in similar terms it is evident that he does not regard them as having no weight; on the contrary, he uses them because he believes them to have good and lawful authority.

MEG. He did not explicitly use any of the ancient prophets. That would be impossible.

b AD. I will demonstrate that the Apostle mentions them in many places; that he does not reject, but confirms them. In the first letter to the Corinthians, he says, "So that no flesh may boast before Him. You belong to Him in Christ Jesus, who became for us wisdom and righteousness, holiness and redemption, so that as it stands written, 'Let him who boasts, boast in the Lord'"[137]. In the same letter he brings it out more definitely still, "Who tends a flock, and does not get sustenance from the milk? Surely I do not say these things by human authority, for does not even the law say these things? In the Law of Moses it stands written, **c** 'You shall not muzzle an ox when it is threshing'. Surely God is not concerned for oxen? Rather, does he not certainly speak for our sakes? It was written for our sakes, because the ploughman ought to plough in hope"[138].

MEG. You know that he spoke of the law of Moses, not of God.

EUTR. I know that he spoke of the law of Moses, but he gave it authority when he said, "Surely God is not concerned for oxen? Rather does he not certainly speak for our sakes? It was written for our sakes". You see, he gave it authority and used it believing that it had been properly given. In providing an argument, no one relies on an obsolete or worthless law for proof, but depends on a better, a valid one. **d** Just as you, in your desire to establish your point, used Paul as a witness, so that

---

[136] The tenses and order of words in this Greek sentence show that the author has in mind a succession of persecuted people: first, the Prophets and Righteous Ones of Old Testament times; next the Apostles of New Testament days; last of all, the followers of Christ in his own age.

[137] 1 Cor. 1:29-31; Jer. 9:23.

[138] 1 Cor. 9:7-10; Deut. 25:4.

your statements might be confirmed, so too the Apostle used the law as a witness.

23   MEG.   I will prove from the Scriptures that there is one God who is the Father of Christ, and another who is the Demiurge. The Demiurge was know to Adam and his contemporaries — this is made clear in the Scriptures. But the Father of Christ is unknown, just as Christ Himself declared when he said of Him, "No one knew the Father, except the Son, neither does anyone know (44) the son, except the Father"[139].

AD.   Your knowledge of Scripture is very small if you imagine that this was said only by the Saviour. Listen to Isaiah: **e** "The ox knows its owner, and the ass its master's stall: but Israel does not know me and the people do not understand Me"[140]. Jeremiah also states that of old He was not known: he says, "All shall know Me from the least even to the greatest of them"[141].

MEG.   What then does Ezekiel mean by saying, "I was known to your fathers in the wilderness?"[142]

AD.   Because Ezekiel says "I was known to their fathers", it does not follow forthwith that they themselves knew Him. Even our Lord Jesus Christ, although He lived constantly with the disciples for such a long time, said, "No one knows the Son except the Father". Although he was seen by all, he was not recognized. **f** When He said, "Depart from Me, you that work lawlessness: I never knew you"[143], surely the Knower of hearts recognized them? But they were not living as He desired.   **818a** By "know" he means "understand", as David indicates: "Your father understood not My wonders in the land of Canaan"[144] — and yet they saw them! Nor is "understand" immediately suggested by "see". Plainly, you are found in opposition, not only to the Prophets, but also to the Gospel, for when Christ, who was openly seen by all said, "No one knows the Son", your

---

[139] Matt. 11:27; Lk. 10:22. Megethius uses ἔγνω instead of ἐπιγινώσκει found in the main recensions. He thus follows Clement of Alexandria, Irenaeus, Origen and Eusebius. He also transposes the clauses with the textual authorities X, N, Irenaeus, Eusebius, and others.

[140] Isa. 1:3. In the Masoretic Text of this verse, the verb here rendering "knows" is best regarded as a Perfect of Experience. The Greek translators of the Septuagint therefore correctly render this Hebrew Perfect by a Greek Gnomic Aorist (ἔγνω). This aorist is properly represented in the English translation by "knows".

[141] Jer. 31:34 (LXX 38:34); but Adamantius has γνώσονται for LXX εἰδήσουσιν.

[142] Ezek. 20:5. There are wide variations from the LXX.

[143] Matt. 11:27; 7:23.

[144] Ps. 105 (106):7. With variations from the LXX.

party considers that the Prophets said the opposite. It is clear that both Christ and the Prophets did make reference to the knowledge of God and to man's[145] ignorance.

EUTR.   Obviously, by "know" the Scriptures mean "understand". The Prophet says, "Israel does not know me and the people do not understand Me";   b in like manner, Christ, although he was constantly with the disciples, said, "No one knows the Son except the Father". But it was in their presence that he made the statement, "I never knew you"[146].

24   MEG.   The proof that Christ is not the son of the (46) Just God is very clear to me: The Christ of the law has not yet come. If he had what David announced regarding Him would be coming to fulfilment: "Why were nations insolent, and why did peoples think vain thoughts? The kings of the earth took their stand, and the rulers were gathered together against the Lord, and against His Christ"[147]. Again, "Ask of me, and I will give you nations for your inheritance"[148].   c And following: "Though wilt shepherd them with a rod of iron"[149]. This proves that the Christ who has come is someone else, for neither kings nor Christ who has come is someone else, for neither kings nor rulers were against Him, nor were Gentiles ruled with an iron rod.

AD.   Those who were supposed to rule and govern in Israel, and who had authority to put to death and to spare, all came against Christ. And that they were ruled with a rod of iron is demonstrated by the prophecy of Daniel: "After the gold, the silver and the brass shall arise a kingdom of iron."[150] This has proved to be the Roman power[151],   d by

---

[145] Lit. περὶ γνώσεως θεοῦ καὶ ἀγνωσίας. Rufinus: *de die agnitione pronuntient* ("speaking with respect to the recognition of God").

[146] Matt. 7:23.

[147] Ps. 2:1-2 (LXX).

[148] Ps. 2:8 (LXX).

[149] Ps. 2:9 (LXX). "Shepherd" translates literally as the Greek ποιμανεῖς, but this word is also used figuratively of protecting, ruling, governing. The main recensions reads תִּרְעֵם, from רָעַע, break, dash in pieces. F. Brown, S.R. Driver and C.A. Briggs, *Hebrew and English Lexicon of the Old Testament*, Oxford, 1953 edn., suggest the pointing תִּרְעֵם, thus deriving the word from pasture, tend, graze. This fits the LXX ποιμαίνω more naturally, although the Masoretic pointing is more suitable for the parallelism of the second line of the Hebrew couplet: "Thou shalt break them in piece like a potter's vessel".

[150] Virtually a paraphrase of Dan. 2:39-40.

[151] Here and in what follows we find an interesting early attempt at the interpretation of apocalyptic. Jewish apocalyptic literature came into existence largely between 200 BC and AD 100. The book of Daniel is one of the chief representatives of it in the OT. Coupled with NT apocalyptic, especially the Apocalypse, the Jewish apocalyptic writings had a certain

which those who opposed Christ were ruled. And the Gentiles have been given Him for an inheritance: Concerning this, David says, "O Lord, remember us in favouring They people: visit us in saving Thy nation; [that we may give praise with Thy inheritance"[152]. It is apparent that this is the inheritance of the Gentiles for which He asked][153].

EUTR.   If there had not existed any authority of kings and rulers, how could Christ have been crucified?

25   MEG.   Daniel says, "I saw, and behold, a stone was (48) cut out of a mountain without hands: and it struck the image and made it like a cloud of dust, and it was blown away by the wind"[154].   e The stone was the Kingdom of God, appearing in glory, and the statue was the kingdom on earth. It is proven, then, through the Law and the Prophets, that Christ has not yet come, for if He had there would not be another kingdom on earth, as Daniel declared. That all the kingdoms do exist shows that the Christ announced through the Law and the Prophets has not yet arrived.

AD.   What has been reasonably stated in the Scriptures you want to interpret unreasonably. The Prophets and the Gospel plainly speak of *two* Advents of Christ — the first in humility, and the one after this, in glory.   f Isaiah spoke in this way of the first: "We saw Him, and He had neither beauty nor form. But His form was despised and more abject than the sons of men"[155]. And again: "Behold by Servant, whom I have chosen, My only beloved[156], in whom My soul has been well pleased. He shall not

vogue within the early Church, since most of the very first Christians apparently regarded the Parousia or Second Advent as imminent. In the latter half of the second century, Montanism flourished with its strong emphasis on millenarian and other apocalyptic ideas derived from the book of Daniel, 2 Esdras, Enoch, etc. Some Gnostic-Christian writers also accepted millenarian-apocalyptic concepts, as did more orthodox writers like Justin Martyr, Irenaeus, and Hippolytus of Rome. Origen did much to destroy such views within the Catholic Church, but works like Daniel and the Revelation have continued to have a certain fascination for Christian Biblical scholars right down the centuries. Under the stress of persecution or other forms of suffering both Jews and Christians naturally began to despair of the present Age, and looked for the cataclysmic intervention of God to end the world order and bring in the Messianic Kingdom, or the reign of Christ. [For later identification of the Danielic Kingdom of Iron with Rome, esp. Jerome, *Comment. in Daniel.*, 2, 2, 31/5; 2, 7, 4-7a, and Sulpicius, *Chronica*, 2, 3. Ed.]

[152] Ps. 105:4-5 (LXX) (106, Heb. Bible).

[153] The enclosed words from the Greek are absent from Rufinus, but are probably original, since they arise naturally out of the preceding statement.

[154] Dan. 2:34-35 (LXX Theodotion), with some variations.

[155] Isa. 53:2-3; cf. also 52:14.

[156] Frequently in profane and Biblical Greek ἀγαπητός came to have the signification "only" or "only-beloved". This is its meaning in Gen. 22:2 (the sacrifice of Isaac) and in the Synoptic Gospels. It would appear to be the best translation here.

contend, nor cry out in the streets. The bruised reed He shall not break; and a spent[157] flax He shall not extinguish"[158].   **819a** Further: "Rejoice, O daughter of Jerusalem, greatly; proclaim, O daughter of Sion, Behold your King comes, meek, and mounted upon an ass"[159]. This is just what has been clearly indicated in the Gospel: that He came into Jerusalem, seated upon an ass[160]. It is plain, then, that He comes in glory, and once in humility. The Apostle Paul also knows about His coming in glory, for he says, "With the commandment of God, and with the voice of an archangel, and with the last trumpet, the Lord shall come down from heaven, and the dead shall rise — these first. Then we who are left to His coming, shall be taken up together with them in the clouds to meet Him"[161]. This is similar to what Daniel says: **b** "I saw One like a son of man coming though the clouds."[162] And in the Gospel it says, "As lightning comes out of the east and appears even (50) unto the west: so shall also the coming of the Son of Man be"[163]. His first coming has been very clearly demonstrated — that it was in humility, and the future coming, that it will be in glory[164]. So as,

---

[157] τετυφωμένον as if from τύφω, to smoke, but the form is perfect passive of τυφόω, possibly 'to be crazy', 'demented'; but more likely 'to becloud', 'choke', 'drown', 'stifle'. The perfect passive of τύφω is actually τέθυμμαι. The text of 'Adamantius' used by Anastasius Sinaita (cf., *infra*, n. 164) also has the form τετυφωμένον, showing that the confusion of the two terms occurred fairly early.

[158] This passage seems to be made up of Isa. 42:1-3; Ps. 2:7, and has an echo of Gen. 22:2. Cf. also Isa. 41:9. Did Adamantius here quote from a Greek version differing from the Septuagint?

[159] Zech. 9:9. Cf. Isa. 40:9f., and 62:11.

[160] Matt. 21:7.

[161] 1 Thess. 4:16-17. There are minor variations from the main recensions.

[162] Dan. 7:13 (LXX Theodotion) with variant wording.

[163] Matt. 24:27, but ἡ ἔλευσις for Matthew's ἡ παρουσία. See also Lk. 17:24.

[164] Anastasius Sinaita (died *ca.* AD 700) quotes, rather freely, this section of the Dialogue: "Meg. Daniel says, I saw... [the] future coming, that it will be in glory". (Migne, *Patrol. Graec.* vol. 89, cols. 77ff). Here I render an English translation of this so that it may be compared with my translation of the Dialogue:

> Megethius says, Daniel says, "A stone was cut out without hands, and it struck the statue and made it like chaff, and it was blown away by the wind". It is proven then that Christ has not yet come, for if He had there would not be another kingdom on earth, as Daniel revealed. From the fact that all the kingdoms do exist, it is clear that the Christ announced through the Law and the Prophets has not yet arrived.
>
> From Origen:
>
> But as it seems, you say the Scriptures are to be understood in the literal sense, and not in the spiritual. The Prophets and the Gospel plainly speak of *two* Advents of Christ — the first in humility, and after this, the second, glorious. Isaiah also speaks in this way of the first: "We saw him, and He had neither beauty nor form. But His form was despised and abject beyond the children of men. Behold also My Servant, whom I have chosen for Myself, My only-beloved in whom My soul hath been well pleased. He shall not contend, nor cry out in the streets. The bruised reed he shall not break; and a spent

when He lived on earth, He announced another coming — the one that is to be in glory — probably you and your party deny both comings. You neither acknowledge His first coming nor expect the other! This is because you do not understand the Divine plan.

c 26 MEG. I will offer you exact proof that the Christ of the Law and the Prophets belonged to another: John did not recognize Him[165] (for it would be impossible for the prophet of the God of Creation[166] to be ignorant of his own Christ): "Now when he had heard in prison the works of Christ, he sent his disciples to Him, saying, 'Are You He who is to come, or look we for another?'"[167]

AD. If John had been inquiring about Christ, he would have said, "Are you the Christ?" whereas he asked, "Are You He that is to come, or look we for another?" In fact, it is nonsense to inquire of those who are present, **d** "Are you here?" The man who said, "Behold the Lamb of God, who takes away the sin of the world"[168], was not ignorant of His presence. However, because he was His forerunner, he inquired whether he was to be that in the abode of the dead also[169]. For he knew that He had stated, "I go

flax He shall not extinguish". Zachariah also: "Rejoice, greatly, O daughter of Sion; proclaim, O daughter of Jerusalem, Behold they King comes to thee, meek, and mounted upon an ass". This is just what has been clearly indicated in the Gospel: that He came into Jerusalem seated upon as ass. And Paul also knows His second and glorious coming, for he says, "With the command of God, and with the voice of an archangel, and with the last trumpet, the Lord shall come down from heaven", just as Daniel says, "I saw One like a son of man coming upon the clouds of heaven". And in the Gospel it says, "As lightning cometh out of the east and appeareth even unto the west: so shall also the coming of the Son of Man be". So his first coming has been demonstrated — that it was in humility, and the second, that it will be in glory.
Apart from the attribution of the words of Adamantius to Origen, Anastasius does not appear to have had a text materially different from the critical one produced by Bakhuyzen — at least, so far as this section of the work is concerned.

[165] That is to say, if Jesus had been the Christ predicted in the OT, John the Baptist, as the prophet of the God of Creation, would have recognized in Him the Christ of OT prophecy.

[166] The Greek text has, προφήτην τὸν ἐκ γενέσεως, which is difficult. Bakhuyzen suggests τὸν τοῦ θεοῦ τῆς γενέσεως, τοῦ δημιουργοῦ (which has been adopted for the English translation); Rufinus renders, *Iohannes namque non cognovit eum, quod utique impossibile erat ut propheta legis ignoraret Christum suum.*

[167] Matt. 11:2-3. See also Luke 7:18-19. Mark and BS2, following X, B, D, W. θ, and other authorities, have "sent through (διά) his disciples". The Vulgate, family 13, family 1 and others have "two" disciples.

[168] Jn. 1:29.

[169] Is this interpretation of John's mission a reference to 1 Pet. 3:19-20; 4:6 (Christ's preaching to the "spirits in prison")? If Christ preached to the dead between His death and resurrection, then it might well be concluded that John was His forerunner there also [but this seems a strange rationalization. Ed.]

away, and I will send the Paraclete"[170] — that is, the Holy Spirit. But there is something truer still to be learnt in the incident: John's disciples were accustomed to reading about two comings of Christ, but they were ignorant that he himself was about to depart from the world; so John, when he was handing over his disciples to the Master (for it was right that those who had been made disciples by John should be transferred to Christ), sent the (52) disciples to learn that **e** the Master was the Christ, lest after his death they should slip. "Go you yourselves"[171], he charged them; "listen carefully to learn whether it is He. Take note of Christ's answers". The master had received the disciples, and wishing to given them proof, he proceeded to perform His works, and then said, "the blind see, the deaf hear, and the lame walk, the dead rise again. And blessed is he who does not take offence at Me".[172] So having received them, He began to instruct them through His works, that they might be convinced that he was indeed the Whole Truth.

820a 27   MEG.   So alien are we to the Christ who has appeared, and the Christ who has appeared to the Creator-god, that Paul says, "Christ has redeemed us".[173] It is clear then that He redeemed aliens, for no one ever redeems those who are his own: he redeems aliens, not his own.

AD.   You and your party argue quite illogically. If you could prove your theories, well and good, but if you are hunting for an argument not yet refuted, then your reasoning is irreverent. You said that Christ is the one who bought: who is he who sold? You must have yielded to the silly fiction that buyer and seller are brothers! If the Devil who is evil, sold to the Good Christ, he is not evil, but good: **b** he who was jealous of humanity from

---

[170] Jn. 16:7; 14:16.

[171] For purposes of comparison, the preceding part of the speech of Adamantius is here given in the rendering of Rufinus: "If John were inquiring about Christ, he would surely have said, 'Art Thou Christ?' But now he says, 'Art Thou He who is to come?' It is certainly not sensible to say to someone present, 'Art Thou here?' He had already said of Him, 'Behold the Lamb of God who takes away the sins of the world!' Well then, he was not ignorant that He existed, but since he had been His forerunner, he asked if he was also to precede Him to the place of the dead. He knew, for instance, that He had said to His disciples, 'I go away, and I will send another Paraclete to you' — referring to the Holy Spirit. Moreover, this question implies also a further point: the disciples of John were not, in fact, ignorant of the two advents of Christ, but they did not know who he might be who should accomplish them both. Therefore, when he was leaving this world, John sent them to the Lord, like a servant handing over what belongs to him. In this way, John hoped to stifle their doubts and strengthen them. Once they recognized in the Lord Christ Him who had not only come, but is still to come, they could not go astray, like sheep wandering in the day time from the true Shepherd. So John said to them, 'Do you go yourselves...'"

[172] Matt. 11:5-6; Lk. 7:22-23. (somewhat abbreviated).

[173] Gal. 3:13.

the beginning is now no longer moved by jealousy, for he has handed over his possession to the Good Christ. In point of fact, he will be just,[174] because he has given up jealousy and all evil.[175] [But even if you say that it was not the Devil who sold, but the Creator God — whom, however, you claim to be just — what better justice will be shown here, if He sold those whom He had Himself made to someone else? For if those who were being sold were good, He who, for ransom money, causes good servants to become the property of others is unjust. But if, actually, He sold bad servants, He will still be unjust, because, for ransom money, He causes his own bad servant to become the bad servant of someone else!][176] The case is rather that men had sinned, and (54) had alienated themselves through their sins, but they were redeemed through God's mercy. The Prophet says this: "You were sold for your iniquities: and for wicked deeds have I put your mother away".[177] Take another Prophet:[178] "You were sold without payment, and you will be redeemed without money". The words *without money* clearly indicate that the redemption was to be through the blood of Christ. c The prophet actually asserts this: "He was wounded because of our sins: by His bruises we were healed".[179] It is fair to say, with you, that he bought, for He gave His own blood; but how, then, did He rise from the dead? If he who received mankind's ransom price returned the blood, it can no longer be said that he sold mankind; but if he did not return it, how could Christ have arisen?[180] By this reasoning Christ's statement is no

[174] This argument is very similar to that used on 805b/3, with which it should be compared.
[175] Following this conclusion there is, in the Greek, "Hence God Himself is found to be the seller!" (αὐτὸς γοῦν ὁ θεὸς εὑρίσκεται πωλήσας). Of this sentence, Bakhuyzen (*op. cit.*, p. 52) says, "I question the correctness of these words. There are two possibilities: that the Devil sold the sinners to Christ, and that the Demiurge did it. We read this also in Rufinus. That 'God Himself' sold them is, in my opinion, inconceivable. It occurs to me that these words are the remains of a lost sentence which had run approximately as the Latin translation".
[176] The passage enclosed is that from Rufinus which Bakhuyzen considers to preserve the original lost sentence in the Greek (see *supra*, n. 175).
[177] Isa. 50:1 (LXX). Adamantius omits ὑμῶν after ἀνομίας.
[178] Although this quotation is from the same book (Isa. 52:3), the author of the Dialogue takes it to come from another prophet, otherwise, as Bakhuyzen points out, he would have written something like καὶ πάλιν. Instead, he puts καὶ ἄλλος πάλιν. This is what Rufinus must have read, for he translates, *Et iterum alius propheta dicit.*
[179] Isa. 53:5 (LXX).
[180] As already indicated (e.g., in Introduction, sect. C, 4), Rufinus is less free in his translation of this Dialogue than in some other writings. However, the following, representing the Latin of the Greek text rendered in English, "It is fair to say ... Christ have arisen?" is an instance of his general method: "Because if you think that He did not, as it were, give His blood for the remission of sins, but in place of a ransom price, and that He did not offer His life for His sheep — suppose that he who received His blood or His life did actually return

longer valid: "I have power to lay it down; and I have power to take it up again".[181] In any case, the Devil holds the blood of Christ instead of mankind's ransom price. What blasphemous folly! The wickedness of it! He arose because He had the power; He *took up again* that which *He laid down*. What sort of "sale" was this? It is contrary to what the Prophet says, d "Let God arise, and let His enemies be scattered!"[182] Where there is a resurrection, there must also be a death.

EUTR.   I think He bought from some other person. But whoever buys what already belongs to him? Explain this, please.

AD.   Christ Himself agrees with the Prophet. He states, "Whoever commits sin is the servant of sin".[183]

MEG.   Did He buy from sin?   (56)

EUTR.   It is obvious that Christ spoke of sin as "lord", and that He "redeemed" — since (straining language to His purpose) He stated that He "bought".[184]

MEG.   He did not say that sin is "lord".

EUTR.   What lack of understanding! By using the words, "Whoever commits sin is the servant of sin", did he not clearly show it?

e   AD.   The Apostle explains the matter very well: "When you were the servants of sin, you were free men in respect of righteousness".[185] [And he says still more clearly, "For sin shall no longer have lordship over us"].[186] [How could sin be called "lord" if he who is being dominated had not submitted?][187]

EUTR.   This point has been fully clarified.

---

it: it would not be a recognized sale. And suppose he did not return it, but retained His blood or His life, how could Christ have risen from the dead?"

[181] Jn. 10:18.

[182] Ps. 67:2 (LXX) (MT, 68:2).

[183] Jn. 8:34; The words τῆς ἁμαρτίας are omitted by D, b, syr(s) Clement A, Cyprian. The BS3 places them in square brackets.

[184] A difficult passage: Δῆλον ὅτι τὴν ἁμαρτίαν κύριον ὠνόμασε καὶ ἐλυτρώσατο, καταχρηστικῶς εἰπὼν ἠγορακέναι. Migne translates, *perspicuum est, eum peccatum Dominum appellasse, et 'redemit', improprie 'emisse' dixit*. Rufinus is no help here. He has something quite different.

[185] Rom. 6:20.

[186] Rom. 6:14. Adamantius has ἡμῶν for ὑμῶν of the main recensions, and οὐκέτι with Marcion X*, and others, for οὐ in the main recensions. The quotation in brackets is absent from the Greek text, but is found in Rufinus, and considered probably genuine by Bakhuyzen.

[187] This second enclosed passage is not in the Latin. Its authenticity is uncertain.

28   MEG.[188]   Christ distinctly says, "No man can serve two masters".[189] Why do you becloud the issue by dragging in irrelevant matters?

AD.   How many "masters" do you think Christ spoke of?

821a MEG.   Just what the Gospel says, "An unsound tree cannot bear
good fruit, neither can a sound tree bear bad fruit".[190] The two masters are
disclosed. You see two natures; two masters.

AD.   Why did you not follow on by giving *all* that Christ said, instead
of picking out and reading only what you think suits your purpose? I will now
read what is actually written: Christ states, "No man can serve two masters. For
either he will hate the one, and love the other; or he will be attached to the one
and despise the other. You cannot serve God and Mammon".[191]

EUTR.   What Mammon does He refer to?

AD.   Wealth-money. This additional[192] passage will (58) convince
you: "By whom each man is overcome,   **b** of him also he is the slave".[193]
Therefore Christ also commands us not to cling to wealth, nor to becoming a slave of mammon, but to rely upon God alone, for, "Whoever commits sin is the servant of sin".[194]

EUTR.   If Megethius insists that mammon is a separate species of
Nature[195] and separate principle — that is, wealth — there will no longer

---

[188] It is difficult to see the exact relevance of this new section. At this point, Bakhuyzen
(*op. cit.*, p. 56) remarks, 'As often, the reasoning is suddenly interrupted, and a new argument
is quite abruptly introduced. Megethius quotes Matthew 6:24 in order to convince his opponent that there are several Principles (ἀρχαί). But what he intends by τί ἕτερα ἀντ 'ἄλλων
εἰσάγετε. [Why do you becloud the issue by dragging in irrelevant matters?] does not clearly
follow from what has preceded. On the other hand, all would be clear if we could allot these
words to Adamantius. He has listened to Megethius' new argument, and replies, "Why do
you confuse the issues and bring in evidence that has nothing to do with the matter? Tell me,
How many masters..." We then read, "Meg. Christ distinctly says, 'No man can serve two
masters.'" "Ad. Why do you becloud the issue by dragging in irrelevant matters? How many
masters do you think Christ spoke of?" If this is right, the mistake must have been already
old, since Rufinus' translation agrees with our Greek MSS.

[189] Matt. 6:24. (some authorities add οἰκέτης with Lk. 16:13).

[190] Matt. 7:18; Lk. 6:43.

[191] Matt. 6:24. *Mammon*.: Greek: μαμωνᾶς, wealth, property, from the Aramaic מָמוֹה
riches, gain; but here personified. For 'ανθέξεται, I read "will be attached to, devoted to".

[192] ἔξωθεν, external, outside of, i.e., "outside of what has already been given and
required", or, "outside of Marcion's *Apostolicon*"?

[193] 2 Pet. 2:19 (Adamantius has ἕκαστος for τις of modern rescensions).

[194] Jn. 8:34. (NEB: "Everyone who commits sin is a slave").

[195] φύσιν. Φύσις: Nature. In Philosophy: elementary substance, principle of growth in the
universe; nature as an originating power. As a concrete term: creature, kind, sort, species.

be two or three principles, but very many. The sun will have its own separate nature and principle; likewise the moon and stairs; air and water. So how can you claim that wealth is a separate nature and principle?

c   MEG.   It was not I who said it, but Christ: "An unsound three cannot bear good fruit, neither can a sound tree bear bad fruit".

AD.   The main emphasis in this passage is not on "natures" but "men"; if Christ had been speaking of natures, He would not have used the term "fruit".

MEG.   ..., for it is impossible for nature to be changed.[196]

AD.   However, I am going to show from the Gospel that Christ is speaking of men possessing free will, and not of principles! He says this, "They come to you in the sheep's clothing, but inwardly they are ravening wolves. By their fruits you shall know them". And again He says "A good man out of the good treasure produces that which is evil. For out of the abundance of the heart the mouth speaks. For from the heart proceed evil thoughts".[197] You see, the Saviour says that from the one human nature both good and evil are brought forth.

MEG.   He does not say this about human beings.

EUTR.   What kind of proof, clearer than this are you (60) looking for?

AD.   You claim, Megethius, that natures are unchangeable.[198] But it reads in the Gospel... "of stones to raise up children to Abraham".[199] The

[196] I translate following a reconstructed text suggested by Bakhuyzen. The main difficulty in the *textus receptus* is with the words ἀδύνατον γὰρ φησι μεταβληθῆναι, where φησι seems to be a corruption of φύσιν. Further, in the light of what Adamantius says a little later ("You see, the Saviour says that from the one human nature both good and evil are brought forth") that it is hard to believe that the author of the Dialogue would make Adamantius state: "It is impossible for nature to be changed". Our oldest MS (B, Venetus) in place of the difficult words above has μεταβληθῆναι· Ἀδαμάντιος ἔτι δείκνυμι... Guided by this, Bakhuyzen reached his conjectural text. However, because Rufinus seems to have had the traditional Greek text before him, Bakhuyzen did not feel at liberty to alter it for his edition. The received text as it stands reads, "Ad. The main emphasis in this passage is not on 'natures' but 'men'; if Christ had been speaking of natures, he would not have used the term 'fruit'. For he [Megethius?] says that it is impossible for it to be changed. However, I am going to show from the Gospel..."

[197] Matt. 7:15-16; Lk. 6:45; Matt. 15:19.

[198] In our text it has been nowhere stated that Megethius had spoken thus. Here we have one of the factors giving credence to Bakhuyzen's emendation adopted in the English translation, for without such alteration Adamantius is charging Megethius with a statement he did not make.

[199] Matt. 3:9.

Apostle Paul also writes, "me, who before was a blasphemer, a persecutor and an insolent man".[200]   e ,What kind of "tree" was he, good or bad? Answer please!

MEG.   I am not inquiring about Paul.

AD.   He was a persecutor at first; after this, he became an apostle. How was it then that the "bad tree" became "good", if a bad tree cannot bring forth good fruit? Moreover, what kind of "tree" was Judas at first?[201]

---

[200] 1 Tim. 1:13.

[201] This is the conclusion of the first debate — that with Megethius. The Latin of Rufinus has a stage note (no part of the original Greek text): "At this point the audience expressed its disagreement with Megethius. Vanquished and confused he temporarily retired from the scene". The second book in Rufinus immediately follows.

SECOND PART[1]

822a 1 MARCUS (a Marcionite): I maintain that there are not three Principles, but two[2] — Good and Evil.

ADAMANTIUS. Are the two Principles self-originate and without beginning, or did none have a beginning of existence, while the other did not?

MK. Both are self-originate and without beginning.

AD. Are the two Principles finite or infinite?

MK. Infinite.

AD. Then the Good and the Evil Principles extend out on every side (for the infinite must be everywhere)?

MK. The Good and the Evil Principles are on all sides.(62)

AD. Well, then, they are intertwined and adhere to one another.

MK. They are not intertwined, nor do they adhere to one another.

AD. But that which stands apart from something is not everywhere. So how can two infinitely great things exist, and yet be separated from each other? We find that things separated one from the other necessarily have an end. Where there is an end, there is also a beginning; and

---

[1] [Rufinus has broken his translation into five parts, whereas the Greek MSS remain undivided. The translation following has been broken up into five parts following the Latin text. Ed.]

[2] Marcus is definitely said in the Greek text to be a Marcionite. As he stands for two ruling principles, not three (like Megethius), he may in this respect represent his master more faithfully. Yet he also would seem to have deviated from Marcion somewhat: Marcus's principles are The Good and The Evil, whereas Marcion himself postulated the Good God and the Inferior God (See Lietzmann, *History of the Early Church, op. cit.,* vol. 1, pp. 251-252, for details, also H.E.W. Turner, *Pattern of Christian Truth, op. cit.,* p.123). It is possible that the author deliberately created this character to indicate that by his time (the end of the third century) the Marcionite movement had developed or split up into a number of sects, each differing from one another, and all deviating from Marcion himself, in some way or another. For the choice of name, see my introduction, A, 3. At the time 'Adamantius' was being composed, most of the Marcionite sects were being absorbed in Manichaeism, although Marcionites were still a force to be reckoned with in the area where the dialogue was probably written (southern Asia Minor or north Syria.)

vice versa. **b** Such things, then, will not be thought of as without beginning or without end. And the area that encloses must needs be greater than the things enclosed.

EUTROPIUS.   If the two Principles exist separated from one another, we shall have to say that God exists in parts. But no right thinking person would believe in a God who exists in parts and has an end. And if Marcus and his party mean that the two Principles pass though one another, one of which is good, and the other evil, needs must be that the Evil shares with the Good, and the Good with the Evil.

2   MK.   Each Principle has its own power.

EUTR.   If each has his own power, presumably each has his own created beings; to whom, then, do you say humanity belongs — to the Good Principle or the Evil One?

c   [MK.   To the Evil One][3].

823a   EUTR.   How did the Good Principle seize those who belonged to the Evil One, if they both have equal powers?

MK.   When the Good Principle saw that humankind was about to be condemned by the Evil Principle, He came and rescued them from the condemnation, and also granted remission[4] and forgiveness of sins.

EUTR.   Against whom had mankind sinned?

MK.   Against the Evil Principle.

EUTR.   Who will swallow your old-wives' tale! Can those who have sinned against their own master receive forgiveness of sins from someone else?

3   AD.   Why do you and your party say that one of the Principles is Good, and the other Evil? Are these mere names, or do the Principles show themselves good or evil by the way each acts?

---

[3] This whole line is absent from the Greek MSS. It is added with justification by Bakhuyzen from Rufinus, for the basis of editions by Wettstein and Picus. The context seems to require it.

[4] ἀμνηστίαν ('forgetfulness', 'disregard', 'neglect') the meaning developing so as to signify 'forgetfulness of injury', 'forgiveness', 'reconciliation' (cf. Eng. 'amnesty'). For examples of its use by the Fathers, see G.W.H. Lampe, *A Patristic Lexicon*, Oxford, 1962, s.v.

MK.   By the very way each acts, one is revealed as Good and the other Evil.

AD.   How is that?   (64)

MK.   Because the Good Principle saves, and the Evil One condemns.

AD.   The Good Principle is so called because it saves?

MK.   Exactly, for it belongs to the nature of the Good to save.

AD.   Thus the cause of this Principle's goodness is the Evil One.

MK.   How is that?

b   AD.   Because, if humanity, belonging to the Creator-God[5], had not sinned, the goodness of this Principle would never have appeared. For if no one had sinned, God would not have been called Good; thus the cause of His goodness has been shown to be the condemnation of sinners. In addition, if you say that He is good because He saves, it is clear that He was not good from the beginning.

MK.   God is always good.

AD.   When did he descend to save humankind?

MK.   As it says in the Gospel: in the reign of Tiberius Caesar, at the time of Pilate[6].

AD.   He descended in the six thousandth year after the Creator God had fashioned man[7].   **c** How could He be good, when He had not saved any one for so long a time?

---

[5] Lit. τοῦ δημιουργοῦ [a usage for the God of the OT not only in Marcionite but also other Gnostic literature (e.g., Tripart. Tract., 105), deriving from Plato's *Timaeus* (21A-31A) (yet cf. also LXX Sap. Sol. 10:1; Philo, *Quod Deus.* 31). Ed.]

[6] [An Adoptionist position seems deliberately suggested, because for the orthodox the Incarnation was placed in Augustus' reign, not from the baptism during Tiberius' rule. Note that the Adoptionist controversy was raging at the time the dialogue was written, Paul of Samosata's views being condemned in AD 268. Ed.]

[7] The early Christian Church computed the age of the human race from the Biblical data, as did the Jews. The actual figure reached, however, varied according to whether the Hebrew or the LXX text was accepted for the genealogical tables of Genesis and the figures in Exodus. The main differences (in *cumulative* chronology) are:

	Hebrew	Septuagint (LXX)
Creation to the Flood:	1656	2242
Flood to the birth of Abraham:	1946	3312
Abraham to the Exodus:	2666	3817

MK.   He was always good.

EUTR.   You said, Marcus, that the fact that He saves causes Him to be called good; you have admitted that He descended in the reign of Tiberius Caesar; it is clear then that He gained the title "Good" from the time onward that He saved.

4   AD.   If this God is called good because He saves, the Creator God must also be considered good, for He also saves many, as the Law and the Prophets promise. So both alike save, but to you and your party one God appears good, and the other evil.

d   MK.   The Good God is good to all, but the Creator God promises to save those who obey Him.

AD.   Does the Good God save all — even murderers and adulterers — or only those who believe on Him?

[MK.   He saves those who flee to Him for refuge][8].

EUTR.   If both Gods save those who obey them, and repudiate the unbelieving, what difference is there between the Good and the Evil God? An equal purpose is found in both!

MK.   The Good God saves those who believe in Him, without, however, condemning those who have disobeyed Him, (66) while the Creator God saves those who believe in Him,   e but judges and punishes sinners.

AD.   So, in your view, the Good god judges no one?

MK.   No One.

AD.   If I should prove that the Good God does judge, would you be convinced that God is a Unity, and that there is not another?

MK.   You cannot prove it.

AD.   Would you be convinced by the Apostle?

The Church and the Hellenistic Jews, however, usually worked from the LXX text, and so favoured the longer period. Some writers attributed the difference between the Hebrew and Greek chronology to Jewish error. The Greek computation to the birth of Christ was as much as 5508 years. Abulpharaj (AD 1226-1286) makes it 5586, and gives the disparity between the Jewish and Greek computation as 1375 years (in his *Hist. Dynast.* [p.72]). Augustine ascribed the divergence to the LXX translators themselves under their prophetic urge, while Jerome imputed it simply to the LXX (Augustine: *De Civit. Dei,* 18, 43; 15, 2, 13; Jerome, *Quaest. in Genes.*) The period stated by Adamantius is, of course, a round figure.

[8] This reply by Marcus is not found in Rufinus, but is likely to be original, in view of its suitability for the context.

824a MK.   I would be convinced by *my* Apostolicon[9].

AD.   I have your Apostolicon here, and I read: "God will judge the secrets of men through Jesus Christ, according to my Gospel"[10].

EUTR.   By speaking of judgement, he refers to the judging of both the good and the bad — to the reward merited by the former, and the condemnation of the latter, the evil and the ungodly. It is evident that the judgement to take place according to the Gospel by Jesus Christ, by which also the secrets of men will be exposed, will confer the reward merited by both righteousness and unrighteousness[11].

AD.   Listen to the same Apostle: "I indeed, absent in body but present in spirit, have already judged, as though I were present, him who has so done,   **b** in the name of our Lord Jesus Christ. When you are gathered together along with my spirit, with the power of our Lord Jesus, you are to deliver such a one to Satan for destruction"[12]. And he says again, "He who troubles you shall bear the judgement"[13]. From whom will be the troubler of the Church bear the judgement? Let Marcus answer: Will it be from the Good God or from the Evil One? If it is from the Evil One, both Christ and the Apostle will be shown to belong to the Evil One. If, however, judgement comes from the Good God the Good God is revealed as judge. Where, then, do we place the Scripture that says, "For whatever a man sows, that also will he reap?"[14]   **c** Where, pray, do we set the Saviour's declaration, "The measure you give will be the measure you get"[15]: and "Whoever denies Me before men, him will I also deny before My Father who is in (68) heaven"[16]. Also, "I came not to bring peace but a sword"[17]. This too: "I came not to bring peace but fire"[18]: and this: "Woe to you scribes"?[19] Take, again, the Apostle: "Seeing it is a just thing with the Lord to repay tribulation to those who afflict you: and to you who are afflicted,

---

[9]   Marcion's Gospel (Evangelium) was an "edited" copy of Luke with the "Judaizing interpolations" removed and the "corrupted" passages, plus ten epistles of Paul (cf. p. 42, n. 29).
[10]   Rom. 2:16.
[11]   Or, (punctuating differently) "the judgement ... by which also the secrets of men will be exposed according to their merit, will confer the reward of both righteous and unrighteous."
[12]   I Cor. 5:3-5.
[13]   Gal. 5:10.
[14]   Gal. 6:7.
[15]   Matt. 7:2.
[16]   Matt. 10:33.
[17]   Matt. 10:34.
[18]   Lk. 12:49, but there the wording is, "I am come to cast fire on the earth".
[19]   Matt. 23:13ff.

rest"[20]. Who then is the One who repays the tribulation?   **d** let Marcus answer, please!

MK.   The Evil One.

EUTR.   If the Evil One gives the tribulation, it is obvious that he also provides the rest [for the tribulation.][21] So since we receive from him both the tribulation and the rest, what need do we have of another God? It has been clearly demonstrated that God is a unity, and that He is Judge. It is therefore needless to take account of empty tales!

6   MEG[22].   *I* will explain this statement of the Apostle more clearly: "Seeing it is a just thing with God to repay tribulation to those who afflict you: and to you who are afflicted, rest": You must remember that I postulated *three* Principles: Good, Intermediate[23] and Evil. Now then, the Intermediate Principle, when it obeys the Good Principle, gives rest, **e** but when it obeys the Evil One, gives tribulation.

AD.   So the Intermediate Principle is servant to both the Good and the Evil Principle; it has no power of its own, because it is subject to both the others. Presumably it does nothing by its own inclination, but only what the Good or the Evil Principle desires. Please tell us then, by whose will the Intermediate Principle created mankind.

MEG.   He created mankind by His own will: "I regret," He said, "that I made Man"[24]. He repented then of making bad people, and wanted to condemn and destroy them. However, the Good Principle did not permit it, **f** but had mercy on the human race.

---

[20] 2 Thess. 1:6-7.

[21] These enclosed words are not given by Rufinus, but he often omits in this way. We cannot be certain of their genuineness, however.

[22] Although already defeated in his own particular debate, Megethius again joins in. In the Greek text, after his name, the words "The first" stand written; the Latin translation has "Again joining in, Megethius says". As Bakhuyzen suggests, the words in the Greek were placed there, either by the author himself, or by a copyist, to indicate that this is the same Megethius as appeared first in the Dialgoue.

[23] μέσην. As Megethius admits further on, this is the Demiurge, or Creator-God. His explanation of the Three Principle teaching is additional proof that he has developed his own views beyond Marcion's dualism.

[24] Gen. 6:6: but a paraphrase. LXX: lit. "And God took it to heart" (ἐνεθυμήθη) that He had made Man upon the earth, and He gave it thought. And God said, I will wipe humans, whom I have made, from the face of the earth ... because I am angry that I made them". The possibility must not be overlooked that Adamantius is quoting from a different Greek version than the one known to us.

EUTR.   This refusal to permit the destruction of what is bad does not belong to a good God. When the Creator God planned to destroy it, the Good God had mercy on the bad! Thus the Good God will be the author of evil. But we claim God to be good (70) who destroys what is bad. He who does not desire the bad to exist is better by far than he who wants 825a to keep and save it.

MEG.   Although they were bad, the Good God rescued humankind from the Evil One, and then changed and made good those who had believed in Him[25].

7   AD.   Since you claim that the Good God rescued and changed mankind into goodness, tell us, then, what it was the Good God came to save: soul and body, or only the soul?

MEG.   Only the soul.

AD.   Does the soul belong to the Good God, or to the Creator God?

MEG.   The soul is a breath[26] of the Creator God; so when He had created it, He saw that it was evil and disobedient, and cast it out. But the Evil One noticed the soul cast out, and brought it back to himself. However, the Good God had mercy   b   and rescued the soul from the Evil One[27].

AD.   After He had rescued the soul from the Evil One, did the Good God give it to the Creator God, or retain it himself?

[MEG. He retained it.][28]

---

[25] In this passage, and in two others (p. 80, "The Good God saves those who believe in Him"; and p. 104, "The Good God is the Father of those who believe"), the ideas of Megethius and Marcus on saving faith are brought to view. These disciples may not fully represent their master in the matter of Faith any more than they are completely true to him in regard to the number and nature of the ruling Principles. If they do, they represent theological conundra in Marcion worth assessment (see E.C. Blackman, *Marcion and His Influence*, op. cit., pp. 108-9).

[26] ἐμφύσημα; Rufinus: *insufflatio*; Migne *inflatus*. The Greek word comes from ἐμφυσάω, "to breathe into or upon; to inflate," and so the noun is literally "an inbreathing, inflation, infusion, swelling". The verb is used, e.g., in Gen. 2:7 (God "breathed into man the breath of life"); Sap. Sol. 15:11; Jn. 20:22 ("He breathed on them"); 1 Clem. 39:6 (quoting Job 4:21).

[27] This is soteriology with a vengeance! It may represent the teaching of Marcion, but it is more likely that Megethius' view is an extension of his master's doctrine (cf. Harnack, *Marcion, op. cit.*, 1921 edn., pp. 68-135).

[28] The enclosed words are from Rufinus, yet are absent from the Greek MSS. They are very probably correct, since the outburts of Eutropius following seems to imply it.

EUTR.   Oh what great goodness — or rather, godlessness![29] Megethius says the Good God took the soul from the Evil One, so that He might rob the Creator God of His own "Breath"!

AD.   Ask Megethius to demonstrate how it was that the Creator God cast the soul out and condemned it.

MEG.   When man ate of the tree from which the Creator God had commanded him not to eat, then the soul fell under judgement, condemnation and destruction.

AD.   Please read, Megethius, how the Creator God condemned the soul.

MEG.   Read yourself what is written in Genesis.

c   AD.   I will read the decree of the Creator God, which shows what it is that was condemned, the soul or the body. He speaks in this way, "Because you have harkened to your wife, and have eaten of the tree concerning which I commanded that from this tree only you were not to eat — since you have eaten from it, cursed is the earth in your labours: with sorrow you shall eat of it all the days of your life. thorns and thistles shall it (72) bring forth to you; and you shall eat the grass of the field. By the sweat of your brow you shall eat your bread   d till I return you to the earth out of which you were taken: for earth you are, and unto earth shall you return"[30]. Is this decree a condemnation of the soul or the body?

EUTR.   The decree shows a condemnation of the body and not the soul, for it says, "Until you shall return to the earth out of which you were taken: for earth you are, and unto earth shall you return".

AD.   What the Creator God condemned, this, Megethius says, the Good God saved!

MEG.   He put a curse upon him: surely this was condemning him?

AD.   He did not curse man, but the ground. That is what it says: "cursed is the earth in your labours".

MEG.   So then, man did not come from the ground?

---

[29] There is a play on words here. The adjudicator exclaims, "Oh what great ἀγαθότητος or rather, ἀθεότητος!"
[30] Gen. 3:17-19 (LXX fairly closely).

EUTR. A moment ago you stated that the soul is a part, a "breath" of the Creator God; e now, however, you seem to have forgotten this, and claim that man[31] was taken from the ground.

AD. So the Good God came to save the soul, although it had not been condemned?

EUTR. Therefore, if the body was condemned, yet according to Megethius and his party, it was not this that was to be saved, but the "breath" of him who condemned — that is, as they say, the soul — it is evident that He saved that which came from God and was part of Him, but gave no assistance at all to that which had been condemned and came from the ground!

8   MK. Your argument seems to have been well stated against Megethius, but it is no proof against *our* teaching. We do not speak of either "body" or "soul", but of "spirit", in harmony with what the Apostle says, "I have delivered such a one over to the destruction of the flesh, in order that the spirit may be saved"[32].

f   AD. The spirit of Man: does it come from the Creator God or from the Good God?

MK. From the Good God.

AD. In that case, the Creator God and the Good God created man together.

MK. How is that?

826a AD. You said that the soul and the body come from the Creator God, but the spirit from the Good God, did you not?

MK. When the Creator God formed man and breathed into him, he could not bring him to perfection; but the Good God (74) above saw the figure turning about and palpitating: He therefore sent some of His own spirit and gave man life. This, then, is the spirit that *we* claim is saved.

AD. Do all humans have some of this spirit, or only those who believe in the Good God?

---

[31] αὐτόν. That is, τὸν ἄνθρωπον. In the margin of MS "C" stands τάχα αὐτήν, i.e., τὴν ψυχήν.

[32] I Cor. 5:5 (παρέδωκα for παραδοῦναι of the main rescensions).

MK.   He comes at the giving of thanks[33].

AD.   How is it then that you asserted that He had come down for humankind's salvation? Now, it appears, He no longer came to save Man, but His own spirit; now, the spirit of the Good God needs salvation!   **b** What shameless presumption! Was the spirit of the Good God condemned by the Creator God along with man?

[MK. No.

AD.   Then He came to save that which had not been condemned?

EUTR.   Either the spirit sent from the Good God was condemned along with man][34], and it is better to obey the Creator God because he is more powerful (for he who is strong enough to condemn the spirit of the Good God will the more certainly condemn the human beings made by himself, because they are not obedient to him); or the spirit was not condemned, and it is absurd to declare that the Good God came for humanity's salvation.

c 9   MEG.   The Good God, when He saw that the soul had been condemned, had mercy and came, but the Creator God decided to plot against Him, hence he resolved to crucify Him.

AD.   Did He choose Himself to die for the salvation of mankind, or was He compelled by someone else?

MEG.   When the Creator God saw that the Good God was annulling his law, he plotted against Him, not realizing that the death of the Good God would be the salvation of humankind[35].

AD.   Did He choose Himself to die for the salvation of mankind, or was He compelled by someone else?

MEG.   He chose it Himself, for He was not injured by death.

AD.   Therefore the Creator God no longer plotted against Him!

---

[33] Ἐπὶ τῆς εὐχαριστίας ἔρχεται. What exactly does Marcus mean by this? Rufinus has *Per eucharistiam venit*. The essential meaning of εὐχαριστία is "thankfulness, gratitude;" then "the rendering of thanks, thanksgiving." Among Christians, it soon came to signify especially "the Lord's Supper, Eucharist." See, e.g., I Cor. 10:16; Didache 9:1, 5; Ignatius: 1 Ephes. 13:1; Phlad., 4; Smyrn., 8:1; 7:1, cf. Justin, *Apol.*, 1, 65; 66; Tertullian, *Adv. Haer.*, 47; Cyprian, *Epis.*, 10. It would seem that Marcus refers to Christian thanksgiving in particular.

[34] [I.e., in Genesis. Ed.] The passage enclosed is absent from Rufinus, but it does not have the appearance of an interpolation, and Bakhuyzen feels that it is genuine.

[35] E. C. Blackman (*op. cit.*, p. 99 and n.) argues that these words (ὁ θάνατος τοῦ ἀγαθοῦ σωτηρία ἀνθρώπων ἐγίνετο) are an example of "modalistic confusion of the Persons of Father and Son," and that the later Marcionites were frequently grouped with Sabellians.

d   EUTR.   Who would be so foolish as to say that what He Himself chose to suffer was plotted? If He Himself chose death, it is absurd to speak of a plot, but if the Creator God (76) compelled Him, then the Creator God himself was the cause of mankind's salvation, and not the Good God.

10   MK.   Our party maintain from the Scriptures that the Christ who has come is not from the Creator God, but from the Good God, for He also abrogated the law of the Creator God.

AD.   From what Scriptures do you propose to prove this?

MK.   From the Gospel and the Apostle, for I do not trust Jewish utterances, which belong to another God.

e   AD.   So if I take my proofs from the Gospel and the Apostle, will you stop speaking blasphemy?

MK.   I do not recognize either Law or Prophets.

AD.   But the Gospel — do you accept that, or not?

MK.   I put faith in that.

AD.   I propose to read and thereby demonstrate that he who does not accept the Law and the Prophets does not accept the Gospel either. Christ says this: "There was a certain rich man   827a who was clothed in purple and fine linen and fared sumptuously every day. Now there was a certain poor man, named Lazarus, who lay at his gate, full of sores, desiring to be filled with what fell from the rich man's table. Moreover, the dogs came and licked his wounds. Now it happened that the poor man died and was carried by the angels into Abraham's bosom. And the rich man also died; and he was buried in Hades. Then, lifting up his eyes when he was in torments, he saw Abraham afar off and Lazarus in his bosom. Calling out, he said, 'Father Abraham, have mercy on me and send Lazarus,   **b** that he may dip the tip of his finger in water to cool my tongue — for I am tormented in this flame'. But Abraham said, 'Son, remember that you received your good things in your lifetime, and Lazarus likewise evil things; but now he is comforted here and you are tormented. Added to all this, between us and you a great chasm has been fixed in order that those here may not be able to pass to you, nor those from there cross over here?' 'Then I beseech you, father, to send him to my (78) father's house for I have there five brothers, that he may warn them, lest they also come into this place of torment'.   **c** He said to him, 'They have Moses and the Prophets. Let them hear them'. But he said 'No, father; but, if someone goes to them from the dead, they will repent!' And he said, 'If they did not heed Moses and the Prophets, neither would they heed anyone though he should rise from the dead'"[36]. Now, who was it who rose from the dead and taught about the Judgement, except Christ alone? As many, then, as did not receive Moses or the Prophets did not receive Him who rose from the dead.

828a 11   MK.   Abraham is said to be in Hades[37], not in the Kingdom of Heaven.

>   **AD.**   Please read that it does not say Abraham was in Hades.

>   **MK.**   The rich man's conversation with him shows where they were.

>   **AD.**   You heard them talking with one another, but did you not hear the great chasm mentioned? The intervening space between heaven and earth he calls a chasm.

---

[36] Lk. 16:19-31. In this extended quotation, there are a number of minor variations from the main recensions, but none that materially affect the sense.

[37] Hades (ᾅδης) was originally the name of the god of the Under-world, hence the Underworld as the place of the dead. By contrast with heaven, it is in the depths, and accessible by gates. Sometimes ᾅδης is personified, and used with θάνατος (death). It is approximately the Greek equivalent of the Hebrew (*Sheol*). The oldest conception is that Sheol is the abode of all the departed — good and bad alike. It is a place beneath the earth, where destruction, forgetfulness and silence reign. All are given the same treatment; all have a bare existence, without joy or experience of God or men (see, e.g., Job 30:23; Num. 16:30, cf. also Job 10:21; Ps. 87: 10-12; 88:48; Isa. 38: 18-19). During the second century, however, the teaching about future retribution and resurrection modified the older concept, and now Sheol was viewed as an intermediate state. A further modification took place when the idea of resurrection was limited to the righteous. שְׁאוֹל was now regarded as the preliminary or permanent dwelling of the wicked. So it came to be virtually equivalent to Gehenna (γέεννα, גֵּיהִנֹּם; lit., "Valley of the sons of Hinnom," a ravine south of Jerusalem. In later Jewish teaching, the last Judgement is to take place there). Gehenna, in the NT, is "hell", while Paradise (παράδεισος) is looked upon as the intermediate abode of the righteous (see Lk. 23:43). The apocalyptic writers (especially Enoch) tended to emphasize the place of Sheol or Hades as the *permanent* habitation of the wicked. However, there was much ambiguity in the use of the terms. E.g., in Enoch 22 the righteous and the unrighteous occupy adjacent areas of happiness and punishment in Sheol. There they all await the judgement. Yet in Enoch 39 the homes of the good are said to be in heaven. This vagueness is noticeable in the passage used by Adamantius from Luke 16. Actually there are two views regarding the nature of Hades as used in this scripture. H.L. Strack and P. Billerbeck (*Kommentar zum Neuen Testament aus Talmud und Midrasch*, München, 1922-1928, vol. 2, s.v.) consider that in this passage Hades means simply the place of the departed, and that Lazarus and the Rich Man are both in Hades, or Sheol, but separated by the "great chasm". On the other hand, such an exegete as J.M. Creed (*The Gospel according to St Luke*, London, 1930, pp. 212f.) thinks that verse 23 suggests the Rich Man only as being "in Hades". In favour of this is the fact that the expression "Abraham's bosom" is not regarded in Jewish literature as a part of Sheol. In any case, Adamantius in our Dialogue clearly does not look upon Abraham as being in Hades or Sheol.

MK.   Can anyone, then, see from the earth to Heaven? That is impossible! It would, however, be possible for someone to lift his eyes and see from earth — or even from Hades — into Heaven, were it not certain that a great space lies between them![38]

AD.   The bodily eyes have been formed to see only things that are very near,   b but the spiritual ones stretch out into the distance, and it is evident that with the body laid aside, the rich man and Abraham see one another with the eyes of the soul. Note how the Gospel says, "Lifting up his eyes," [the rich man "saw Abraham". Without doubt, he who lifts up his eyes][39] naturally lifts them up towards Heaven, and not towards the earth[40].

EUTR.   I think that Christ here brings forward the case of the Rich Man and the Poor Man in order to teach the difference between the just and the unjust. What else would the Kingdom of Heaven be except, very clearly, good? What else would Gehenna[41] and the sentence of condemnation be except bad? This is just what was read in the Gospel; "Son, remember that you received (80) your good things in your lifetime, and Lazarus likewise evil things: but now he is comforted here and you are tormented".   c Obviously he declared that those who do not believe Moses and the Prophets do not believe Him who rose from the dead, either.

12   MK.   We do not accept the Law and Prophets, nor do they come from our God. We do, however, accept the Gospel and the Apostle.

---

[38] The text of Marcus' reply is probably corrupt: Δύναται οὖν τις ἀπὸ τῆς γῆς ἕως οὐρανοῦ ὁρᾶν; ἀδύνατον. ἐπάρας τοὺς ὀφθαλμοὺς αὐτοῦ ἰδεῖν δύναται τις ἀπὸ γῆς, ἢ μᾶλλον ἀπὸ τοῦ ᾅδου εἰς τὸν οὐρανὸν ὁρᾶν. εἰ μὴ δῆλον ὅτι φάραγξ ἦν ἐν μέσῳ αὐτῶν. Rufinus is not much better. Bakhuyzen offers a conjectural emendation (while admitting we cannot get certainty without a better text): Δύναται οὖν τις ἀπὸ τῆς γῆς ἕως οὐρανοῦ ὁρᾶν ἀδύνατον, "ἐπάρας τοὺς ὀφθαλμοὺς αὐτοῦ εἶδεν". εἰ μὴ δύναται τις ἀπὸ γῆς ἢ μᾶλλον ἀπὸ τοῦ ᾅδου, εἰς τὸν οὐρανὸν ὁρᾶν, δῆλον ὅτι φάραγξ ἦν ἐν μέσῳ αὐτῶν. (Can anyone then see from earth to heaven? That is impossible! 'Lifting up his eyes he saw': if no one could see from earth — or even from Hades — into heaven, it is certain that a great space lay between them").

[39] The bracketed words are absent from the Greek, and are inserted from Rufinus. Fitness for context suggests their authenticity. [There is also a probably allusion here to Ps. 121:1. Ed.]

[40] In the critical text of Bakhuyzen, there is a lacuna from the words "*Lifting up his eyes*" to "*towards heaven*". Comparing the Textus receptus with Rufinus, it seems likely that words have fallen out of the Greek. Hence Bakhuyzen's conjectural emendations in n. 38 *supra*. The English translation is an adaptation of this with the addition of the bracketed words from the Latin.

[41] γέεννα. The valley of Hinnom was from very early times used as a place for human sacrifice (cf. 2 Kgs. 16:3; 21:6). Later Jews regarded it as a place specially appointed by God for the punishment of apostates and other great sinners (cf. Ethiop. Enoch 27:2f; 90:26f; 2 Esdras 7:36-38). Thus Gehenna is used in the NT for the place to which the wicked go for torment after the Last Judgement (e.g., Matt. 5:29; 10:28; 18:9; Jas. 3:6.)

AD.　Which Apostle? Christ had many apostles.

MK.　Paul.

AD.　How did you know that Paul is an apostle? If you find his name written in the Gospel, point it out, but if you do not find it written anywhere there, how did you learn that he is an apostle?

d　　MK.　He writes concerning himself, "Paul, an apostle of Jesus Christ"[42].

AD.　No one witnessing about himself is to be trusted. Even Paul himself says, "It is not he who commends himself who is approved"[43]. No one else, nor the Gospel, witnessed to him. How then is it known that he was an apostle?

MK.　How do *your* party know that he was an apostle? It is not written in the Gospels.

AD.　Ask for the Acts of the Apostles and the Epistles to be read. There you will find him borne witness to: first, as "a chosen instrument"[44] acknowledged by Christ; then by the Apostle Peter when he wrote, "according to the wisdom given to　e my brother Paul"[45].

EUTR.　Does your party, Marcus, accept the "Acts of the Apostles and those called Disciples" as genuine, or not?

MK.　*We* do not accept anything beyond the Gospel and the Apostle.

EUTR.　From which apostles do the Acts and Epistles come? I remember that in the Gospel there are twelve and seventy-two of them[46].

AD.　The Acts, Epistles and Gospels are from those who have been recorded in the Gospel. If you wish, I will read how they were sent to preach the Gospel.

EUTR.　Read, please.　　　　　　　　　　　　　　　　　　　(82)

---

[42]　2 Cor. 1:1; Ephes. 1:1; Col. 1:1.

[43]　2 Cor. 10:18. Adamantius has συνιστῶν, with Marcion, ψ, D, pl., etc; Main recensions have συνιστάνων. (Cf. J.H. Moulton and G. Howard, *Grammar of New Testament Greek*, Edinburgh, 1929, vol. 2, p. 205, n. 1, for variation in spelling).

[44]　Acts 9:15.

[45]　2 Pet. 3:15 (rather free).

[46]　See *supra*, sect. 806c-d/I, 5.

AD.   I am reading from the Gospel: "Then, calling together the twelve apostles, He gave them power and authority over all demons and to cure diseases. And He sent them to   **829a** proclaim the kingdom of God and to heal". A little further down it says, "And going out, they went through town after town and village after village, preaching the Gospel and healing everywhere"[47].

EUTR.   How is it, Marcus, that your party do not accept those who were sent out by Christ to preach and proclaim the Gospel, yet you do accept one for whom you offer no proof? Why is it that you disparage Matthew and John, whose names are recorded in Scripture, and whom Christ sent out to preach and proclaim the Gospel, but accept Paul, for whom you have no proof? Surely this is ridiculous? Tell us this at least: Did they proclaim and preach the Gospel or not?

MK.   They proclaim the Gospel.

b   EUTR.   Was their proclamation and preaching of the Gospel recorded or unrecorded?

MK.   It was unrecorded.

EUTR.   It is quite absurd to assert on the one hand that those who were sent out to preach and proclaim the Gospel did so unrecorded, and on the other to claim that Paul, who had not been sent out, taught and was recorded! Presumably then, the apostles used to proclaim salvation only for listeners of their own day, but for those who came afterwards they gave no thought! (For speech that is unrecorded passes away in a little while, because it has not been published.)

13   AD.   Further, how do the party of Marcus know that Christ is the Son of God? Let them answer that, please! If they accepted the Law and the Prophets, which proclaimed Him beforehand, **c** it would be well enough, for these announced that the Word of God would take on human form, be crucified, and save the human race. But if they do not accept those who announce and give proof of Him beforehand, how do they know that Christ Jesus is the Son of God?

EUTR.   How did your party, Marcus, learn that he is the Son of God?

MK.   From the Gospel and the Apostle.

AD.   And yet in the Gospel He does not call Himself Son of God, but Son of Man!

---

[47] Lk. 9:1-2, 6.

MK. In the Gospel, Christ says, "'Who do men say (84) that I, the Son of Man, am?' The disciples said, 'John the Baptist: but some say Elijah, **d** while others claim that one of the prophets of old has arisen'. And He said to them, 'But who do you say?' Simon Peter, answering, said, 'The Christ'"[48].

AD. Because he was a Jew and had been taught in the Law, Peter was expecting the Christ announced by the Law and the Prophets. He had heard about Christ before, and now acknowleged Him as such.

EUTR. Peter did not call Him "Christ" because he had himself given Him that title, nor because Christ was unknown to him, but because he had already heard about Him. But I would like to ask you this question Marcus: Is Peter the one who wrote the Gospel?[49] How is it then that you claimed that the apostles taught without being recorded?

MK. It was not Peter who wrote the Gospel, but Christ.

EUTR. Then it is false what is read in the Gospel, that Christ sent out the Twelve to preach the Gospel. **e** In addition, you have no proof that Paul was an apostle, nor that Christ is called the Son of God. Surely, then, the words spoken by Adamantius must be true: things that had been promised long ago, that had been given acceptance — these things were now expected[50].

14 AD. Marcus claims that Christ was unknown, and had never come into anyone's mind. He says that the Christ who has come is not the One announced by the prophets[51], but the One who was not known to

---

[48] Matt. 16:13-16; Mk. 8:27-29; Lk. 9:18-20.

[49] One is reminded here of the statement of Papias of Hierapolis (*ca.* 130) that Mark was the "interpreter of Peter" (Eusebius, *Hist. eccles.*, 3, 39). In this sense only could Peter be truly said to have written the Gospel; but it is unlikely that the Papias saying is in the minds of the speakers in the Dialogue of Adamantius [and perhaps this apparent neglect of Papias tradition will add fuel to the fire of those who reject it altogether. Ed.].

[50] Bakhuyzen considers that the words "things that had ... now expected," (τὰ πάλαι γὰρ ὑποσχεθέντα καὶ πρὶν ἢ γενέσθαι κηρυσσόμενα καὶ πιστευόμενα ἢν προσδοκώμενα) do not make sense. Admittedly they are difficult yet clearly they refer to the remark of Adamantius previously that Peter had expected the Christ because he had been announced beforehand. Rufinus has, "Things that have been promised of old, or had been announced before they happened, possess a sure faith when they are fulfilled." This seems little better, and implies a somewhat different Greek text.

[51] The Textus Receptus has the words "He says that the Christ ... by the prophets" is ὁδὲ χριστὸς οὐχ οὕτως οὐχ ὁ ὑπὸ τῶν προφητῶν, φησί, κηρυχθείς ἐστιν. Bakhuyzen conjectures that in place of οὐχ οὕτως there was originally ὁ ἐληλυθώς. This has been accepted for the English translation.

anyone. We must first, then, carefully consider the question, in whom we should believe, and whose orders we are to accept. According to Marcus and his party, no one who has fully instructed them bears witness about Him[52], f nor would the Unknown One be worthy of credence if he spoke of Himself, as he Himself said: "If I bear witness about Myself, My testimony is not true"[53]. Nor must credence be given indiscriminately — to anyone at random who speaks on his own behalf — otherwise we should (86) be justified in believing each and all who do this. By the view of Marcus and his party, the Gospel would be thought of[54] as proclaiming an Unknown Word,   830a One neither hoped for nor expected![55] What right has Marcus to say that Christ wrote the Gospel? The Gospel writer did not refer to himself; he refers to Him who he is proclaiming — Jesus Christ. Nor does the writer, after he has come to know Him, proclaim One who is (according to them) unknown. Nowhere among them[56] will it be found that the Saviour taught anyone, "I Christ am unknown".

15   MK.   If Christ and Paul had been sent by the Creator God, they would not have abolished the law and the Prophets.

AD.   In what way do Christ and the Apostle annul them? Let him explain this, please.

b   MK.   He annuls the Law, destroys the punishment and (88) cancels the judgement.

AD.   Well then, since no one will be punished or judged, what need is there to flee from the Creator God, who neither judges nor threatens to punish? How comes it that these words have been repealed, "Woe to that man through whom the cause of stumbling comes"[57], or this, "He who is troubling us shall bear this judgement, whoever he be?"[58]

MK.   He abrogates His commands.

---

[52] The Greek literally translated is, "The things about Him are not borne witness to by anyone who has fully instructed them" (i.e., the party of Marcus?).

[53] Jn. 5:31.

[54] "Would be thought of" (νομισθείη, standing here for the more classical νομισθείη ἄν).

[55] Of this last sentences, Bakhuyzen says, "How these words connect with the preceding ones is not clear". Perhaps the sense is, "If we were to accept evidence about Christ in this haphazard way, and had only His testimony to rely on, then indeed He would be what Marcus and his friends say — virtually unknown!"

[56] αὐτῶν. The plural here refers to Marcus and his fellow Marcionites.

[57] Matt. 18:7.

[58] Gal. 5:10 (Adamantius: ἡμᾶς; Rufinus: nos; main recensions: ὑμᾶς).

AD. It is evident then that Marcus wants things to exist that
are opposed to what has been commanded. But to commit adultery is
opposed to the command, "You shall not commit adultery"; murder
opposes "You shall not murder"; and in the same way, stealing is against
the command not to steal[59]. Presumably, then, the rest of the commandments have been abrogated. But how could it be that Christ abrogated
the Law? Let Marcus explain, please.   c For in the Law it stands written,
[You shall not murder][60]; you shall not commit adultery; you shall not
bear false witness[61]. Let him say, then, which one of these Christ abrogated? Whom does He order to commit adultery — He indeed who had
actually rejected the more lustful look as unchastity? Whom did He
command to kill — he who directed not to resist the evil man? Whom
did the Saviour teach to steal, in order that He might oppose the Law-
maker? These commands of the Saviour are not new, but are from the
Law and the Prophets. The Saviour asserts, "But I say to you not to resist
evil"[62], while the Old Scripture says,   d "Say you to those who hate and
detest you, 'You are our brethren'"[63]. When the Law again said, "do not
steal", the Saviour said, "Sell your possessions, and give to the poor"[64].
But giving to the poor is not new teaching, for it was comanded in the
Old Testament: "Do not refrain from doing good to the needy one
whenever your hand can help"[65]. The Saviour's 'Love your enemies'[66] is
not new, but required in the Prophets: "If your enemy be hungry, give
him to eat: if he thirst, give him to drink"[67]. But why must we prolong
the discussion? It is at least clear that although the Saviour came to fulfil the Law[68], Marcus' people asset that He came to destroy it!

[59] Exod. 20:13-5.
[60] Enclosed words added from Rufinus, where they appear to indicate a Greek original.
[61] Exod. 20:16.
[62] Matt. 5:39 (τῷ πονηρῷ could also be "the evil man").
[63] Isa. 66:5 LXX (ἡμᾶς Rahlfs; ὑμᾶς B,L,Cp). Varying widely from Masoretic Text: אָמְרוּ
אֲחֵיכֶם שֹׂנְאֵיכֶם מְנַדֵּיכֶם לְמַעַן שְׁמִי ("Your brethren who hate you and cast you out on account
of My name have said").
[64] Matt. 19:21.
[65] Prov. 3:27 (LXX for ἐνδεῆ, "the needy one"; the Masoretic Text has, בְּעָלָיו lit., "its
owners"). In this context, presumably "one to whom good is due" (as in RSV). The Jewish
commentators explained this to mean "charity upon which the poor have a claim". This
would seem to be the sense in which the LXX also understood the Hebrew.
[66] Matt. 5:44; Lk. 6:27.
[67] Prov. 25:21 (LXX, but Rahlfs' text has τρέφε, for the ψώμιζε of Adamantius, MS "B"
and Romans 12:20). In speaking of Proverbs as among the Prophets, Adamantius is nearer to
LXX arrangement of OT books than to the Hebrew Canon.
[68] See Matt. 5:17.

MK. The Judaizers[69] wrote this, "I did not come to destroy the Law, but to fulfil it"[70], but Christ did not speak in this way. He says, "I did not come to fulfil the Law but to destroy it"[71].

831a AD. It is like your party's audacity — to reverse (90) this statement, just as you have tampered with others! However, let the Apostle come forward to reprove your dishonesty.

16 MK. The Saviour clearly says, "A new commandment I give to you"[72]. The new one is not the same as the old, for the Saviour says again, "New wine they put into new wineskins, and both are preserved"[73]. The new commandment is not the complement of the old one, for the Saviour says again, "Nobody puts a patch of unshrunk cloth on an old garment"[74]. Neither Christ nor the Apostle is the complement of the Law.

---

[69] οἱ Ἰουδαϊσταί; a group of Jewish Christians who still adhered to the Levitical laws of the Old Testament, believing them to be binding upon all Christians. Among these laws they particularly insisted on the rite of circumscision and the observance of the distinction between clean and unclean meats. It was against such as these that Paul fought one of his hardest battles, as a careful reading of his letters to the Galatians and Corinthians will show. In the context of our Dialogue, the term seems to mean, however, the writers of the Gospels of Matthew, Mark and John (and Luke also until Marcion had 'purified' his text). In Marcion's belief, none of the disciples had really understood the Master's teaching; all of them viewed Him as the Messiah of the OT and God, and the 'Four Gospels' of the Catholic Church were full of Judaizing interpolations. Christ had had to reveal His true Gospel once more — this time to Paul, who alone among the apostles was able to grasp the genuine content of the Christian Faith. There was only one Gospel, after all, and therefore the 'Gospels' accepted by the orthodox Church were 'Judaizing' ones, not to be relied on for conveying the true teaching of the Lord. Paul's writings, along with Marcion's doctored copy of the Lukan Gospel, were the only writings that accurately, and without Jewish interpolation, presented the Master's actual message (see Lietzmann, *op. cit.*, vol. 1, pp. 253-255, and our Dialogue sects. 806c-808c/I, 5-7).

[70] Matt. 5:17. For the variations from main recensions, cf. next note and the Introduction *supra* sect. D, p, iii.

[71] Marcus here reverses the words καταλῦσαι and πληρῶσαι. Is this the result of Marcion's "purging" of 'the OT Gospels' of 'Jewish interpolations', or is Marcus himself responsible? In favour of the latter conclusion is the fact that Marcion himself did not acknowledge the Gospel of Matthew: his only Gospel was a mutilated Luke. It should not be forgotten, however, that "the Marcionite text of the gospel went through many changes" (Lietzmann, *op. cit.*, vol. 1, p. 255), and it is reasonable to suppose that Marcion's disciples might well continue this process for some time after their founder's death.

[72] Jn. 13:34. Intriguingly Marcus again quotes from a Gospel outside Marcion's Luke, as he does further on; cf. the next notes. [This may be an inconsistency created unwittingly, but possibly deliberately — to weaken Marcionite arguments — or it may reflect an attempt by a Marcionite, or one represented in the Dialogue, to adapt to orthodox arguments. These appeals to non-Marcionite texts raise important questions as to how the Dialogue was constructed. Ed.].

[73] Matt. 9:17; Mk. 2:22; Lk. 5:37.

[74] Matt. 9:16.

AD.   Observe as judge, noble Eutropius, how my opponent, hunting after words[75], takes in a wrong sense instructions so clearly laid down! Please request the Gospel to be read,   **b** and it will be revealed what new commandment the Saviour has enjoined.

EUTR.   Let it be read!

AD.   I will read: "A new commandment" He says "I give to you: that you love one another, as the Father has loved you"[76].

EUTR.   It is plain that He designated Love as a new commandment.

AD.   Yet the new command is no stranger to the old one previously existing.

MK.   The old command of the Law belongs to the Creator God, but the new one comes from the Good God, for He says "Nobody puts unshrunk cloth on an old garment".

AD.   How can the new cloth possibly be foreign to the old garment, when it is one and the same substance[77] natural to sheep from which woollens are made?   **c** But even the art of working in wool had to do with one and the same thing, for it makes both the old and the new. But then, even wine is from the same vine that produces both the old and the new. Yet, so that I may the more clearly establish the fact that the Saviour did not enjoin anything unheard of before when He said, "A new commandment I give unto you: That you love one another", let me read what is hidden in the Law: "You shall love the Lord God with your whole mind"[78]; secondly, "Your neighbour as yourself"[79].

MK.   How is it then that the Apostle says, "If anyone is in Christ, he is a new creature; the old things have passed away. Behold, all things have become new?"[80]

---

[75] Δεξιθηρῶν. Θηρεύω is a word used in the hunt, meaning "to hunt after, chase, catch". So in Lk. 11:54; "seeking to catch something from his mouth". Δεξι - θηρέω therefore signifies here, "chasing and hunting after words with which to ensnare Adamantius".

[76] Jn. 13:34; but καθὼς ὁ Πατὴρ ἠγάπησεν for the main recensions' καθὼς ἠγάπησα, perhaps with Jn. 17:23 in mind.

[77] οὐσία is used here: a word to become prominent in the Arian controversy [in fact, its usages in this text are of precursory importance for the Nicene formulations. Ed.]

[78] Deut. 6:5 (LXX: MS A has καρδίας for the διανοίας of MS B [rescriptor] and Adamantius).

[79] Lev. 19:18 (LXX).

[80] 2 Cor. 5:17. Marcus adds τὰ πάντα with Marcion and others.

d   AD.   Please show, Marcus, what new creature He (92) created; what new heaven or earth, and what new human being. Surely you realize that old things renewed are called 'new' although the same substance still exists?

EUTR.   The new things are not different from the old ones in material or kind. The case is like that of a man who should want to remodel one of his vessels that has become old. Using his skill anew, he remoulds and reworks the silver, but would not claim that the new vessel is made out of a piece of material different from that of the old. So what you thought to offer, Marcus, as fresh, new proof, will be found written in the Law, and to assert that there is a God previously unknown who lays down decrees previously unknown is inconceivable.

e 17   AD.   Paul will demonstrate to you very clearly that love is the fulfilling of the Law. With your permission, I now read the passage referring to this: for "'You shall not murder. You shall not commit adultery. You shall not steal.' and, if there be any other commandment, it is comprised[81] in this word: 'You shall love your neighbour as yourself'. Love works no evil to one's neighbour. Love therefore is the fulfilment of Law"[82].

MK.   The word 'comprised' shows that the former law has been annulled.

832a   EUTR.   I have listened to the Apostle speaking of the fulfilling of the Law. If what is lacking is made up, what is already there is not different from what is supplied, but is united with it, and the completed whole[83] will not be different from what was there before.

AD.   The Saviour will more clearly convince you of this in the Gospel. Someone came to Him and asked, "'Good Teacher, what shall I do to inherent eternal life?' And Jesus said, 'Why do you call Me good? None is good except One — God.' And he said, 'I know the commandments, "Do not murder. Do not commit adultery. Do not steal. Do not bear false witness. Honour your father and your mother"'. And he said, 'All these things have I kept from my youth.'   **b** When Jesus had heard this, He said to him: 'One thing you lack: Sell everything you have, and give to the poor; and you will have treasure in heaven'"[84].

---

[81] ἀνακεφαλαιοῦται, with the meaning, "is summed up".

[82] Rom. 13:9-10 (slight variations with main recensions).

[83] ἀνακεφαλαιούμενον, signifying 'is being summed up' that is, 'being brought to a head, embraced, comprehended, included' (see *supra*, n. 81)

[84] Lk. 18:18-22; Matt. 19:16-21; Mk. 10:17-21. For οἶδας of the main recensions, Adamantius has οἶδα, with Marcion.

EUTR. See, Marcus! All the audience is astounded at your incredible proofs! He who came, as you said, to annul (94) the Law, and to lay down decrees previously unknown, stated, "You still lack one thing so that you may receive treasure in heaven?" Therefore the "one thing" is quite clearly revealed as a 'fulfilling' of the others. The Apostle is in complete agreement with this statement when he sets forth "one thing" as the fulfilling of many, that is Love.

c 18   AD. The Apostle regards the Law as a foreshadowing[85] of the Gospel. He says, "now these things happened to them as a type, but they were written for our admonition"[86].

MK.   It is not so written, for it says, "These things happened to them without a type[87], but they were written for our admonition".

866e[88]   EUTR.   What continuity of thought can be preserved (96) by using this expression? There must be a preceding type or example, so that those who see it may be warned. A warning without type or example **867a** would never be offered.

AD.   If, Sir, I may presume on your wisdom, bear with me a little, and hear what the Apostle, whom my opponents have brought foward, really does say. You will then perceive their want of understanding. The wretched Marcion, although he corrupted the statements of the Apostle, did not completely erase them[89], but these people, right up to the present,

[85] πρωτότυπον: an archtetype, original, prototype, and so the first or the earliest type of anything. Also a pattern, model, standard, exemplar. Rufinus: *typum, id est, figuram vel formam.*
[86] 1 Cor. 10:11. For Adamantius' τύπος the main recensions have τυπικῶς. MSS A, D G, and many later MSS have τύποι συν-έβαινον. Vulgate: *in figura*; Rufinus: *in typo*; NEB: "symbolic".
[87] ἀτύπως, "without a type". Our Dialogue is actually the only authority for this reading, which would seem to come from the Marcionite Apostolicon. Cf. the Introduction, sect. D, p, iii. Rufinus has *sine typo.*
[88] At this point, from the words "Eutropius: What continuity" to "had blinded the minds of unbelievers" (sects. 866e — 833b), we have that section of the Dialogue which comes much later in the Greek manuscripts, but which corresponds to the Latin text of Rufinus in this place. Bakhuyzen believes that here, as well as at sects. 816e/I, 21 and 817a/I, 21 (the references to persecution), the Latin gives the more original text. His view is that, at some time after Rufinus completed his translation, but before our available Greek MSS were written, these pages became misplaced. In support of this is the fact that the argument of the Dialogue does run much more smoothly if the Greek text is emended to agree with the Latin. For a full discussion of the matter see Bakhuyzen's notes to his text, *op. cit.*, pp. 94, 110, 236; cf. also his *Einleitung*, sect. 9.
[89] This is interesting as indicating something of Marcion's methods in 'editing' Holy Scripture. Lietzmann, *op. cit.*, vol. 1, p. 256 states that Marcion excised "foreign" passages

remove anything that does not agree with their opinion. So whatever it may be that they do not understand, and have abandoned because it opposes their views — all this I have gathered up (like small grapes left for gleaners) from the apostolic and prophetic utterances, and I will clearly expound it for your understanding. The Apostle speaks thus, "Let the women keep silence in the Church; for permission has not been given them to speak, **b** but to be subordinate, as also the Law[90] says"[91]. Again he says, "This is the third time I am coming to you. By the evidence of two or three witnesses shall every word stand"[92]. In similar manner, here also the Apostle, without question, is seen to follow the Law when he says, "Then shall come into effect the saying that is written, 'Death has been swallowed up in victory. [O death, where is thy victory']"[93]. Let my opponents indicate where this statement is written, except in the Law and the Prophets! When the Apostle says that the word written in the Law[94] will come to pass, does he believe the Law has been abrogated, or that it will be fulfilled? It belongs to things impossible to abrogate the Law and yet to assert that what is written in it will come to pass!   **c** Writing to the Ephesians he says, "Remembering that once you, the Gentiles who are called uncircumcision by that which is called circumcision in the flesh, made by hands; that you were at that time apart from Christ, being aliens from the commonwealth of Israel and strangers to the covenants of promise, having no hope and without God in the world. But now, you, who once were afar off, have been made near by the blood of Christ"[95]. Now what promise does the Apostle here remember, to which those who were without Christ were (98) strangers? What promises did God make — this God who is, according to my oppo-

from Paul's writings "with a high hand amd much self-confidence," and let his imagination "run riot". It is obvious from Adamantius' remark in our text, that we must exercise care here. That Marcion altered and reconstructed is not to be doubted (see Harnack's discussion of Marcion's "Apostolicon" in his *Marcion, op cit.*, Beilage III, pp. 54-62), but Adamantius says that "although he corrupted the statements of the Apostle, he did not completely erase them" (οὐ παντάπασιν ἀπήλειψε). It may well be therefore that Marcion began a process which, seen in moderation in his own hands, became more and more radical in the hands of his followers, and ultimately went far beyond what he had originally intended.

[90] A possible reference to Gen. 3:16.

[91] 1 Cor. 14:34. 'Adamantius' follows Marcion and others in writing ἐπιτέτραπται for ἐπιτρέπεται, and ὑποτάσσεσθαι for ὑποτασσέσθωσαν, thus going against main recensions.

[92] 2 Cor. 13:1 (see Deut. 19:15; 17:6; Num. 35:30).

[93] Bracketed words not in Rufinus, perhaps as a result of homoeoteleuton (repetition of νῖκος). The quotation derives from 1 Cor. 15:54-55; Isa. 25:8; Hosea. 3:14.

[94] Adamantius appears to use the term 'Law' in two ways: (1) referring to whole OT (2) indicating the Pentateuch — called "the Law" (*Torah*) in the Hebrew Canon. See also *supra*, n. 69.

[95] Ephes. 2:11-13 (minor variations from main recensions).

nents, strange and unknown?[96] **d** When did He who had never appeared prior to the time of Tiberius Caesar make a promise? How could He who spoke and promised in former times be unknown to them? The Apostle plainly teaches that those who were strangers to the covenant of Israel were without God[97]. Yet again he says, "For all God's promises are in Him, Yes!"[98] So if the strange God, who has now appeared for the first time, was not known to anyone previously, neither had made any promises, it is evident that He who promised is none other than the Creator God. But I want to establish more positively that Christ was announced by the Law and the Prophets, just as the Saviour Himself claimed concerning John. He said, "This is he of whom it is written, **e** 'Behold I send my messenger before your face, who shall prepare your way before you'!"[99] Since then this promise came through the Prophets, so that the forerunner of the Lord was sent before His face — John, who was to prepare the way of God — can Marcus and his party show someone else before whose face John sent? If someone else came prior to Christ, sent by the Creator God, let them prove it[100], but if no one else appeared except our Lord Jesus Christ alone, and John went before His face, **f** it is apparent that the promise previously given was fulfilled then, and that Christ is from no other God than the Creator, from whom the Law and the Prophets also came. Does not the Apostle very clearly proclaim Christ out of the Law when he tells the Corinthians "that our fathers were all under the cloud; and all passed through the sea, and all were baptized into Moses in the cloud and the **868a** sea; then all ate the same spiritual[101] food; and all drank the same spiritual drink; for they drank from the spiritual rock that followed them; and the rock was Christ?"[102] Who would not marvel at the folly of Marcus' people, who read these things indeed, but do not understand them? And suppose someone should add to (100) this the statement,

---

[96] ἄγνωστος. A favourite word of the Gnostics, who used it to designate the supreme God, distinguished from the Demiurge; or God as the Father of Christ; or Christ Himself. [Yet see also Acts 17:23, cf. E. Norden, *Agnostos Theos*, Leipzig and Berlin, 1913. Ed.].

[97] In the printed editions of the Dialogue, the comma is placed after Ἰσραὴλ, not διδάσκει. The translation is then, "The Apostle plainly teaches those who were strangers to the covenant of Israel that they were without God".

[98] 2 Cor. 1:20. An alternative translation is, "However many are God's promises, in Him they find their 'yes'". NEB: "He is the Yes pronounced upon God's promises, every one of them."

[99] Matt. 11:10; Mal. 3:1. Cf. Lk. 7:27.

[100] But Megethius, the colleague of Marcus, had already denied that the Christ of the Law (and therefore of the Creator-God) had come. See sects. 818b/I, 24 of the translation *supra*.

[101] πνευματικὸν. RSV and NEB render this, "supernatural".

[102] 1 Cor. 10:1-4.

"Christ our Paschal Lamb was sacrificed?"[103] This is the very Paschal lamb decreed by the Creator God!

19[104]   MK.   You have given attention to those words of the Apostle; surely you will heed these too: "The first man, Adam, became a living being, the last, the Lord, a life-producing spirit.   **b** The first man was of the earth, earthly; the second, the Lord was from heaven?"[105]

AD.   Clearly the Apostle shows that both the first man, Adam, and the second, the Lord came from the same God, and not from some other. If it is written, "the first man was from the earth, earthly — Adam, and the second was from heaven — the Lord"; there is no point in fabricating fictitious arguments[106], for what is written here will not be found different from what is written in the Law, and the heaven from which the Lord came is seen to belong to none other God than the Creator.

EUTR.   Does the Good God own the heavens?

MK.   Not the heaven of the Creator God.

EUTR.   He lives, then, close to the Creator God?

c   MK.   The Good God has His own heavens.

EUTR.   So it has been proved that the Good God is also the creator of the heavens.

MK.   The heavens of the Good God are not made with the hands; they are uncreated.

AD.   Then, if they are uncreated, they cannot be described; for what is uncreated cannot be described. In any case, my opponents are laying down the dogma that they came by chance — which is the teaching of Epicurus[107].

---

[103] 1 Cor. 1:7.

[104] From here to the end of the pages misplaced (sect. 833b/II, 21 of the translation) the name Marinus appears in the place of Marcus in many of the MSS, but not in the Latin of Rufinus.

[105] 1 Cor. 15:45, 47. In the two places where the dialogue has 'Lord' (κύριος), the main recensions have 'Adam' and 'man' respectively. In the second case, the dialogue follows Marcion and MSS A, P, etc.

[106] μυθοποιία ('making of fables, composing of fiction').

[107] Epicurus (342-270 BC) taught the materialistic atomism of Democritus (born *ca.* 460 BC), according to which the universe was brought into being by the chance union of atoms or of elementary particles infinitely small. Dionysius of Alexandria (died *ca.* AD 265) in his

MK.   How is that?

EUTR.   The apostle said, "The second was from heaven — the Lord" (according to the textual reading of your party). So inquiry must now be made as to which heaven is meant. If it is that of the Creator God, then Christ is also seen to have come from the Creator God; but if He is from another heaven (as you, Marcus, claim), we must ask if [it is from an uncreated one, and if][108] it is possible for one uncreated thing to have an identity distinct from another uncreated thing[109].

d   AD.   This is probably their view — [but if is an impossible one.][110] Even if Christ did not avail Himself of the heaven of the Creator God, He did at all events use the (102) name. Where did Marcus and his party get the name 'heaven' from? Is it not found clearly in the Law? This is what it says: "And God called the expanse Heaven"[111]. Observe now, this impious audacity, how they have corrupted the Scripture. Wishing to expunge the teaching about the birth of Christ in the flesh, they changed the words, "the second man", and made it read, "the second, the Lord". They do not see that they must either admit the birth of the spiritual Christ also in the flesh, or acknowledge that He came into existence at a later time than Adam.   e When we read, "the first was", and "the second was", what else are we to understand but this, that if Adam was first, and the Lord second, it logically follows that the Lord came into existence at a later time than Adam? [Thus it will be found that, in harmony with their falsification of the Scriptures, and their rejection of Christ's nativity in the flesh, Marcus and his party avow that a spirit, produced previously, came afterwords in a man][112]. Again, writing to the Corinthians, the Apostle says, "For it is

treatise περὶ φύσεως (On Nature) describes the theory of atoms thus: "They say that these atoms, as they are carried along in the void by chance, fall in together with one another because of their disorderly rush, and become mingles together through being of many shapes. They seize hold of one another, and thus produce the world and things in it; and far more — worlds without limit" (*apud* Eusebius, *Praep. Evang.*, 14, 23).

[108] The words "it is from an uncreated one, and if" are in the Latin, but not the Greek text, and have the effect of making the argument somewhat smoother. Bakhuyzen, however, is uncertain as to their genuineness.

[109] Lit.: "If what is uncreated can differ from what is uncreated". Bakhuyzen suggests that in the light of the Latin, the text should be rendered as in our English translation.

[110] Words enclosed not in Rufinus. Their relevance suggests their authenticity, because in sect. 839d/III, 13 *infra*, Eutropius says quite definitely, "Two uncreateds are impossible".

[111] Gen. 1:8.

[112] The bracketed passage is given by Rufinus, but not the Greek MSS. It is extremely corrupt, so that its genuineness cannot but be questioned. Of the argument of Adamantius in this place, Bakhuyzen (*op. cit.*, p. 103) writes, "The reasoning ... is in my opinion as

the God who said 'Let the light shine out of darkness', who has shone in your hearts, to give the light of the knowledge of His glory in the fact of Christ"[113]. Upon careful inquiry as to whom the God is who commanded light to shine out of darkness, to whom He spoke, and when; we shall also discover the God whom the Apostle proclaims, and the origin of the light that was given to us from the face of Christ. **f** If it is the Good God (as Marcus and his party imagine) who is discovered to have said this to someone or ones [although He is 'unknown'][114], it must be shown when, what and to whom He spoke[115]. If He spoke, it is false to claim that He is 'unknown', and has never appeared, nor ever came into anyone's mind. If He used to speak and make promises in former times, He was not unknown, nor did he make His first appearance (as they **869a** claim) when he came down and appeared in Capernaum, during the reign of Tiberius. But if He was not the One who promised the light, but the Creator, it is clear that we who are being enlightened belong to Him, and also Christ, in whose face the light from the Creator shines. In writing to the Ephesians, the Apostle says, "And when he came, He preached (104) peace to you who were far off; and to those who were near. For through Him we both have access by one Spirit to the Father"[116]. From whom were we "far off", and to whom were the Jews "near"? Was it, indeed, the strange and unknown God of whom Marcus and his party speak? And how is it that the Jews were nigh to Him of whom (equally with us) they were ignorant; whom they neither obeyed nor followed, since (according to the Marcus party) **b** they served another god, one who is opposed to the purpose of the Good God? The Apostle goes on, "through Him we both have access to the Father". To what Father? Is it not clearly to Him who has created us? We will offer, furthermore, an incontrovertible statement from the same Apostle, that there is one God of all things, who has created us and all creatures, the only Good God, to whom belong the world and all things: Paul says, "One God, Father of all. [Who is above all, and through all,][117] and

follows, 'While the Marcionites falsify Paul's words, they do not notice that they must either recognize the bodily nativity of Christ, or teach that He was created later than Adam. Since they deny the bodily nativity, only the second part of the dilemma remains'".

[113] 2 Cor. 4:6, with slight variations from the main recensions.

[114] The enclosed words found in the Greek MSS only, and their trustworthiness is doubtful.

[115] The passage "If it is the Good God ... He spoke", is difficult. The rendering adopted is from a conjectural reconstruction of Bakhuyzen. Rufinus has, "If, according to their accounts, the good God said this, it must be shown to whom or when He spoke ..." The translation of ἀναπλάσσω by 'imagine' is parallelled in Justin, Eusebius, etc, see Lampe, *op. cit.*, s.v.

[116] Ephes. 2:17-18.

[117] In the Latin of the quotation, but not in the Greek; its genuineness being uncertain.

in us all"[118]. **c** So the Father of all is God. But who might he be thought to be according to Marcus and his party? The One who, in their view, is the Good God, who did not create any of us, nor made anything at all, or the Creator God? Of whom will be be the Father? It is impossible of us to be children of one from whom we have not sprung! but the Prophet says, "Has not God created us, and is He not the Father of us all?"[119]

MK.   The Good God is the Father of those who believe, for Paul says, "We have been received into adoption"[120].

EUTR.   Look Marcus! The audience are smiling at your ignorant argumentativeness. The Apostle did not say, "One Father of the faithful," but, "of all, and through all, and in us all."

d   MK.   But he did say, "We have been received into adoption"[121]. Who ever adopts his own children?

AD.   Actually he who has seized what belongs to someone else against the owner's will is evil, while he who has given it up is good. That Paul indisputably proclaims the Creator God can be gathered from what he says here, "God has composed the body by giving greater honour to the inferior part"[122]. Now take (106) this still clearer passage. He says, "therefore, let no one boast in men: for everything is yours, whether it be Paul or Cephas, the world, life or death, things present, or things to come, everything is yours; and you are Christ's; and Christ is God's"[123]. This statement from the apostolic discourse will, of necessity, force my opponents to speak the truth, even unwillingly.   **e** To which God do they want Christ to belong? Let them answer, please!

MK.   To the Good God.

---

[118] Ephes. 4:6. ἡμῖν being omitted by the main recensions, with Adamantius following Marcion, D, and some other authorities in inserting it.

[119] Mal. 2:10 (LXX; Adamantius omits εἷς after θεὸς and after πατὴρ).

[120] Gal. 4:5 (Adamantius has ἐλήφθημεν for ἀπολάβωμεν of the main recensions), cf. also Ephes. 1:5.

[121] Adamantius does not, in his following speech, deal directly with the doctrine of general Adoption. He is content to say, in effect, God would accept only what was voluntarily given to Him in adopting humanity, else He would not be good. From this it may be implied, though it is not stated directly, that as adoption is a voluntary arrangement, the good God could not have adopted from the creator God, for the latter would not voluntarily have given up his own. Therefore the good God and the creator God must be one and the same.

[122] 1 Cor. 12:24.

[123] 1 Cor. 3:21-23.

AD.   Well then, we also, who belong to Christ, belong to the Good God, along with our possessions — that is, the world; life and death; and things present and to come.

MK.   The world belongs to the Evil One.

EUTR.   Christ, Paul, Cephas, and life as well, will according to you belong to the Evil One. Plainly, argumentativeness leads to impiety.

20   AD.   I will not hesitate to bring forward yet another statement from the Apostle: He says, "To God be thanks who always causes us triumph in Christ,   f and makes apparent the sweet odour of His knowledge through us in every place. For we are a fragrance of Christ among those who are being saved and among those who are perishing. To the one indeed an odour of death unto death; but to the others a perfume of life unto life"[124]. From whom, therefore, we have all things, also comes — it is clear — the good odour of Christ existing unto life in them that are saved, and odour bringing death in them that perish. Now since the hawkers   **870a** of so much nonsense read these things, how can they be so wicked, attempting to argue that the Good God and Father of Christ is one God, who saves, while the other is the Creator and Master of the world, who judges? For if all things — ourselves, the world, death and life, and all other things — are from one God, and Christ is to some an odour of life, and to others, an odour of death, the imposition of the other God will be needless. How shameless they are, when Paul says, "To me, the least of all saints, was given this favour, to preach among the Gentiles the unsearchable riches   **b** of Christ; and to enable all people to seek what is the plan of the mystery hidden from eternity with God who created all things"[125]. If indeed this was the dispensation or plan of the unsearchable riches of Christ (108) hidden from eternity, and this is the mystery which Paul brings to light and preaches among the Gentiles, it is plain that he who brings to light the dispensation hidden in Him and who says that the unsearchable riches of Christ come from none other than the God who created all things, is an apostle of the Creator of all things. Yes, and it is clear and indisputable that he knew the law and its ordinances, for he says, "Therefore the Law indeed is holy; and the commandment holy, just and good"[126]. **c** And again, "Sin, that it may appear sin working death in me, through that which is good"[127]. Well then,

---

[124] 2 Cor. 2:14-15.
[125] Ephes. 3:8-9.
[126] Rom. 7:12.
[127] Rom. 7:13.

since the commandment in accordance with the Law is good (as it is written), it is evident that He who gave it will, of necessity, also be acknowledged as good, inasmuch as the tree is known by its fruit. Yet again, "circumcision is indeed profitable, if you keep the Law"[128]. If circumsion is profitable to those who keep the Law, it is obvious that it is found to be good for them, for who is so senseless as to deny that profitable things are good? Further, the Rock given through Moses was Christ, as Paul has shown,   d so my opponents either declare that Christ is not good, or they will acknowledge that he who gave the Rock is good. When Paul says, that "the cup of blessing, and the bread which we break, is a sharing in the blood and body of the Lord"[129], does he not, at all events, want it to be understood that he is referring to good things? If not, the partaking of the blood and body of Christ Jesus will be regarded as wrong, and the question, "What fellowship has light with darkness?"[130] will be a futile one. If Marcus and his party read what is written in the Gospel: "looking up to heaven, the Lord gave thanks,"[131] surely they will see that he gave thanks to the Creator? When He took and blessed the bread and cup,   e did He then give thanks and praise another god for what had been made by the Creator God, or did he give praise to Him who had made and supplied them?

MK.   We have learned from the Apostle and the Gospel that the Creator God and what he has created are evil.

AD.   What Christ recognized as good you, Marcus, call evil!

MK.   He does not call the world nor its creatures good. He says, "If you were of this world the world would love its own"[132].

AD.   I will give you the Saviour's own words, as (110) recorded in the Gospel: "Would any of you, if his son should ask for bread, give him a stone?   f [If he should desire a fish, would you give him a serpent?][133] If he should want an egg, would you give him a scorpion? If you then, though you are evil know to given good gifts to you children..."[134]. Since Christ acknowledges the bread, the egg, and the fish,

---

[128] Rom. 2:25.

[129] 1 Cor. 10:16.

[130] 2 Cor. 6:14.

[131] Matt. 14:19; Mk. 6:41; Lk. 9:16 (Adamantius has εὐχαριστεῖ for the εὐλόγησεν of the main recensions).

[132] Jn. 15:19.

[133] Enclosed passage not in Rufinus. But the mention of fish further down seems to imply that it stood in the original just as it stands in the present Greek text.

[134] Matt. 7:9-11; Lk. 11:12-13.

which are products of the Creator God, to be good gifts, most certainly He desires their Maker, through them, to be thought of as good also, for a tree **871a** is known by its fruit. When, again the Saviour says, "The Kingdom of heaven is like a grain of mustard seed", or, "leaven", or, "a drag-net"[135], or to some such things, which are products of the Creator God, and which, the Lord says, the Kingdom of God resembles, let Marcus and his friends ponder what sort of conception they have of the Kingdom of God, if they stigmatize these things as evil! If the grain of mustard seed and the other products are evil (as they claim a product of the evil god is), it is obvious that the Kingdom of Heaven, which resembles them, must be likewise. Then why do we desire it, if it is evil? But if the Kingdom of Heaven is good, the grain of mustard seed, and all the other products that the good Kingdom of God resembles,   **b** must be good, too.

21   MK.   I will produce a clear statement of the Apostle proving that the God of the World is a different God: He says this,   **832c** "With regard to these, the God of this world has blinded the minds of unbelievers[136], that the light should not enlighten them"[137]. Note that he calls the God of this world evil—the God who does not cause the light to shine!

AD.   When a soul has been seized and possessed by (112) evil, it is scarcely willing to lift up its eyes[138], consequently, what the Apostle expresses so well my opponents *will* misunderstand.   **d** What the Apostle said was meant, not to prove the existence of another God, but to refer to unbelievers. His words — which are in the form of an hyperbaton[139] through the preconceived ideas of your sect, but, if you want to know their

---

[135] Matt. 13:31, 33, 47.

[136] With the words "minds of unbelievers" (τὰ νοήματα τῶν ἀπίστων) the end of the pages misplaced in reached. Bakhuyzen points out that after they had strayed, a copyist attempted to join up the following pages with the preceding ones so as to cover the gap. To do this he had to insert the later words to make the connection. Bakhuyzen restored the pages that had wandered, eliminated the copyist's words and alterations, and brought order once again to the reasoning. See also *supra* n. 88.

[137] 2 Cor. 4:4 (with the omission interestingly, of τοῦ εὐαγγελίου τῆς δόξης τοῦ χριστοῦ, ὅς ἐστιν εἰκὼν τοῦ θεοῦ, and also with διαυγάσαι [Marcion, A, 33, *et al.*] for αὐγάσαι of the main recensions.

[138] ἀνανεῦσαι. Ἀνανεύω is used by Athanasius of 'looking up to the truth'; Clement of Alexandria uses it of looking up to the clear sky, or heaven (see Lampe, *op. cit.*, s.v.).

[139] ὑπέρβατον. "To assume *hyperbaton*, i.e., an artificial misplacement of a word (or words) as opposed to natural word order, is a very old exegetical expedient. Plato has Socrates use it (*Protag.*, 343, E) in order to force Simonides the poet to express what Socrates regards as correct. It has been employed in the same way and with scarcely more warrant by NT exegetes" (thus F. W. Blass and A. Debrunner, *Greek Grammar of the New Testament*, (trans. and rev. R. W. Funk), Chicago, 1961, p. 252, sect. 477).

true meaning, listen: The Apostle is to be understood in this way: "With regard to these the God of the unbelievers of this world has blinded their minds". It is the people who do not believe in God who are blinded, [lest, when they do **833a** understand the message, they should treat it with contempt. The Lord says, "The servant who knew and did not shall be severely beaten, but he who knew not and did things worthy of stripes shall be lightly beaten"[140]. So God, wanting to spare them, blinds the minds of unbelievers, and, because He is good, also says, this, "If you will not believe, you shall certainly not understand"[141]. But if you still want to argue the point, listen to these words, which are also from Christ:][142]

MK.   Is it a characteristic of the Good God to cause blindness?

AD.   The Creator God blinds these who come to Him without faith. Now observe how Christ (who, you say, is superior to the Creator)[143] orders unbelievers to be cast out "into the outer darkness, **b** where there will be weeping, and gnashing of teeth"[144]. Again, note how the Apostle, who belongs to the Good God, delivers people to Satan: "I have delivered such a one to Satan for destruction"[145]. Which is better, then: for unbelievers to be made blind, or for them to be cast into the darkness and delivered to Satan?

EUTR.   He who was made blind endured then the brief pain of only one member, yet had all his other members sound; but he who has been cast into the outer darkness, where there is weeping and gnashing of teeth, and he who has been delivered to Satan, endures the injury of all the members at once. **c** So it is better to put up with the injury of a single member, than for the whole body to be delivered to torments.

AD.   Listen to the Saviour Himself in the Gospel: (114) "If your right eye causes you to stumble, take it out and cast it from you, for it is

---

[140] Lk. 12:47-48 (with omissions).

[141] Isa. 7:9 (LXX; but Masoretic Text has, אִם לֹא תַאֲמִינוּ כִּי לֹא תֵאָמֵנוּ: "If you will not hold by it, you will not be held firm"; Vulgate (Six. et Clem.) reads, *Si non credideritis, non permanebitis.*

[142] The enclosed passage ("lest, when ... from Christ:") is not in Rufinus. Its authenticity is not established, but it contributes to the argument, and the practice of Rufinus to abbreviate must not be overlooked. This may be one of many places where he has done this.

[143] ἀγαθώτερον, which can hardly here have reference to moral goodness, for Marcus has already spoken of the Creator-God as evil (See sect. 868b-c/II, 19). The word is best translated 'better than' in the sense of 'superior to'. Ἀγαθώτερος as part of the vernacular speech is not found in the NT, nor the LXX proper (Jud. 11:25; 15:2 have it only in MS B and its satellites), though it later takes on the form we have here as a regular one.

[144] Matt. 22:13; and 8:12.

[145] 1 Cor. 5:5.

better for you that one of your members should perish than that your whole body be cast into hell-fire"[146].

EUTR. [Rising to give his decision, the adjudicator said to the audience:][147] I am convinced that Megethius and Marcus, and their companions, hold the same foolish opinions. **d** The Greek Tragedies are far more plausible than their theory. Megethius has argued for three Principles — the Good, the Just and the Evil, but has failed to do more than use them as mere names, for, on examination, the Evil Principle of which he speaks was found to be more just than the Just Principle, while what he called the Just Principle was shown to be good to a higher degree than the Good Principle. Marcus declared for two Principles — the Good and the Evil, but when his hypothesis was examined, the Evil Principle was seen to be good to a higher degree, and wealthier, than the Good Principle. **e** I consider that the only sound argument is that of Adamantius insisting on One God, Creator, and Maker of all things, who has an Active Word, and a Holy Spirit. He it is who rules over all things, whom nothing can oppose, whose will nothing has withstood, and to whom the Catholic[148] Church, the guardian of sound doctrine, is justly devoted[149]. Would that I might be reckoned a member of her community, for I believe and think as she does!

[146] Matt. 5:29.

[147] The stage note in brackets is found in the Greek only. Rufinus has merely, 'Eutropius said'. The note is not certainly genuine.

[148] By this time ἡ καθολικὴ ἐκκλησία had mostly come to mean 'orthodox' as against the various heterodox or heretical groups. Cf. W. Walker, *History of the Christian Church*, Edinburgh, 1959 edn., p. 57; K. Latourette, *History of Christianity*, London, 1954, p. 130.

[149] Compare with this 'confession' of the heathen adjudicator that of Adamantius (sect. 804c-d/I, 2), and the similar statement of Eutropius at the end of the Dialogue (sect. 871f/V, 28). The phraseology in some places is reminiscent of Dan. 4: 31-32, 34. Taken together the three statements offer a fair sample of a Trinitarian-looking Christian creed as it might have been formulated at the end of the third century.

THIRD PART[1]

834a 1 MARINUS (a follower of Bardesanes)[2]: Please bear with me while I make a brief effort to establish the soundest teaching.

EUTROPIUS. Speak, by all means.

MAR. Simple folk, and those who do not understand the Scriptures, always seek to give them an interpretation different from what is written — contrary to reason. Here, therefore, in the presence of Eutropius, I propose to show whether I and my party understand the teachings of the Scriptures correctly, or you and your party, Adamantius.

ADAMANTIUS. First explain what teaching it is that you are putting foward, and then set out the Faith according to your views, so that the debate may begin without further delay. **b** Were you only to look for the divine teachings out of a love of truth, and not from a love of argument, you would discover that the truth shines brilliantly clear[3]. What then

---

[1] This is the beginning of the third part of the Dialogue as Rufinus divides it in his translation, there being five parts altogether. Bakhuyzen considers, though, that Rufinus himself probably had only one unbroken dialogue before him, for the words *incipit tertius* and similar expressions at the head of the various divisions found in his translation may well derive from mediaeval scribes, or editors. The various manuscripts, translations and editions of the Dialogue of Adamantius all show differences of divisions, most having either 3 or 5 (Migne has five). Examination of contents suggests a division into two parts: Part One with the Marcionites; Part Two with speakers holding Gnostic or similar views (see Introduction, sect. A, 2). This is supported by the fact that the adjudicator rises on only two separate occasions to close the discussion: once just before this point (sect. 833c-e/II, 21) and once at the end of the whole Dialogue (sects. 866e-872a/V, 28).

   In spite of this natural division, it would seem that the author designed his work to be a unity, for (1) there is only one adjudicator for both parts — Eutropius; (2) The book is always designated as διάλογος (Dialogue), never διάλογοι in the plural; (3) There is only one introduction for the whole work; (4) Megethius and and his companions take part as witnesses in the second part; and (5) in his final summing-up Eutropius includes *all* the speakers in his judgment (sect. 866e/V, 28).

[2] Sometimes written Bar Daisan (the Syriac form of his name). For summary of his teaching see our Introduction, A, 2, s.v. Marinus, and H. Lietzmann, *History of the Early Church, op. cit.*, vol. 2, pp. 260-265; H.E.W. Turner, *Pattern of Christian Truth, op. cit.*, pp. 90-94; F. Haase, *Zur Bardesanischen Gnosis (Texte und Untersuchungen zur Geschichte der altchristlichen Literatur 34/4)*, Leipzig, 1910.

[3] The words "Were you only ... brilliantly clear" form a conditional clause in the Greek, with optative in the protasis, and future indicative in the apodosis. The optative is best regarded as potential.

is this (116) doctrine that you say you have found to be the soundest of all? Proceed to answer, please, so that, after testing by both sides, the argument of greater brilliance may plainly appear, like gold by fire.

MAR.   I think it is outrageous for you and your party to say that evil was brought into existence by God, for God is not the cause of evil. Wrong-headed, too, are your assertions that the Word of God assumed human flesh, and that this flesh in which we have been clothed rises from the dead. It has been appropriately called a weight, a tomb, and a chain, because the soul, when it sinned, was enclosed within this body. Thus Paul, the Apostle of Christ, longing to be delivered from the body, says, "Wretched man am I! Who will deliver me from this body of death?"[4] These, then, are the three matters that I would have discussed.

EUTR.   First of all, set out your conception of faith in God, and then these matters will be examined.

MAR.   I, for my part, say that there is One God,   835a as does Adamantius, and I agree that God is a Unity. However, there are three issues in regard to which I and my party are not in agreement with the Catholic Church.

EUTR.   What are they?

MAR.   We deny that God created the Devil; that Christ was born of a woman; and that the body will rise from the dead.

2   AD.   We must take up the discussion at the point where you began. You set out to accuse us of saying that evil was created by God. However, what we do actually claim is that the only evil is to be deprived of what is good[5].

MAR.   Evil most certainly does exist, for the Scripture says that in the beginning the serpent made the suggestion to Eve. Why, everywhere in

---

[4] Rom. 7:24.

[5] The explanation of Evil as the absence of Good is very ancient. Here our Dialogue anticipates the classic Christian defence of this view in Augustine. Thus Augustine's *Enchiridion* 4, 12: "Where there is no privation of the good, there is no evil. Where there is evil, there is a corresponding dimunution of the good"; and also his *Confessions* 7, 12, sect. 18: "Evil, then,... has no substance at all; for if it were a substance, it would be good. For either it would be an incorruptible substance, and so a supreme good, or a corruptible substance, which could not be corrupted unless it were good". Augustine connects this view to the moral will and (as in *Enchiridion* 8, 23) he writes, "The cause of evil is the defection of the will of a being who is mutably good from the Good which is immutable."

the Scriptures the Devil is called Satan, Evil One and Evildoer. How can you say then, "There is no evil". Please explain this.

b   AD.   What is evil?

MAR.   Do you consider murder to be evil?

AD.   Judged by the views you have enunciated, murder is the greatest good of all!

MAR.   How is that?

AD.   You said that the body is the prison of the soul; you also adduced Paul as a witness: "Wretched man am I! Who will deliver from this body of death?" Now murder, that you call (118) an evil, is the separation of the body from the soul[6]; evidently then, murder is good, since it removes the prison-body from the soul. So by your theory, murder is a good, because it liberates the prisoner   **c** and delivers the soul from its burden.

MAR.   The matters I designated — these are the ones I want discussed.

AD.   Do not confuse the matters under debate. What point do you want discussed first?

MAR.   Concerning the Devil.

3   EUTR.   Both of you first define the terms of your argument, please.

AD.   I maintain that there is nothing uncreated, except God alone; everything else whatsoever is created and made.

MAR.   I consider the Devil to be self-existent and self-originated. I also confess two root-causes — Good and Evil[7].

---

[6] Cf. Plato, *Gorgias*, 524b: διάλυσις τῆς ψυχῆς καὶ τοῦ σώματος ("separation of soul and body").

[7] As a follower of Bardesanes, Marinus would hold that evil is "hostility towards God," and that it arose from causes inherent in the world order outside the influence of the will of the Good God, who, of course, was not the creator of the world. Nevertheless, God organized the world, and showed humans how to free themselves from evil by cultivating a good will — one submissive to the Divine Logos. God could not be held responsible for evil; on the contrary, He provided a means by which humans, using the moral powers within their souls, could liberate themselves from the darkness. It is interesting to compare this teaching with that of Manes. As against Bardesanes, who at least recognized light and splendour in the world, the founder of Manichaeism put forward the pessimistic doctrine of an absolute Evil,

EUTR.   You claim, then, that there are two uncreateds — Good and Evil?

d   MAR.   I say, two root-causes.

AD.   You stated that there are two uncreated root-causes; tell me, please, are they changeable, or unchangeable?

MAR.   In what way do you mean?

EUTR.   Can the evil root be changed and become good?

MAR.   No, for it is evil by nature.

EUTR.   Obviously the good root cannot be changed and become evil, either.

MAR.   No, for they are two separate root-causes — good and evil.

4   AD.   As you have laid it down that there are two unchangeable root-causes, please tell us what the nature and the action of each entity[8] are?

MAR.   The nature and the action of the Good produce light, goodness, happiness, mercy,   **836a** piety, justice and whatever else makes for happiness. The nature and the action of the Evil produce darkness, evil, unhappiness, cruelty, impiety, injustice, and whatever else makes for unhappiness.

AD.   Are the things you speak of perceived by the mind or by the physical senses?

MAR.   We must begin by discussing the things perceived by the physical senses.

AD.   The light of the Good, and the darkness of (120) the Evil — do you say that they are perceived by the senses, or by the mind?

MAR.   I am going to speak first of the things which are visible.

---

eternally opposing the absolute Good. Like Bardesanes, Mani believed that there was that in the human which could be liberated, but unlike him he taught that marriage must be avoided at all costs, for to bring children into the world would mean that more souls of light would be imprisoned in human bodies. The debate in the Dialogue of Adamantius in this section has to do with the subject of the origin of evil, but from the point of view of Bardesanes rather than that of Manes (cf. also the summary of the argument of Marinus in my Introduction, sect. A, 2, s.v.).

[8] ἑκάστης οὐσίας; Rufinus: *uniuscuiusque substantiae*.

EUTR.   Are darkness and light, day and night, included in the things visible?

[MAR. Yes.]⁹

AD.   Did the Good and the Evil create the light and the darkness by mutual agreement?

b   MAR.   No, for the Apostle says, "Light has no fellowship with darkness, nor Christ with Beliar"¹⁰.

AD.   How then do the light and the darkness come into harmony?

MAR.   They do not come into harmony at all, nor do they have anything in common with each other.

[AD.]¹¹   Have the light and the darkness a precise number of hours?

MAR.   Light and darkness have twelve hours each.

AD.   If the light and the darkness do not have a common origin, the one cannot succeed the other, unless the darkness were to succed the light, and the light the darkness by the common consent of their creators. Yet one cannot yield to the other when their creators are not in agreement. c But so that I may force my opponent into difficulties even more extreme, 5 let me respectfully request, Sir, permission to explain the matter to you more fully. The very darkness itself will not allow Marinus and his friends to introduce two creators.

EUTR.   How is that?

AD.   If, as they claim, the light and the darkness had twelve hours each, this would show¹² that they both come from the same God. But this is not the case in the present instance, for at the winter solstice, the dark-

---

⁹ Added from Rufinus, as it is implied by the context.

¹⁰ 2 Cor. 6:15 (abbreviated).

¹¹ The name Adamantius is absent in Rufinus, but Bakhuyzen points out that it is in the style of the Dialogue for Adamantius to seduce his opponents through a question to give an answer that must reveal their folly.

¹² In this conditional clause, εἰ δώδεκα ὥρας ἔχει τὸ φῶς, we should expect imperfect indicative in both protasis and apodosis (ἄν in the apodosis already ceasing to be necessary), but as often happens, we have a mixed construction, with the present (ἔχει) in the protasis.

ness lenghtens and has more hours; and again at the summer solstice the light is prolonged, as (122) it takes over from the darkness.

MAR.   Light is from one source, and darkness from another.

EUTR.   If the light and the darkness are not from one and the same creator,   d how can the light give way at all to the darkness, and the darkness to the light? If Evil is the opposite of the Good, and the Good of the Evil, yet no opposition is found between the light and the darkness, it is obvious that both light and darkness have a single creator.

AD.   Marinus said that the essential substance[13] of the Good is light, and that its nature is goodness and happiness. It happens also to be uncreated and incorruptible. Let him tell us, please, is the Good opposed to the Evil?

MAR.   In every way, Evil opposes the Good.

6   AD.   It is evident, then, that this opposition holds with regard to essential substance, nature and contingency. In essential substance, darkness is the opposite of light; by nature, Evil is the opposite of the Good,   e and if the opposition holds with regard to contingency, the created will be the opposite of the uncreated, and the corruptible of the incorruptible.

MAR.   How is that?

EUTR.   You laid it down that the two substances are uncreated. But the uncreated is also by nature immortal, so of necessity, if the two substances are uncreated, they are immortal by the very fact that they are said to be uncreated. But consider the matter a little futher: If the Evil is uncreated, the Good is not uncreated, because it is not the Evil, and by the same reasoning we say that, if the Evil is by nature created, the uncreated is the Good and not the Evil.

7   AD.   Are the two substances corruptible or incorruptible? Or is one incorruptible?

MEGETHIUS.   The two substances are incorruptible

f   AD.   You should keep quiet and listen, since the subjects of the previous debate have already been fully discussed.

MEG.   In this matter, I agree with Marinus.

---

[13] Ὀυσίαν.

EUTR.   You both say that the two substances are uncreated and incorruptible. They must then be of the same essence[14], and similar[15]. — which is impossible!

AD.   Are they both equal in power?

MEG.   They are not equal in power. By no means! (124) Christ says in the Gospel, "No one can enter into the evil man's house and plunder his goods, unless he first bind the stronger man"[16]. It is evident then that He was stronger, and bound the Devil and took his goods. The Lord thus showed clearly that He rescued us who belonged to the Evil One.

837a   AD.   If He had simply said, "The evil man" and not "the evil man's goods", you would have reason to speak, but actually He says, "the evil man's goods", showing that the goods of the evil man had their use, but that they did not belong to him. The reference is not to making nor possessing, but to use, i.e., to the evil man's carrying off by force[17] the property of some-one else. Paul confirms this, when he says, "As you have yielded your members as servants to wickedness and impurity for lawlessness, so yield your members to God as servants to righteousness"[18]. Now you, Megethius, said that the evil substance is incorruptible and uncreated; therefore   **b** if the nature of the Evil One is incorruptible, Jesus labours in vain when He tries

---

[14] 'Ομοουσίους, this being the word that became famous in the Arian controversy. 'Ομοούσιος was given to Greek Christology by Origen (*In Hebr.*, frag. 24, 359; cf. Quasten, *Patrology*, Westminster, 1962, vol. 2, pp. 78, 81; J.N.D. Kelly, *Early Christian Doctrines*, *op. cit.*, pp. 129-30), thus anticipating Nicaea. It was introduced into the Creed of Nicaea, with the purpose of excluding Arianism, in AD 325. Although many disliked it because it had been used by the Gnostics and Paul of Samosata (the Neo-Platonists, Plotinus, Porphry and Iamblichus had also employed the term), a number preferring ὁμοιούσιος, the word impelled and endured in expressing the relationship of Christ to the Father within the God-head, Athanasius maintaining this with remarkable force and clarity in his long fight against the teaching of Arius (cf. *supra*, pt. I, n. 12). In our Dialogue, of course, written before the Council of Nicaea, ὁμοούσιος is being used, not to determine the nature of Christ's relation-ship to God, but to indicate what (possible or alleged) relation Good has to Evil.

[15] ὁμοίας. This could also be rendered "alike"; Rufinus: *et similes atque eaedem ambae sunt.*

[16] Matt. 12:29. The Dialogue has τοῦ πονηροῦ for τοῦ ἰσχυροῦ of the main recensions.

[17] βιαζομένου. Bakhuyzen points out that it is extraordinary to find this word joined here with αὐτοῦ ἦν. He thinks that Adamantius means to say that "from Matthew 12:29 it does not emerge that we were the property of the Evil One; he has neither created the goods nor legitimately acquired them; he merely makes use of them while he takes them by force from someone else". [The debate here responds to an interesting piece of 'Marcionite' exegesis that Megethius is made to inject into the discussion here. Ed.].

[18] Rom. 6:19. Adamantius has ἀδικία for ἀνομία of the main recensions. He also adds τῷ θεῷ before δοῦλα τῇ δικαιοσύνῃ.

to destroy evil, for it cannot be destroyed. Why then did He suffer so as to put down death, when it is not to be put down? You said that both are uncreated and incorruptible. So one, then, submits to the other to be annihilated? But, if the Good One did not prevent this Evil One from perpetrating his many dreadful deeds, the Evil One would not permit his goods to be destroyed either — that is, accepting your assumption that both Good and Evil are uncreated and incorruptible[19].

[EUTR. If the first Principle were uncreated and the second created, it might be reasonably expected that the created one would submit to the uncreated. We should also have to say that the one is necessarily stronger, because he is (126) uncreated and incorruptible, while the other is weaker because he is created (for it is the uncreated that is stronger)][20].

c   AD. As Megethius has had the audacity to enter the debate, let him tell us, please, whether the two substances mix with or meet one another.

8   MEG. They do not mix with one another. By no means!

AD. How then did the Good One reach the goods of the Evil One, and how is it that, when the substances do not meet, a meeting took place, although they are opposed to one another? [If the world does not belong to Jesus, but to the Evil One, how could it come to Jesus, when He was not the stronger one? As both are equally powerful, neither can attack the other, because both are uncreated and incorruptible][21].

MAR. I claim that God only is incorruptible.

AD. Therefore the Devil is corruptible.

---

[19] This speech of Adamantius is not without its difficulties, and it is by no means certain that the translation does justice to the author's thought.

[20] The words of Eutropius in brackets are not found in the Latin, but are not necessarily inauthentic, for Rufinus often abbreviates. The speech in the Greek is rather typical of the adjudicator, who likes to recapitulate the argument of Adamantius. Bakhuyzen (*op. cit.*, p. 124, n.), considers Rufinus reflects a Greek original.

[21] The lines enclosed have also no counterpart in Rufinus, but the reply of Marinus implies their presence in the original text. [In this reply we see how Adamantius could easily be thought here to be attacking the Manichaean position, with its strong divarification of Good and Evil Powers. Marinus, as defender of the eastern Bardesanes is seen to hold a not dissimilar view. Ed.].

d   [EUTR.][22]   If there is created and uncreated, the uncreated could be incorruptible, and the created corruptible[23].

9   MAR.   Well now, answer, will you, while I ask some questions?

AD.   What are your questions?

MAR.   Does Good exist?

AD.   Yes.

MAR.   Does Evil exist?

AD.   I hold that Good exists as essential Being[24], and that Evil is an accident[25]; that the Good is incorporeal, but Evil is perceived by the physical senses. I maintain, therefore, that Evil does not happen to what is intrinsically Good, but only to that which is good by adoption or circumstance, and that it is the result of the exercise of free will[26].

MAR.   I would like to know exactly what you mean by "intrinsically", and "by adoption or circumstance".

AD.   Even though you ask in a tone charged with irony, listen to me, just the same. God is intrinsically good, and no evil can happen to Him.   **e** But the human is called good by adoption or according to circumstance. In the same way, we say that the Word of God is instrinsically Son, while the Scriptures, making use of similarity of terms, speaks of mankind as "sons" by adoption or circumstance. So Evil does not happen to the (128) intrinsically good, but to what is good by adoption or circumstance, and as the result of the exercise of free will[27].

MAR.   According to you, even the Devil has free will! And that which has freedom of choice is also self-existent and self-originated.

AD.   You do not seem to know the difference between one who possesses all power[28], and one who has the power of free will[29]. I hold that

---

[22] Rufinus omits the name Eutropius. This may be because his copy of the Greek text did not have it. The copyist could have left it out by mistake owing to the following εἰ.

[23] In place of this sentence, Rufinus has (but attributed to Adamantius): "for from two uncreateds, there cannot be one unchangeable and one changeable" (*Non enim potest ex duobus ingenitis unum esse immutabilem et unum mutabilem*).

[24] κατ 'οὐσίαν, used in a philosophical sense.

[25] ἐπισυμβαῖνον, another philosophical term. Cf. also *infra*, pt. 4, n.50.

[26] διὰ τὸ αὐτεξούσιον; good being substance and evil 'accident'.

[27] αὐτεξουσιότητος; Rufinus: *pro arbitrii libertate*. The Greek term is used in the Fathers of the Son, the Holy Spirit, the Devil and of Man (cf. Lampe, *op. cit.*, s.v.).

[28] τοῦ παντεξουσίου; Rufinus: *habere onmium potestatum*.

[29] τοῦ αὐτεξουσίου; Rufinus: *habere arbitrii sui potestatem*.

God has all power, but I believe the apostate angel called 'Satan' has free will, and that mankind has also.

838a   MAR.   You claim that the Devil and humankind have free will?

10   AD.   I maintain that God has made the angels and men with the power of free will, but not with omnipotence.

MAR.   You stated that free will was given by God, but that evil came as a result of the exercise of free will, therefore evil is seen to come from God. Now tell me this. Surely God knew when he gave free will that the apostate angel and man would turn for the worse?

AD.   Well, here is wisdom aspiring to be above God! You would make humans and angels to be equal with God — unchangeable![30]

MAR.   In what way unchangeable and equal with God?

b   AD.   Because God is unchangeable, but humans are changeable; God is immortal, but humans mortal, so you blame God for not making another like Himself.

MAR.   How is that?

AD.   If humans did not have free will, they would be unchangeable; but the unchangeable is immortal, and the immortal is God. Surely it was enough that, in the goodness of God, angels and men were created, without making them equal with God? This would have been to strip away all God's pre-eminence.

MAR.   How would it do that?

AD.   Mention the qualities produced by God's activities[31].

MAR.   Goodness, justice, mercy, piety, holiness — there they are.

AD.   If there had been no free will, all this activity would have been stripped away from God.

---

[30] Of this passage, Bakhuyzen says "the text is corrupt, and not easy to emend." Rufinus has: "As I see it, you want to be wise beyond God, for you think that angels and men ought to be equal with God".

[31] The Greek word is ἐνεργείας, "operative, active powers." The context, however, seems to require some such rendering as is offered in the translation.

c   MAR.   How is that?   (130)

AD.   If mankind is unchangeable, how was God shown to be good, when people do not have need of His goodness?

MAR.   Explain yourself more fully.

AD.   God's activities of which you spoke, are they mere names, or are they actual deeds?

MAR.   He deals in deeds, and not in mere names.

AD.   Upon whom does He work?

MAR.   Upon humanity.

EUTR.   If mankind came into existence unchangeable, these activities were unnecessary. Was God, then, going to show mercy so some who were not sinners? To whom was He going to be good, when there were none who needed God's goodness?

d 11   AD.   Why do you speak on the one hand of an evil root-cause, and on the other of a good one?

MAR.   Because the good root-cause saves and the evil one destroys.

AD.   What is the reason for the salvation or the destruction of humankind?

MAR.   The cause of humanity's salvation is God, but the cause of his destruction is the Devil.

AD.   Why did you say then that God is just?

MAR.   And I *am* still claiming that God is just.

AD.   Is God a just judge, or not?

MAR.   God is a just judge.

AD.   Whom does He judge?

MAR.   He judges the Devil and his angels; also those people who flee for refuge to Him.

AD.   Why does He judge the Devil?

MAR.   Because he leads mankind astray.

e   EUTR.   This judgement is very unjust; if the Devil has free will, and has the power to become either good or evil, he is properly judged, on the grounds that, when he could become good, he did not do so; but if he cannot be good, because his evil nature will not permit it, it would have been better not to allow the Devil to exist at the beginning, than to judge him (132) unjustly after he had come into existence!

MAR.   He is judged because he is evil.

EUTR.   But the judgement is unjust!

MAR.   Why?

EUTR.   Good, surely, cannot change and become evil?

MAR.   No.

EUTR.   Why not?

MAR.   Because it is such by nature.

839a   EUTR.   Neither can evil change and become good. So as there are two unchangeable natures[32] one would be unjustly judged by the other, or, if Evil is justly judged, then Good will also be justly judged.

MAR.   The Good does the judging.

EUTR.   Now it has been clearly shown that one is uncreated, and the other created; and that one is incorruptible, and the other corruptible; that one is unchangeable, and the other changeable; and that one judges justly, but the other is judged.

12   AD.   Marinus stated that mankind is justly judged by God. Let him explain then, please, how, if people do not have free will, they are judged justly.

MAR.   They are justly judged by God because they yield obedience to the Evil One.

EUTR.   Now you plainly admit that humans have free will, for to yield obedience to Evil or to Good belongs to freedom of the will, and not to compulsion.

AD.   Please answer a few questions I would ask?

MAR.   Make your inquiries.

---

[32] οὐσιῶν.

b   AD.   Do you believe that he is almighty or not?

MAR.   I believe that He is almighty.

AD.   Does He encircle all things, or is he Himself encircled?

MAR.   It is obvious that He encircles all things, and is not Himself encircled.

AD.   By what power is the heaven or the earth, the sea or the world as a whole, encircled and held together? By Whom is it encircled and controlled?

MAR.   Obviously, by God.   (134)

EUTR.   By the good or the evil God?

MAR.   *I* know only one — the Good God.

EUTR.   Where then do you think the Evil One is?

MAR.   On the earth, for Christ says, "I saw Satan fallen like lightning from heaven"[33].

c   EUTR.   Presumably then, Satan is kept under control on earth by Him who controls the earth, and he will not escape[34]. Thus the Good God, who keeps the Evil One under control, is blameworthy for one of three things: permitting him to exist; inability to destroy him; or ignorance that he does exist.

13   AD.   Since Marinus mentioned the Gospel and the falling of Satan, it is opportune to treat briefly of this matter, so that you may understand the truth of the Divine teaching. The Saviour, when He wanted to teach that Satan was formerly an angel created by God, who shared in light, but afterwards turned for the worse by free will, and fell from rectitude[35] (one cannot fall from a prostrate position, but only from an upright one) **d** said, "like lightning", to show clearly that Satan shared in light before he

---

[33] Lk. 10:18, but with εἶδον for ἐθεώρουν of the main recensions.

[34] καὶ οὐ φεύξεται. Bahkuyzen thinks that the subject of φεύξεται must be ὁ Θεὸς (understood), and that perhaps the author actually wrote, "Will not the Good God escape blame?" (φεύξεται). ("He who keeps the Evil One under control will then be one of three things: He permits him to exist; He cannot destroy him; or He does not know of his existence", Migne having a rendering similar to this).

[35] Cf. esp. 2 Enoch, 29:4.

changed and fell — for lightning stands for light.

EUTR.   Two uncreateds are impossible[36].

MAR.   Therefore Good is the cause of Evil.

AD.   It is not unreasonable to make use of an illustration from the world around[37] to clarify the argument: supposing a sculptor makes a statue, polishes the silver (136) (naturally bright), and then gives it to you. Because, through your neglect of the article, corrosion sets in, would you say that the sculptor is the cause?

MAR.   Well, what then?

EUTR.   The corrosion is not natural, but accidental, brought about through the negligence of the owner. In the same way, God is not responsible for evil, for He gave reasoning power bright and gleaming, along with free will,   e to angels and humans. He Himself will be found to be without blame, for evil is shown to be not natural, but accidental, or by concurrence. [It is also very evident, from what Adamantius has put before us, that there is only One God, unbegotten and uncreated, and whether it be humans or angels, they are fittingly judged by His just judgement, for it

---

[36] For this line see Methodius, *De lib. arbit.* (*Schriften*, ed. G. N. Bonwetsch), Erlangen and Leipzig, 1891, p. 15.

[37] Or, "an earthly example" (κοσμικοῦ παραδείγματος).

[38] In Rufinus we find an addition to the speech of Eutropius (enclosed in brackets in the translation). It sounds rather like a short summary of the previous argument advanced by Adamantius, before a new speaker comes on the scene, and would therefore be in keeping with the duty of an adjudicator. However, it must be noted that in the Latin text the words immediately preceding this bracketed passage are attributed to Adamantius, leaving Eutropius without anything to say prior to the entrance of Droserius. A later scribe, therefore, may have felt the need for a speech by the judge at this point, added the words for Eutropius, and adjusted the previous words to fit Adamantius.

FOURTH PART[1]

840a 1 DROSERIUS[2] I have listened to Marinus and his friends for a long time, and condemned their ignorance. Let me now match my strength against my son, Adamantius, for a little.

ADAMANTIUS. You must first of all define your terms, and explain what teaching you are presenting; then begin the debate.

DR. I present the teaching of Valentinus[3], a man very upright, and well able to convince you where the Devil and evil come from. I have the views of Valentinus here, and, with your permission, will read them out.

b EUTROPIUS. If the views put forward by Valentinus should be refuted by your opponents, will *you* answer what they put forward?

DR. I think that when the views of Valentinus have been read, they will not be open to contradiction, for their author was no ordinary man. However, if anyone should contradict them, I will answer.

---

[1] The Fourth Book in the Latin Text of Rufinus begins here.

[2] For the character Droserius see sect. A, 2 of our Introduction. The author of the Dialogue evidently intends him to present the view of Valentinus with regard to the matters under discussion. If his information is accurate, what Droserius says here should be carefully considered alongside the statements of other writers on Valentinianism, such as Irenaeus, Tertullian, Clement of Alexandria, Hippolytus, and the Coptic Gnostic texts from Nag-Hammadi.

[3] Valentinus (second century) seems to have been one of the most outstanding of the Christian Gnostics. New light has recently been shed upon Valentinus and his system by the discoveries at Nag Hammadi, on the eastern bank of the Nile, of Gnostic texts written in Coptic. Among them is the *Gospel of Truth*, written very probably by Valentinus himself. (Irenaeus claims that a work with such a title had been composed by this Gnostic, although much found in the Nag Hammadi *Gospel of Truth* does not harmonise with what Irenaeus tells of the teaching of Valentinus. There are absent from it, e.g., the pairs of Aeons that figure so prominently in the accounts of Irenaeus and others). Valentinus seems to have differed from most Gnostics in postulating three class of mankind: the 'pneumatics' to whom alone is given the saving Gnosis by which entrance in the *Pleroma* is gained; the 'psychics' (or Catholics) who are capable of reaching only to the middle range of the Demiurge; and the 'hylics' (the remainder of the human race) who are eternally lost. Valentinus had a very large number of disciples. In spite of his heterodoxy, there are elements in his teaching that reveal a mind of high quality, and it is not surprising that to defeat the very real error in the system of doctrine propounded by Valentinus, the Church had to call upon some of here finest thinkers. For fuller treatment of the Valentinian school, see H. Lietzmann, *History of the Early Church*, *op. cit.*, vol. 1, pp. 287-295; F.L. Cross, *The Early Christian Fathers*, London, 1960, pp. 32, 36-38; H.E.W. Turner, *Pattern of Christian Truth*, *op. cit.*, pp. 83ff., 111f., 115ff.; W.C. van Unnik, *Evangelien aus dem Nilsand*, n.p., 1959; H. Jonas, *Gnostic Religion*, *op. cit.*, ch. 8.

EUTR.   Let the teaching of Valentinus be read!   **2** []⁴

("So thinking in some such way on how well the world was ordered, I was returning home. But on the next day [that (138) is, today]⁵, when I arrived, I saw two men — of the same race⁶, let me emphasise — wrangling among themselves,   **c** and abusing each other! Another, again, was trying to strip his neighbour. Some were beginning to dare things even

---

⁴ At the beginning of the next paragraph, most of the manuscripts have the name Droserius, but it is absent from the oldest (the Venetus), from two others, and also from Rufinus. As Bakhuyzen suggests, the author seems to be chiefly concerned to present the opinions of Valentinus, and is little interested in indicating the particular person who expresses them. It may well be therefore that the original document of our Dialogue contained no name at all.

With the quotation begins the fairly extensive use of the writings of Methodius of Olympus. In the translation, with the exception of smaller phrases and sentences, the extracts are indicated generally by rounded brackets, with the quotation marks in the first instance reflecting a quotation from Valentinus read to the participants in the dialogue. Page references to the work of Methodius are given at the end of such quotation.

Of Methodius himself, little is known. As a writer he is considerably better as a stylist than the author of the Dialogue of Admantius, and in some respects resembles Plato, whom he strove (not altogether successfully) to imitate. He appears to have been bishop of Olympus in Lycia, southern Asia Minor, was one of the first to oppose certain teachings of Origen, and died as a martyr in the last great persecution under Diocletian, *ca.* 311. Methodius is distinguished chiefly for his writings, of which the main ones are: *The Symposium*, modelled on Plato, in which ten virgins extol the virtues of virginity; *On the Resurrection*, insisting on the resurrection of the earthly body, and attacking the doctrine of the pre-existence of souls held by Origen; *On Free Will*, which opposes the Valentinian dualism and determinism. The whole of the *Symposium* is extant; considerable parts of the other two works also exist in the Greek, while there is a Slavonic version of the *Free Will*, complete except for a few gaps. The author of 'Adamantius' quotes first of all from the *On Free Will*, which, from the fact that it is less severe in its treatment of views attributed to Origen, may be regarded as having been written somewhat earlier than the *On the Resurrection* — even as far back as AD 270 (so A. Robinson, *Philocalia, op. cit.,* p. xiv). Later in the Dialogue of Adamantius there appear quotations from and references to Methodius' other work, *On the Resurrection*, but this book is so antagonistic to the Origenistic view of the Resurrection that the historian Eusebius, *ca.* 308, exclaimed "How is it that Methodius dared to write against Origen, saying this and that about Origen's teachings?" (Cf. *Ibid,* p. xiv for references and discussion). But while our author used Methodius to advance his own arguments, it may well be doubted whether he shared his strong opposition to Origen's doctrines as such. The Dialogue does not seem to be aimed particularly at Origen himself, but rather at certain Gnostic and Marcionite teachings, and passages from Methodius (and perhaps from a number of others whom we cannot now distinguish) are chosen simply because they are felt to deal adequately with the author's themes, and quite irrespective of the sources from which they came. For the possibility that the author of the Adamantian Dialogue may have been a follower of Methodius, see our Introduction, sects. B, 4; C, 1-2.

⁵ The enclosed words are absent from Rufinus, but are part of the original in Methodius. They are therefore likely to be authentic.

⁶ [ὁμογενεῖς This passage is the more interesting for what it implies about the ancient history of 'race relations', and the expectation that small-scale violence against those of a different ethnic group (as part of a minority, let us say) would be more likely in the Roman empire of later Antiquity than between people of the same *ethnos.* Ed.].

more terrible, for a man plundered a buried corpse, dragging it to the sur-
face and the light of the sun, thus insulting a form like his own, and leaving the dead as food for dogs. Another man bared his sword and attacked a
person similar to himself. The latter tried to save himself by flight, but his
assailant kept on pursuing him, and would not restrain his wrath. I do not
need to say more: the pursuer reached the fugitive and struck with the
sword.   d Although his victim held out supplicating hands, the attacker did
not abate his anger. Showing no mercy to one of his own race, nor recog-
nizing himself in the image of the other man, he was like a wild beast, and
began his devouring by means of the sword. So great was his wrath, that
even now he was putting his mouth to a body like his own. Another could
be seen despoiling an injured man; he had stripped him of his clothes,
without even covering the body with earth.   841a On top of all this, a fellow came forward with the intention of fondling[7] his neighbour's wife, thus
robbing another man of his marriage. Refusing the husband the right of
lawful fatherhood, he was urging her to an illicit union. So now I began to
believe the Tragedies… [It seemed to me that the Thyestean Banquet[8] had
really happened][9]. I credited even the drunken lust of Oenomaus[10], and no
longer doubted the rivalry by which brother drew sword on brother[11]. Having witnessed so many things just like these, I began to investigate their origin, the (140) source of their activity,   b and who is the one who devised
such great evils against mankind, to learn where they were discovered, and
who teaches them. To dare to say that God is their maker was not possible.
It could not be said either that they have the subsistence of their being from
Him, for how could anyone think these things of God? He is Good, and

---

[7] παίζειν; used of Abraham and Rebecca in Gen. 26:8 LXX.

[8] The reference is to the old Greek legend in which Thyestes, in ignorance, ate the flesh
of his own two sons at a banquet. The food had been prepared by his brother Atreus, who
had slain the sons, and served their flesh to his brother in revenge for the rape of his wife by
Thyestes (Cf. Athenagoras, *De Resurr.*, 4).

[9] The enclosed passage is absent from Rufinus, but probably original, since it is found in
Methodius.

[10] Who, in Greek legend, was the grandfather of Thyestes and Atreus, and king of Elis
and Pisa.

[11] The reference is probably to the strife between Eteocles and Polynices, sons of Oedipus and Jocasta. The brothers attempted to rule Thebes after the departure of their father,
but quarrelled, and finally died fighting against each other. The tragic story of Oedipus and
his sons has been immortalised by Aeschylus (*Septern contra Thebas*); Sophocles (*Antigone*),
and Euripides (*Phoenissae*). The charge of "Thyestian banquets and Oedipodean inter-
course" was often made against the early Christians, especially in times of persecution,
and was strongly refuted by the Apologists and Fathers. Cf., Athenagoras, *Legat. pro Christ.*,
1-3; Justin Martyr, *Apol.*, 1, 26; Irenaeus, *Adv. haeres.* I, 25, 3; Eusebius, *Hist. eccl.* 4, 7;
5, 1.

the Maker of the Best[12]; nothing bad belongs to Him. It is not His nature, indeed, to rejoice in such things. He prohibits their production, rejecting those who do find joy in them, but accepting those who flee them. It is most surely wicked to claim that God is the creator of these things when He rejects them. He would not want them to go out of existence were He first of all their Maker! c He wants those who draw near to Him to become His imitators, so I think it is unreasonable to fasten these things upon Him, either on the grounds that they had their existence from Him, or — if it were definitely agreed that something existing can come out of things that do not exist! — that He Himself made evil[13]. He who brought them into existence from non-existence would not blot them out of existence again, but if He did, it must be said that there was a time once when God rejoiced in evil, but that He does so no more. This is exactly what I think one cannot say of God,   d for it is incongruous with His nature to fix this on Him. Therefore I think that there co-exists with Him something that is called "matter"[14], from which He created existing things, separating them with wise skill, and arranging them well, and that it is from this "matter" that evil seems to come. Thus, when it was inert and formless, moving about without any order, and lacking God's skill, He bore it no ill will, nor did He leave it (142) to exist constantly in this state. Instead, He began to create, wanting to separate the best elements from the worst. In this way then, God created. However, He had to leave as they were all those elements that were unsuitable for the process of making,   e because they were — so to speak — turbid and impure. They were in no way fitted to His

---

[12] τῶν κρειττόνων ποιητής. This use of the comparative degree may represent the later tendency to level down the degrees in Hellenistic Greek. Cf. Blass and Debrunner, *Greek Grammar, op. cit.*, p. 32 (sect. 60); p. 126 (sect. 244). This last expression shows that the Valentinian Gnostics, at least, held with orthodox Christianity a high conception of God as Creator. They differed from it of course in the view taken of the relationship of the Supreme God to matter and the created order.

[13] This is a difficult passage, and there are variations between the MSS of Methodius and 'Adamantius'. Bakhuyzen considered it to be "scarcely intelligible". For the last sentence, the translation of the Methodian text by W.R. Clark (Methodius, *Symposium* [*Ant.-Nic. Lib.*], Edinburgh, 1867, vol. 14, pp. 124f) has, "though it must certainly be granted that it is possible for something to come into existence out of what has no existence, in case He made what is evil".

[14] ὕλη. Aristotle was the first, as far as is known, to use this term in the philosophical sense. In the philosophy of a later time, it was mostly used to denote that which is opposite to the νοῦς, the intelligent and formative principle. It is found with this meaning in the writings of Proclus (fifth century AD) and Iamblichus (fourth century AD). In the NT and earliest Christian literature ὕλη is mostly used to denote earthly, perishable matter, of which both humans and idols are composed. Sometimes, therefore, it has the idea of that which is sinful and at enmity with God (as in Philo and Gnostic literature). See e.g., Ignatius (1 Romans 6:2) and Barnabas 46.

purpose. It is from these, I think, that evil now streams out on mankind. It appeared to me that this was the best way to understand the matter")[15].

3   DR[16]. I think that an absolutely correct and impartial explanation has been offered by the wise Valentinus. Yet, if anyone should want to argue against it, let him come forward,   842a for I am ready to answer all opponents.

AD.   Please put aside your preconceived ideas, and give an answer calmly to all the questions I am going to ask you.

DR.   I intend to debate in a calm and orderly way; I have no desire to gain the victory by false means, but only to discuss matters fairly.

AD.   I appreciate your willingness and sincerity. However, you deceive yourself, Droserius, when you dispose of the issue in such a way that God is said to have created existing things from some existing substance[17]. As a matter of fact the question of evil has caused many to deal with the issue after that manner[18]. There have been a large number who have taken the view you do, but there have been others again who declared that God *is* the creator of evil,   b because they feared to admit a substance as coeval with Him. Still others, fearing to call God the maker of evil, felt that they *must* assume matter to be coeval with Him. It happened that in both cases they were in error, because their fear of God was not based on (144) knowledge of the truth[19]. Nevertheless, as you are so much in earnest,

---

[15] The end of the quotation from Methodius (following *Schriften* in Bonwetsch edn., 1891, pp.7-12; cf. Migne, *Patrol. Graec.*, vol. 18, pp. 243ff.).

[16] With the following speech of Droserius we leave this extended excerpt from Methodius, but there will be others to take its place, from mere words and phrases to longer pieces. In the Greek original, the difference of style when we pass from Methodius to 'Adamantius' is easily perceptible, although it cannot be brought out in the English translation. Though the former falls far short of Plato, both in thought and expression, the fact that he emulated the great Greek philosopher reveals itself in his writing, even in the composition of the passage attributed to Valentinus. It shows that Methodius had really read Plato for himself (unlike most of his contemporaries), and accounts for Jerome's praise of his ability and style (*Comment. in Daniel.*, 12, 13; *De vir. illustrib.*, 3, 38).

[17] οὐσίας.

[18] As has been already pointed out (pt. III, n. 5), the problem of evil has busied thinkers' minds from very early times. The chief aim of most explanations has been, of course, to absolve the Supremely Good God from all responsibility. If matter (ὕλη) be considered as the source of evil, then the easiest way out of the difficulty naturally appears to be to deny that God had anything to do with it. In this case, matter, with its evil, must be the work of an inferior God, or is co-eternal with the Good God. This last is the position taken by Valentinus (as presented by Methodius) and endorsed by Droserius in the Dialogue of Adamantius.

[19] The passage "I appreciate ... knowledge of the truth", is also from Methodius, with one or two alterations.

I will turn to the subject under discussion. If you will answer carefully all the questions I shall ask, you will know the truth and I shall not have reasoned with you in vain[20].

DR.   I am ready to defend the views of Valentinus.

c 4   AD.   What proofs have you that Matter is coexistent with God?

DR.   Does it not say in Genesis, "that the earth was invisible and unformed?"[21]

EUTR.   Does it not say that the earth *was*, and was not made by God?[22]

DR.   With your permission, I will read.

AD.   Many people dream in their sleep that they possess great riches, only to discover on waking up, that their hands hold nothing — the dream was but a vain hope. Droserius is like that. Ask therefore that the Scripture dealing with the Creation be read, and you will learn whether it was the earth that pre-existed, or matter.

EUTR.   Let the Scripture be read. "In the beginning God created heaven, and earth.   d And the earth was invisible and unformed"[23].

AD.   You see, Sir, the wicked scheme of Droserius, when the Scripture says that first God made heaven and earth, and then it had existence. It did not say, In the beginning was the earth, but, "In the beginning God created heaven and earth", and then a little lower down, "And the earth was invisible".

EUTR.   The Scripture plainly shows that heaven and earth are a work of God. It clearly places the deed first, and then adds, "It was...". The state of existence necessarily has to follow the act of bringing into existence.

---

[20] The passage is also from Methodius, but Methodius has: "If I truly seem to you to speak reasonably about what is more excellent, answer to each and all of the things that I ask", etc.

[21] Gen. 1:2 (LXX; ἀόρατος for Hebrew תֹהוּ, formlessness, confusion, unreality; cf. for similar expressions in Scripture and the Patristic writers, Col. 1:16; The Symbol of Nicaea, *apud* Theodoret, *Hist. eccl.*, 1, 12; Origen *Comment. in Johan.*, Frg. 1). Has the use of ἀόρατος in the LXX of Gen. 1:2 thus influenced the early Greek Fathers when referring to Creation?

[22] [Here, briefly, we seem to have a hint that Eutropius is, after all, a Pagan adjudicator, and is represented as accepting the eternity of the world (with the Platonic, Peripatetic and Stoic Schools). Ed.].

[23] Gen. 1:1-2 (LXX).

5   AD.   Let us return to the question under discussion: Valentinus
wants to affirm that Matter is coexistent with God so that he may demonstrate that God is not the cause of evil?

e   DR.   Yes.

         AD.   Was God separated from this Matter, or united with it?

843a   DR.   He was separated from it.   (146)

         AD.   What then was between God and Matter, separating them?

         DR.   Nothing.

         AD.   Then He was united with Matter, for there was nothing sep-
arating them. But looked at from another angle, your statement makes God
exist only in part — He cannot thus be everywhere.

         EUTR.   It is impossible for something to be separated from some-
thing else if there is nothing to separate them. And that which separates
must needs be stronger than that which is being separated. So there will be,
above all, a third part — the God who holds them together! What do you
say, then, Droserius? Is God in a part only, and not everywhere?[24]

         DR.   I do not claim that God is in a part only; but that He is not
responsible for evil.

         AD.   You want to say that He is not responsible in theory, but in
practice both Valentinus and you have taught that   b He is the creator and
reservoir of evil.

         DR.   How is that?

         AD.   The discussion, as it advances, will reveal this teaching.
"Now, I do not think you are ignorant that two uncreated things cannot
exist together, although you appear to have intended this is the previous
discussion. Quite clearly, we must say one of two things: either that God is
separated from Matter, or that He is inseparable from it. If anyone should
really want Him to be united to it, he would speak of only one uncreated
body, for each of them will, in that case, be a part of the other. But as they

───

[24] [As a Pagan, Eutropius is here made to reflect the concerns of the philosophic schools
for the ultimate unity of the Divinity. Ed.]. In the Latin of Rufinus, the words "what do you
say then, Droserius? Is God in a part only, and not everywhere?" are attributed to Adamantius. Bakhuyzen thinks that this is probably correct.

are parts of one another, there will not be two uncreateds, but one, composed of diverse elements". **c** "If, however, someone should say that God is separated from Matter, there must be something between them that shows the separation". "And if anyone says that God is neither separated from Matter, nor joined to it, but that God is, as it were, where Matter is, or Matter where God is, let him (148) hear what this involves: if we say God is where Matter is, we shall also have to say that He must be able to be contained, and to be enclosed by Matter; in fact that, like Matter, He must be carried about in disorder[25].   **d** In addition, we must say that God has come into even worse straits, for if Matter was once without order, and, deciding to change it into a better state, He put it in order, there was a time when God was within disordered elements. I might, indeed, properly ask whether God filled Matter, or existed in some part of it. If one were to say that God is in some part of Matter, how much less than Matter does he make Him — that is, if part of it contained the whole of God! If, however, one were to say that God is in the whole of Matter, and permeates it all, let him explain how He created it. It would have to be said that God underwent some contraction, and that when this had taken place, He created that from which He had withdrawn; or, that He worked together with Matter, because He had no place to which He could withdraw. But if someone says that Matter is in God, then it is equally right to ask whether He created by being separated, as it were, from Himself, and (life creatures living in the air) by dividing and distributing Himself for the purpose of receiving the beings produced within Him, or, whether He worked, as it were, in some place — that is, like water in the ground.   **844a** Now, should someone say that God acted like creatures in the air, he would have to admit that He is divisible, but if he said that God worked like water on the ground, because Matter was without order and arrangement — and besides this, contained evil — he would also have to say that the place of the disorderly and the evil is God. Now, I think this is not only irreverent, but — worse still — dangerous"[26].

---

[25] After the words "in disorder," Methodius continues "and he must neither stand nor remain by himself". These words possibly also stood originally in 'Adamantius'. In sect. 844d/IV, 6 of our Dialogue, Adamantius (in the Greek MSS) again uses words from Methodius: "we shall also have to say" and "nor remain by Himself," but as they are largely a repetition of the preceding statement, and are not found in Rufinus, Bakhuyzen eliminates them as very probably spurious.

[26] The sections within the quotation marks are from Methodius (cf. Bonwetsch edn. pp. 14f., 17, 19). There are some minor variations from the original.

6   DR.   In order to show that God is not responsible for evil, Valentinus fastened it upon Matter, so that Matter, not God, might be responsible.

AD.   You desire the coexistence of Matter with God, so that you may avoid saying that God is the maker of evil, but, although you plan to escape this, you appear to do so only (150) in word;   **b** actually, when the position is thoroughly examined, you demonstrate that God is the reservoir and creator of evil. If then you want to make the guess that Matter exists uncreated from subsisting things …,[27] but since you say that the origin of evil is the cause of your guess, I think I ought to proceed to examine this question. Once it has been clearly shown how evil exists, and that it cannot be claimed that God is not[28] the cause of evil simply by substituting Matter for Him[29], I think such a guess will be refuted. You say, then, that Matter [without qualities][30] coexists with God, and that out of this He created the world at the beginning[31].

c   DR.   That is what I claim.

AD.   So if Matter is without qualities, and God made the world, yet qualities are in the world, God made the (152) qualities. I heard[32] you read earlier that nothing can come into existence from non-existence; will you then answer this question: do you think that the qualities of the world have not come from existing qualities?

DR.   That is how it seems to me.

AD.   And that they are distinct from the substances themselves?

DR.   I say that they are distinct from the substances.

---

[27] The hiatus can be filled in from Methodius: "I would have produced arguments to prove that it is impossible for it to exist uncreated". Something like this may have been written by the author of our Dialogue.

[28] "not the cause": The Greek manuscripts of the Dialogue of Adamantius, and also the ordinary Greek Text of Methodius, have αἴτιον. However, Eusebius, *Praep. Evang.*, 7, 22, (cf. Origen, *Philocalia* 24, 1 [Robinson edn., p. 215]) quotes the Methodian passage with ἀναίτιον; and Rufinus has *causa non esse*. Bakhuyzen therefore places ἀναίτιον in his edition of the Greek text of the Adamantian Dialogue.

[29] Rufinus has: "And note that God is not shown from this not to be the cause of evil, on the ground that matter is substituted which seems able to accept the responsibility for evil" (*quae mali posse causam suscipere videatur*).

[30] ἄποιον. Absent from Rufinus, but suitable to the context, and so probably original.

[31] τὴν τοῦ κόσμου γένεσιν: "the origin of the world".

[32] The Imperfect: ἤκουον, "I was listening".

AD.   Therefore, if God did not create the qualities from existing qualities, nor do they arise out of the substances, because they are not substances, we must say that they have been made by God out of Non-existence.   d Thus you seem to say too much when you assert that it is impossible to believe that anything has been created by God from nothing[33].

7   VALENS[34]   said, on this subject, Droserius has reached an absurd conclusion by maintaining that Matter is without qualities.

AD.   Well, what do *you* say? That the qualities coexist with Matter?

e   VAL.   (I consider that Matter has qualities that are eternal[35]. I claim also that evil comes thus from its own outflowing[36] so that God may not be held responsible, but that Matter may be recognized as the cause of them all)[37].

AD.   Valens does not even believe in Valentinus, his own teacher, for he refutes his doctrine.

845a   VAL.   What have I refuted?

AD.   Valentinus answered that God is the creator of Matter[38], but *you* say that Matter has the eternal qualities of substances. Of what then is God the Maker and Creator?

VAL.   God is the creator of the world.

EUTR.   Valens is willing to admit that God is Creator in word only.   (154)

VAL.   How is that?

EUTR.   You say that Matter coexists with God, and that the qualities also coexist. If Matter was pre-existent, and the qualities also coexisted, it is pointless to say that God was creator. So either Valentinus will be found to have given an unsatisfactory explanation, or Valens — but more likely, both of them.

---

[33] This concludes the quotation from Methodius (Bonwetsch edn., pp. 19-21). On this and the following pages, various words and phrases are taken from Methodius which it has not been thought necessary to indicate. Minor variations in the longer extracts have also not been noted.

[34] For the little that can be said about this character, see the Introduction, sect. A, 2.

[35] ἀνάρχους, "without beginning".

[36] ἀπορροίας, "emanation, effluence".

[37] This portion is based mainly on Methodius (Bonwetsch edn., p. 28).

[38] Cf. the Dialogue, sects.841a-d/IV, 2 and our Introduction, sect. A, 2.

8   AD.   Will Valens please answer a few questions?

b   VAL.   Mention them.

AD.   (In what sense do you say that God was creator? Did He change the substances so that they were now no longer what they had been before, but had become something different, or did He retain the substances, but change their qualities?

VAL.   I do not think that He made any change of the substances, but I do say that there has been some change of the qualities, and I claim that it is with respect to these that God is creator. Just as, if someone should say that a house had been built out of stones, it would not, therefore be said that stones were no longer in the house before they had become a house ... c so I think that, while the substance remained, God brought about a certain change of its qualities. It is by virtue of this, I maintain, that God made the world).

AD.   Since you say, then, that a certain change of qualities was brought about by God, please answer a few questions I want to ask?

VAL[39].   Ask your questions, by all means.

AD.   (Do you think that evil things consist of qualities of substances, or of substances?)[40]

VAL.   It consists of qualities of substances.   (156)

AD.   Were these qualities in Matter from the first, or did they have a beginning?

VAL.   I believe that these qualities were eternally[41] coexistent with Matter.

AD.   But do you not claim that God made a certain change of the qualities?

VAL.   That is what I assert.

AD.   Did He change them for the better or the worse?

---

[39] The names, Valens and Adamantius are placed in brackets by Bakhuzyen. He points out that in the parallel passage in Methodius, the Orthodox speaker continues on after the words "a few questions I want to ask".

[40] Rufinus is somewhat similar. Yet the division of the words as given in the Greek MSS of 'Adamantius' is not out of harmony with the style of the Dialogue, and so the name attached to this question may be genuine.

[41] ἀγενήτως.

d   VAL.   Clearly is was for the better.

AD.   Well then, if evil consists of qualities of Matter, and God changed its qualities for the better, we must seek the origin of evil, for the qualities did not remain what they once were by nature. If formerly the qualities were not evil, and (you say that through God's changing them, the first of such qualities came into existence with respect to Matter, it is plain that God is the cause of evil; since he changed qualities that were not evil into evil ones)[42].

VAL.   You are disposed to forget the explanation of Valentinus. He said that Matter was disorderly and formless. God changed some elements of this for the better, but all the others that were turbid and impure, since they were not useful for the process of making, He had to leave, because they were in no way fitted to His purpose. It is from these, I think, that evil streams out.

e   AD.   It was only the good elements of Matter that, as you say, God changed. He left the evil ones alone?

VAL.   That is so.

EUTR.   The theory advanced by Valentinus and Valens is extremely difficult to follow, and unreasonable. We must seek [to learn?][43] (whether, although God had the power, He did not wish to destroy evil, or whether He did not have the power. If you and your party say that He had the power, but did not wish to destroy it, you are bound to say that He is responsible for evil, because, when He had the power to blot evil out, (158) He permitted it to remain as it was, especially when He began to work on Matter. If He had taken no interest at all in Matter, He would not be the cause of what He permits to remain. However, since He left a part of it untouched, although He had the power to change it for the better, He is responsible for evil, for the reason that He left   **846a** a part of Matter in an evil condition, which resulted in the destruction of the part on which He worked.

---

[42] This sentence is corrupt in the Greek and we have to rely on Methodius who has at the end of this passage, "God is the cause of evil, since He changed qualities that were not evil into evil ones" (a conclusion resembling Rufinus' translation). Cf. Bonwetsch edn. of Methodius, p. 29.

[43] There is a lacuna here in the Greek text [and a conjecture has been added. Ed.]. In place of "Eutropius: The theory… we must seek," Methodius has, "Orthodox: How is it then that you say that He left remaining the qualities of the bad things as they were?"

Actually, I think, in regard to this part of Matter which God arranged in a state of order, that it was injured most of all by the fact that it shares in evil[44]. For if anyone were to investigate the situation carefully, he would discover that now Matter has suffered a more grievous misfortune than the first disorder. Before it was divided, it had no perception of evil, **b** but now each of its parts has that sense[45]. So this, what you claim God did to benefit Matter, is actually found to have made it worse. But if you say that evil is still in existence because God is powerless to destroy it, you thereby assert that He is impotent. This lack of power[46] will be the result either of natural weakness, or of surrender to fear, and enslavement to someone stronger. Above all, you thus affirm that evil is greater than God, since it overcomes the strength of His purpose. I think it is wicked to say this about God! Moreover, will not these things which, according to the views of Valentinus, **c** are able to conquer God, really be gods — that is, if we mean by God the One who has power over all things?)[47]

9   DR. The origin of evil must be sought on more secure grounds, for if we say that evil is coeval with God[48], many wrong-headed ideas will follow in the wake of truth. Consequently, if evil does not come from either Matter or God, we must seek its origin.

        AD.   [If it has now become clear to you that Valentinus' views are contrary to sane reasoning, please accept the true explanation:][49] Evil does

[44] Migne's translation of the Greek text here is, "In fact, I think that the part which He made has received the greatest injury from this part [i.e., the evil part], since it desires evil". The crucial word in the Greek text is ἀντιλαμβανόμενον, which may also signify "lay hold of, share in, practise, perceive, assist," according to context. [This is Eutropius' longest speech in the Dialogue, and seems to reflect an attempt by the author of the dialogue to show on what ground philosophic Pagans concerned with the Divinity's problematic relation to matter and changeableness would disagree with the decided dualism of the Valentinians. Ed.].

[45] After the words "has that sense," Methodius continues, "Let me now take a human example: before it was moulded into form and made a living creature by the skill of the Creator, it had no inherent apprehension of evil, but from the time that it was made into a human being by God, it gained perception of approaching evil".

[46] From here on Methodius has variant readings and additions.

[47] From the words "whether, although God had the power" to "power over all things," the passage is from Methodius (Bonwetsch edn., pp. 32-35).

[48] Droserius here appears to modify his previous approval of the dictum of Valentinus that matter is coeval with God. He can no longer accept the view that there was ever a part of matter which was evil ("turbid and impure"), and which God could not use when He created the world. Thus, little by little, the opponents of Adamantius are forced into an untenable position as the argument in our dialogue proceeds.

[49] The enclosed words are found in Rufinus only. Bakhuyzen feels that they are an attempt by the Latin translator to improve the continuity of the narrative.

not arise as part of the nature, essence or substance of being, but by means of free will.

DR.   On the contrary, I maintain that evil does (160) arise as part of the essence and substance of being. The manner of its coming is 'accidental'[50].

847a AD.   Please explain clearly what you mean by the expression, "as part of the essence and substance of being".

DR.   All that the Law forbad I call evil, such as murder, adultery, theft, immorality, and whatever the Law forbids.

AD.   (All these things are of an 'accidental'[51] nature. Murder is not substance, nor again is adultery, nor are any of the similar evils. But just as the grammarian is named from Grammar and the rhetorician from Rhetoric...[52], yet neither Rhetoric nor Grammar is substance, but it receives its name from those things which are 'accidental'[53] to it, and from which it seems to be thus named, although it is none[54] of them, so, it seems to me, the substance receives its name from what are considered to be evil results, though it is none of them.   **b** The producer of evil results is called evil; yet what a man produces is not himself, but his actions, and it is from these that he receives the designation "evil". [Should we say that he is himself what he does, when he commits murders, adulteries, thefts, and all such like things, he will himself be these things. Now if he is these things, and they have existence only when they are committed, but cease to exist when they are not committed; and furthermore if they are committed by men,

---

[50] ἐπισυμβαίνων ἐστίν: "happen besides, come into existence afterwards, supervene"; Rufinus: *accidens res est*. Origen uses the word ἐπισυμβαίνω (in *Comm. in Ps*. 36) of evil as not being an ultimate principle.

[51] τῶν συμβεβηκότων: "chance events, contingencies." In philosophy the expression sometimes means a contingent attribute or 'accident' in the modern sense. Rufinus: *accidentia sunt*.

[52] In Methodius the text runs more fully, "(just as) the grammarian is named from Grammar; the rhetorician from Rhetoric, and the medical practitioner from Medicine, although neither Medicine, nor Rhetoric, nor Grammar is substance, but the latter receives its name from what is accidental..." Rufinus in his translation of the Adamantian Dialogue has somewhat similar. In view of this similarity, Bakhuyzen thinks it probable that the composer of Adamantius originally copied Methodius fairly closely, at this point [and the translation compromises between the incomplete Greek MSS and these two longer versions. Ed.].

[53] Again, τῶν συμβεβηκότων; Rufinus: *accidit*.

[54] ὁπότερον. This word generally signifies "either of two," or "which of two," but here (and in similar contexts) it must have a wider connotation. Cf. sect. 848d/IV, 11, Bakhuyzen, *op. cit*., p. 164, ln. 28.

men will be their own makers, and conversely, the cause of their own non-existence!][55] But if you affirm that these vices are his actions, then Man is held to be 'evil' because of what he does, and not because of what he is in substance. We said that a human is called evil from things that are "accidental"[56] to his or her substance — things which are not the actual substance just as a craftman takes his name from his craft.   c Now if Man is evil as a result of what he does, and what he does has a beginning of existence, then Man himself began to be evil, and these evil things also began to be; but if this is so, Man (162) was not originally evil, nor are evil things uncreated, for they prove to be created by him)[57].

10   DR.   You claimed that evil is in conduct[58], and not in substance; but evil proves to have existence through substance. Please, then, explain more fully how evil is in conduct, and not in substance.

AD[59]. (I affirm that at first there is nothing naturally bad; but that it is called bad according to the manner of its use. The term 'adultery' refers to the union of man and woman.   d Now, if a man should have union with his wife for the procreation of children and the continuation of the race, such union is good[60]; but if he forsakes and insults the lawful marriage by illicit union, he is guilty of a great wrong. The union itself is the same,

---

[55] The bracketed section is not found in Rufinus, but is in fact taken from Methodius, and so must be genuine. Bakhuyzen conjectures that the omission by the Latin translator may be due to his feeling that the reasoning is "too strange" (*Ibid.*, p. 163).

[56] Once more τῶν συμβεβηκότων. Rufinus: *substantiis accidentia*. In all three places where the word occurs, we have rendered the Greek by 'accidental' as the term most likely to convey the meaning of the original, if 'accidental' be understood, not in the popular, but the philosophical sense of something which is not the result of the essential nature of a thing, but an external, casual, chance happening or contingency. Cf. the use of ἐπισυμβαίνω in the perfect participle neuter plural to express "accidents, accidental properties" (cf. *supra*, ns. 50, 51, 53).

[57] The section "All these are of an 'accidental' nature ... prove to be created by him," is taken from Methodius (Bonwetsch edn., pp. 25-27). There are, as is usual, minor variations from the text of 'Adamantius'. [The non-inclusive language has been left because the argument hinges on the Adamic Fall. Ed.].

[58] τρόπῳ εἶναι τὰ κακά. Rufinus: *voluntate vel actibus esse mala* (evil is in will or actions).

[59] Here begins another long extract from Methodius. It is not found in Migne's edition of the *De lib. arbit.* (*Patrol. Graec.*, vol. 18), nor is it included in the *Philocalia*, for it belongs to a part of the Methodian work not used by Eusebius (cf. our Introduction B, 4, c). It is given, however, by Bonwetsch in his edition of 1891 used by Bakhuyzen.

[60] The Anglican Book of Common Prayer (Preface to the Marriage Service) indicates a threefold purpose for marriage: 1. the procreation of children; 2. the avoidance of sin; 3. mutual society. Of these aims, it is the first two (especially the first) that tend to be emphasized in the Fathers. In the Dialogue of Adamantius, the procreation of children receives approval; in Augustine the avoidance of sin (as in *Confess.*, 6, 12-13).

but the circumstances of its use are not. The same thing can be said of
unchastity in general. Sexual union, then, considered apart from the circumstances of its use, is not evil. It becomes evil only when a wrongful use
is apparent. I point out that it is the same with murder. Should a man
desire the death of someone caught in adultery,   **848a** demanding the
punishment of his shameless act, he does no crime. Yet, if a man kills someone who has done nothing illegal, on a mere pretext, or for the purpose of
removing his household property — that is, his money or goods — he does
wrong[61]. The act is the same in both cases, but the circumstances of the act
make the difference. To this may be added the (164) taking of money from
someone, where it is the circumstances of the taking that make it bad.
Should anyone, out of a desire to share, make a gift from his possessions,
the recipient does no wrong in taking it, but on the other hand were someone to seize it from another against his will, or secretly, he would do something evil.   **b** Taking what belongs to another is common to both parties,
but it is the circumstances of the taking that cause the latter to be called
bad. In the same way, the worship of God can become wrong by the circumstances of its performance. If a man worships the true God, he per-
forms a good deed, but if he forsakes Him, and worships a god that does
not exist, desiring to bestow the honour due to the Almightly on objects of
wood or stone, he does wrong. The act itself is indeed 'worship', but the
conditions governing its conduct alter what is done.

11   DR.   Well, as you brought the argument forward, endeavouring to
prove how evil exists,   **c** and how humans are the makers of it, may I ask
briefly whether they received the means of action from themselves — that
is, whether they themselves were the discoverers of such use, or whether
they were made such people by God, or again, whether there is someone
else who impels humans to such actions?

---

[61] This sentence is far from clear in the Greek. We could turn to Methodius for guidance
(since Adamantius is copying him here) were it not that in this place all that we have is the
Slavonic translation of the Greek original of Methodius. This runs, "Because of nothing but
the taking of his property, that is, his possessions and riches" (Bonwetsch edn., p. 44). After
the words, "someone who has done nothing illegal", Rufinus has, "in order that he may
fall upon his goods". This, however, is not in the Greek text, which has, οὐδενὸς ἄλλης
προσφάσεως λόγου χάριν. Bakhuyzen conjectures that perhaps the original of Adamantius
read, "should kill for the sake of nothing but a pretext, for the sake of removal of his household possessions;" or, "should kill for the sake of some other motive, because of the removal,"
etc. Migne renders, "But if anyone should kill him who has done none of the things that have
been forbidden for the sake of no other cause, nor because of private property (that is, either
money or possessions) taken for himself, he does wrong".

AD.   I do not claim that humans were made people of such a kind by God; I believe that they possess free will, and that this supreme gift was conferred them by God[62]. [All other things obey the Divine command out of necessity.   **d** If you speak of Heaven, it has its Master, and does not move from its appointed place; should you desire to discuss the sun, this body completes its appointed movement, without deviating from the course, and obeys the Master by some compelling force. You also see the earth similarly fixed and carrying out the behests of Him who gave the orders. It is the same with the other created bodies: they are compelled to obey their Maker, and not one of them can do anything except that for which it was created. Nevertheless, we do not compliment these bodies because they thus obey their Master, nor can they expect any future (166) advancement on the grounds that their obedience to orders has been voluntary][63].   **e** But Man received the power to obey whom he would, and brought himself into subjection[64]. He is not bound by the compulsion of nature, nor is he deprived of strength. Consequently, I claim that he is a free will agent in the interests of his future advancement — that he may receive from the Almighty something extra; something that is the reward of obedience, and which he begs as his due from his Maker. I believe that Man was made, not to suffer injury, but to achieve a higher position[65]. If he has come into existence as one of the heavenly bodies or the like, and served God from compulsion, then he can no longer receive the reward that his exercise of free will merits. He will be but a passive instrument of the Creator…[66] He who used Man was also the cause of these things. Did Man

[62] This statement by Adamantius is, of course, taken from Methodius. As given in the edition of G.N. Bonwetsch (*Griech. Christ. Schrift.*, vol. 27, Berlin, 1917), the Methodian text reads, "That human beings have become such from God I do not think it at all right to say. I say that the first man came into being as a free will agent (that is, free), from whom the successors of the race inherited the same freedom. Therefore I claim that the human was made free, and I do not want him to be a slave. I say that this was the best gift, graciously conferred on him by God. For all other things…"

[63] The passage is omitted by Rufinus, but it belongs to the original text (cf. Methodius, *Schriften*, Bonwetsch edn., pp. 46f).

[64] Cf. Augustine: "Thus it was fitting that Man should be created, in the first place, so that he could will both good and evil — not without reward, if he willed the good; not without punishment, if he willed the evil". "For it was in the evil use of his free will that Man destroyed himself and his will at the same time…" *Enchirid.*, 18, 105; and 9, 30.

[65] The Dialogue teaches that Man was created free so that by obedience to the will of his Creator, he might progress to higher things. [The non-inclusive language is kept with the translation of this passage because the text points to the Adamic situation. Ed.].

[66] There is a lacuna in the Greek text here. In Methodius, the gap is filled by the words "suffering unfairly the blame for that which he did wrong". The Slavonic translation has, "receiving neither praise for the good he did, nor blame for what wrong he committed".

know nothing more than that with which he was (168) born, he would never know the greater Good. Consequently I say that God honoured Man by providing him with the means of deliberate choice and a knowledge of the greater Good[67], and that He gave him the power to do what he wishes)[68]. [But if you (167) offer this objection, that as God knew beforehand that through free will Man would choose rather to do wrong, He ought not to have made him the kind of being He knew would fall, I reply first that we must recognize that it is not a just judgement to condemn because of foreknowledge anything which has not yet been committed in actual fact. Secondly, the objection infers that God ought to have been restrained by fear from making that which He had anticipated might go wrong, whereas, in fact, if anyone erred and fell, be would not at any time drift entirely from His divine Providence, nor is there anything that becomes completely lost to Him[69]. Above all, we must add to this that Man is a part — however great or small — of all rational nature, inasmuch as he was given, like all other rational[70] creatures freedom of choice, yet, like a sheep wandering over the mountains and hills of ignorance, he was brought back on the shoulders of the Good Shepherd, and restored to the ninety and nine sheep that had not wandered. When you look at the matter in this way do you think that the advancement and renown of the ninety and nine sheep ought to have been hindered so that one little sheep might not stray? There would indeed have been a hindrance if free (169) will, by which the

[67] τῶν κρειττόνων. In Hellenistic usage this could mean "the greatest good".

[68] The extract from Methodius ends here (cf. Schriften, Bonwetsch edn., pp. 43-48). In the Latin translation of our dialogue, however, the following enclosed section is found. Bakhuyzen points out that certain Greek loan words (e.g., stadium, agōn) might lead to the conclusion that the Latin addition represents a genuine Greek original now lost. Against this is the fact that there appears in it a question that has already been brought forward at 838/III, 10. But of course this repetition may be due to differences in the sources, and we cannot rule out the possibility that the Latin may after all be authentic.

[69] si labitur quis et decidat, a divina eius providentia nusquam prorsus abscedat, nec omnino aliquid sit quod illi penitus pereat. This is reminiscent of Origen's teaching regarding the possibility of ultimate salvation for all (De Princip., I, 6, 3; cf. Quasten, Patrology, op. cit., vol. 2, pp. 87-91). Jerome, in Ep. ad Pammach. et Oceanum. 7, claims that Origen taught that "after many ages and the one restoration of all things, Gabriel will be in the same state as the devil, Paul as Caiaphas, and virgins as prostitutes". The teaching (known as ἀποκατάστασις) that at last all may be saved (cf. J.N.D. Kelly, Early Christian Doctrines, op. cit., pp. 473f., 486), is also found in Clement of Alexandria, and in Gregory of Nyssa. It was strongly opposed by Augustine, and was at length condemned by anathema of a Church Council — probably that which met at Constantinople in 543 (cf. Quasten, op. cit., vol. 2, p. 42). [Rufinus, as defender of Origen's view and the translation of his works, will be interested in this insight, if indeed he does not accentuate it. Ed.].

[70] [Presumably animals are not intended in this reference, but orders of rational beings other than humans, e.g. angels. The flavour is Origenist. Ed.].

ninety and nine had continued on to the very peak of progress, had not
been granted to the rational world[71]. And the Divine Purpose has not overlooked the salvation of those who have wandered in any way, for He has
arranged this present visible world as a kind of racecourse.   f By this means
He offered a return to the pristine state as a reward of the struggle of con-
testants and adversaries in a limited combat. Throughout this struggle, the
human can, by the exercise of free will, choose the things   **849a** that make
for that goal[72], and at the same time reject those which do not].

12   EUTR.   The arguments of this unquestionably right (168) teaching can not only convince a foolish person, but can also refute one lacking
in understanding. I think it is quite wrong for Droserius and his colleagues
to keep on prolonging the debate with their ideas when the discussion has
made the matter clear to us. As decisive proof of this I think it appropriate
to take as an example what lies before us[73]: I liken the Truth and the Teaching of the Catholic Church and her shielder to an ever-flowing spring
which fills up as if with joy whenever her water is drawn off[74]. The more
Droserius draws water, expecting her to be exhausted,   **b** the more she

---

[71] This is a noble teaching, based on the parable of the Lost Sheep (Matt. 18: 12-14; Lk.
15:4-7); but it is also in harmony with Jesus' injunction in such passages as Lk. 13:24 ("strive
to enter by the narrow gate"); Mk. 8:34 ("let him deny himself and take up his cross and follow Me".); Matt. 10:22 ("he who shall persevere unto the end, shall be saved"). The author
of our dialogue would, in effect, say that free will was granted to us so that by
making the right choice we might begin the struggle upwards to higher things, and ultimately
reach the top of moral and spiritual achievement. But it could be only through strenuous
effort to the very end, as Jesus points out in the Gospel.

[72] So Origen: "This also is laid down in the Church's teaching, that every rational soul is
possessed by free will and choice ... we are not, however, compelled by necessity to act either
rightly or wrongly, as is thought to be the case by those who say that human events are due
to the course and motion of the stars, not only those events which fall outside the sphere of
our freedom of will but even those that lie within our own power" (*De Princip.*, 1, Praef., 5).
For Augustine, to note the determinative Western view, "freedom" meant "unimpeded activity", not freedom of choice, which was lost at the Fall. However, as A.C. Outler ("Introduction" to *Augustine: Confessions and Enchiridion (Library of Christian Classics 7)*, London 1955,
p.14) says, "He never wearied of celebrating God's abundant mercy and grace — but he was
also fully persuaded that the vast majority of mankind are condemned to a wholly just and
appalling damnation. He never denied the reality of human freedom and never allowed the
excuse of human irresponsibility before God — but against all detractors of the primacy of
God's grace, he vigorously insisted on both double predestination and irresistible grace".
Augustine's later writings are not always consistent with his earlier ones, but it is these later
works which we must accept as his mature opinions, and it is these which have done much
down the centuries to determine the theology of the Church on such issues.

[73] The Greek of this passage is not perfectly clear. Rufinus does not translate it.

[74] Migne translates this sentence, "I think that the teaching of the Catholic Church, and
he who defends her, are like an everflowing spring which, made to conduct water, flows constantly, gushing out increasingly as if with joy".

overflows with the rains again[75]. Therefore I think it is right that Droserius and Valens should retire from the unequal contest. However, if Marinus should desire, let him discuss his two remaining propositions[76], for they seem to be lacking in his previous exposition[77].

MARINUS.   With reference to Christ, I want to conduct an inquiry to determine whether (as you, Adamantius, and your friends claim) He assumed flesh from our substance[78]. I consider it perfectly outrageous to

[75] The passage beginning with the speech of Eutropius ("The arguments of this unquestionably right teaching...") down to this point ("...with the rains again.") contains a number of words that are *hapax legomena* so far as the Dialogue is concerned. They are of a metaphorical character, and contrast with the rather ordinary language of much of the rest of the Adamantian work. Nor do they seem to be taken from Methodius' writings that have come down to us. It could be, therefore, that the author of our dialogue has borrowed them from other writers, or from works of Methodius no longer extant. I refer to such expressions are: "ever-flowing"; "fills up as if with joy"; "overflows with the rains again"; "her water is drawn off".

[76] See sect. 835a/III, 1: "that Christ was born of a woman, and that the body will rise from the dead".

[77] With the following words (of Marinus) Picus and Humfrey in their Latin translations make a new section. The former gives it the title, "Concerning the Incarnation of Christ". In Greek codex "E" we have the heading, "Another Godless Doctrine of Marinus".

[78] ὑποστάσεως. This word, in Christian thought, underwent a development in meaning. Among its main significations are, substantial nature, substance, actual existence, reality, essence. It could thus be taken as almost a synonym of οὐσία (substance, essence, stable being, immutable reality). In fact Origen did use it in this way, while the anathemas attached to the Creed of Nicaea, 325 also contain ὑπόστασις with the same meaning. However, by about AD 350, the term was coming to be used in Christological discussions within the Church in the sense of 'person', i.e., 'individual reality'. Finally, largely under the influence of the Cappadocian Fathers, ὑπόστασις came to be defined as the equivalent of the Latin *persona* with the meaning fixed by Tertullian: objective modes of being, condition, status, function. Οὐσία was then reserved for the concept of the Latin *substantia* (substance, essential being). Until this clear-cut definition became current, however, there was much confusion within the Church in Christological controversies. For instance, long before the Cappadocian Fathers, and three quarters of a century prior to the beginning of the Arian controversy, Dionysius of Rome and his namesake of Alexandria (about the middle of the third century) had misunderstood one another's use of the term ὑπόστασις. Dionysius of Rome and his fellow-Westerners translated the Greek ὑπόστασις by the Latin *substantia*, not by *persona*, since at that time this Greek word was often regarded as almost identical with οὐσία. He therefore thought that when Dionysius of Alexandria spoke of three ὑποστάσεις in the Godhead, he meant three 'substances', and was thus teaching Tritheism. Dionysius of Alexandria and his Eastern friends were, by this view, proclaiming "in a way three Gods, since they divide the holy Monad into three separate substances (ὑποστάσεις) wholly foreign to one another" (cf. C.L. Feltoe, *The Letters and Other Remains of Dionysius of Alexandria*, (Cambridge Patristic Texts), Cambridge, 1904, p. 178). However, Dionysius was really using ὑπόστασις in a sense somewhat like the Latin *persona* (mode of being, condition, status, function). He says, "If, since there are three Persons (ὑποστάσεις), they say that they are separated, there *are* three, even though they may not wish it, otherwise, let them do away with the divine Triad altogether" (*ibid.*, p. 196). As a matter of fact, for the Westerners, using Latin, Tertullian in his *Adv. Prax.* (written sometime after 213) had defined the Godhead in terms that almost anticipated the results of

attribute this to the Immaculate Essence[79], especially as the Scriptures assert that He assumed heavenly flesh.

AD.   You realize that he who really wants the inquiry to be directed to its conclusion by wisdom will discreetly (170) lay aside an argumentative manner and his preconceived ideas. Thus he will discover the truth. So first please explain clearly what it is that you wish to have discussed.

MAR.   The inquiry is about Christ: I maintain that He took a heavenly body. Please indicate now what it is that you believe.

AD.   I claim that His body was of the substance[80] of Adam, who was the first to be formed. We also are of this substance.

MAR.   The teaching of Christians stands by faith and the Scriptures, so we must convince or be convinced from Scriptures.

AD.   Please bring your proofs from Scripture.

MAR.   First let me ask whether it is not a shameful thing to say **d 14** that the Word[81] of God Himself assumed flesh from a woman?

AD.   The Word of God experiences some passion if the Godhead feels shame[82].

Nicaea and the work of the Cappadocian Fathers: "All are of one, by unity of substance". The unity is distributed "into a Trinity" (the first use of the word as applied to the three Persons of the Godhead); the three are placed in the order, "the Father, the Son, and the Holy Spirit; three, however... not in substance but in form; not in power, but in appearance, for they are of one substance and one essence and one power". These three distinctions within the Godhead are called 'persons' (*personae*), by which Tertullian meant objective modes of being (cf. Quasten, *op. cit.*, vol. 2, pp. 285f., 324f.). Nevertheless, the confusion remained between East and West until Athanasius, who had himself used ὑπόστασις sometimes in the Western sense of 'substance', and sometimes in the Eastern sense of 'person', investigated the matter at the Council of Alexandria (AD 362) and found both sides really "in agreement". It was left to the Cappadocian Fathers and the Council of Constantinople of 381 to define terms and produce the formula, "One Substance in Three Persons" (μία οὐσία ἐν τρίσιν ὑποστάσεσιν). Cf. P. Auvray, P. Poulain and A. Blaise, *The Sacred Languages*, London, 1960, pp. 113f., Kelly, *op. cit.*, pp. 133-136.

[79] τῇ ἀχράντῳ οὐσίᾳ.

[80] τῆς ὑποστάσεως.

[81] αὐτὸν τὸν τοῦ θεοῦ λόγον. This was the great scandal to the Gnostics, that One who was the very Word of God — a Divine Being — should have any essential contact with Matter, and therefore with a human body. To be born of a woman would mean the very closest relationship with that which was evil — a negation of all deity and so a denial of the Supremely Good. To overcome the dilemma, the Gnostics and Marcion postulated a Docetic Christology, whereby Christ, the Word of God, did not really assume a real human body, nor die. Either He temporarily inhabited the human Jesus, or His 'body' was but a 'phantom' appearance. In the Dialogue of Adamantius, Marinus argues for the latter.

[82] In the Received Greek Text, the 'if' (εἰ) comes before the clause "The Word of God experiences some passion". This makes a difficult argument. Bakhuyzen, therefore, places it in

MAR.   Well?

AD.   Because you stated that it is shame to say that the Word assumed flesh. But the Godhead does not feel shame; it does not grasp at glory; nor does it experience desire. These things are passions, but the Godhead is not susceptible to passions[83]. I want now, to ask you a few questions.

850a   MAR.   Let me hear them.

AD.   Who created Man?

MAR.   God.

AD.   The Father of the Word — that is, of Christ?

MAR.   The Father together with the Word.

AD.   How did He create him?

MAR.   Just as the Scripture says: "Let us make Man," it says, "according to our image and likeness; and God took soil from the ground and fashioned Man"[84].

AD.   When God took soil, did He change it into something better or something worse?   (172)

MAR.   Obviously into something better.

AD.   If God was not ashamed to take soil and fashion Man from something inferior, was He ashamed to assume that which He had fashioned?

MAR.   How do you arrive at that conclusion?

---

front of the second clause ('the Godhead feels shame'). Thus the 'being ashamed' of which Marinus speaks would be a 'passion', but the very nature of the Godhead is inaccessible to passion (πάθος); and the 'being ashamed' has therefore been excluded from consideration. In the Latin of Rufinus, we find a question,"Can some passion (*passio aliqua*) happen to the Word of God, or something shameful to the Divinity?"

[83] The doctrine of the impassibility of God is here raised. The teaching has been held in three forms: 1) God is not passible as a result of external influences; 2) God is incapable of changing the emotions from within; 3) God is free from experiencing feelings of pain or pleasure caused by another being. It would seem that most of the Fathers of the Early Church held the doctrine, in one form or another. It was an essential element of religio-philosophical thought among the Greeks, from whence, presumably, the Greek Fathers took it, or at least were influenced by it. It was also asserted of Christ insofar as His divine nature is concerned. In our Dialogue, besides the passage on this page, we have the doctrine enunciated in sects. 855d, e/V, 8. The Council of Chalcedon (451) asserted the impassibility of the Godhead, distinguishing between the passibility of Christ's human nature, and the impassibility of His divine. The teaching has been fairly generally maintained in certain theological circles within the Church up to modern times, among the earliest writers opposing the view being James Hinton, in his *Mystery of Pain*, London, 1866.

[84] Gen. 1:26; 2:7 (after LXX, but free, especially in 2:7).

b   EUTR.   Did you say that Man has been created out of soil or not?

MAR.   I did.

EUTR.   Which then is the more honourable and glorious: soil, or Man?

MAR.   Man.

EUTR.   Then it is nonsense to say that He is not ashamed of the inferior product, but is ashamed of the superior one. If God was not ashamed to take soil, how could He be ashamed to take Man, who was made in His likeness?[85]

15   AD.   Does not Nature herself prove that the Word of God fashions humans, right up to the present day — or do you believe that the human is moulded into a living creature in the womb quite apart from God? [Further, how will He give a rational and heavenly spirit to those whom He has not Himself fashioned?][86]

MAR.   I believe that the power of God makes the human to be as a living creature.

AD.   Listen to what the Apostle says: "Christ, the power of God and the wisdom of God"[87].   c Hear John the Evangelist: "Through Him all things came into existence; not one created thing came into existence apart from Him"[88]. But in fact, Jeremiah the Prophet also declares God to be Man's Maker. He says, "Before I fashioned you, I knew you from the womb"[89]. David too confesses, "Thy hands have made me and fashioned me"[90]. Yes, in Genesis as well it says, "God took soil and fashioned

---

[85] With these words, Eutropius passes affirmative judgement on the preceding argumentation, begun in sect. 849c/IV, 13, as to whether Christ really assumed human flesh. Adamantius now turns to show that the power of God in His Word has been active in the creation of mankind generally, and that this makes it still more possible to believe that the Word actually did take a human body, for it is He who operates with God to form human bodies.

[86] The enclosed words are found in Rufinus only. They look rather like the insertion of a copyist who felt that they added strength to the reasoning. This may be doubted, although they are not at variance with the trend of the argument.

[87] 1 Cor. 1:24.

[88] Jn. 1:3. Adamantius follows the textual authorities EHK, fam.1, sy^h, bo, Chrysostom, Nonnus, Jerome, the Textus Receptus, in placing the full-stop after the second "was made" (γέγονεν). However, in favour of putting it after "nothing" (οὐδὲ ἕν) are C^x(D) GLW al lat sy^c.p sa fa as well as Clement of Alexandria, Irenaeus, etc.

[89] Jer. 1:5 (LXX).

[90] Ps. 118:73 (LXX).

man"[91]. [And the Apostle again: "But when it pleased God, who separated me from my mother's womb".][92] If then the Scriptures show that the Word of God moulded Man into a living creature,   **d** how is it that God accepts what is considered shameful (for you people claim that the Godhead can feel a sense of shame!), while you on your side disparage something higher and even more glorious?[93]

16   MAR.   What have you to say to the clear assertion of the Scriptures which state that Christ assumed a heavenly body? For instance, John the Evangelist says, "And the Word became flesh, and dwelt among us"[94].

AD.   The Evangelist has expressed the matter in a (174) completely orthodox[95] way; he shows that the Word dwelt among us, that is, in our flesh.

MAR.   But the Word was made flesh[96].

AD.   If it had said that the Word "was" flesh, you would have gained a point, but the "was made" shows clearly that what did not exist had been added, and that what did not previously have existence was now made.   **e** What has been made is not spoken of as 'existing', but as "made", since it had no existence before it was made. So the flesh of the pre-existent Word was made. Now what is made is later in time than that which exists.

MAR.   The Word Himself was made flesh; He did not assume anything external to Himself.

---

[91] Gen. 2:7 (after LXX, but not identical).

[92] Gal. 1:15. The enclosed passage is found only in the Greek. It does not seem to add anything vital to the argument, and may have been omitted by Rufinus for this reason, or else his Greek manuscript may not have contained it.

[93] The reasoning would appear to be, "If God, who (you say) can feel the passion of shame, accepts, in accordance with the Scriptures, humanness and the birth process (which is considered a thing of shame), why do you refuse to accept something much more glorious than human birth — the birth of Christ in a human body?"

[94] Jn. 1:14.

[95] ὀρθοδόξως. The adjective corresponding to this adverb, ὀρθόδοξος, denotes 'orthodox in religion', the compilers adducing the *Codex Justinianus* (AD fourth-sixth cents.) and others for its use in this way. The term was originally taken by the Eastern Church to distinguish its position from those of the Monophysites and Nestorians. Later on it was sometimes used by historians to mean the opposite of 'Catholic'. Here in the Dialogue, written at an earlier date, ὀρθοδόξως could signify either 'in an orthodox manner,' or simply 'correctly'.

[96] σάρξ ἐγένετο. Presumably Marinus interprets John 1:14 to mean that Christ existed originally as 'flesh': i.e., there was no need for Him to assume flesh by any external means. [This seems a curious position to ascribe to Marinus but it shows that Gnostics had to wrestle with the usage σάπξ in John's prologue and put their own special mystical-looking meaning on it; as the argument following indicates when Eutropius interprets Marinus as referring to 'heavenly flesh'. Ed.].

AD.   Is the Word of God capable or incapable of change?[97]

MAR.   Incapable.

EUTR.   By trying to show that the Word of God did not assume flesh and by evading this conclusion, you are piercing yourself with a very terrible and ungodly blasphemy.

MAR.   How is it blasphemy?

EUTR.   Well, first, because by your exegesis, this Word of God has no coherence;   f second, because the Word will be found capable of change if He was made flesh in the way you say. For that which is changed from what it was by nature will no longer be what it was, but what it has been made. Therefore it is futile to say that Christ is the Word of God, for by your view He is not Word but flesh. It is also futile to assert that He had heavenly flesh.

17   AD.   If Marinus believes that the Word was made flesh, and did not assume human flesh, will he please state what it was that suffered on the cross?

MAR.   He suffered in appearance[98].

---

[97] ἄτρεπτος (immutable, unchangeable), used of the Divine Essence. When used of the Logos, it means "one in essence with the Father, and remaining so when incarnate ... and suffering no change in the Incarnation". The adverbial form of this word has been made famous from its use by the Council of Chalcedon, which decreed that Christ was "revealed in two natures without confusion, without change, undividedly, inseparably" (ἐν δύο φύσεσιν ἀσυγχύτως, ἀτρέπτως, ἀδιαιρέτως, ἀχωρίστως γνωριζόμενον).

[98] I.e., that he supposedly, or was 'thought to suffer', rather than 'He did suffer'." With this answer, the Latin translator concludes his fourth book, and commences the fifth and last.

FIFTH PART

1   EUTROPIUS.   In appearance — that is, in fancy, but not in reality![1]

851a   ADAMANTIUS.   If He suffered in appearance, and not in reality, Herod sat in judgement only in appearance; in appearance Pilate washed his hands of Him, and in appearance Judas betrayed Him. Caiaphas[2] likewise delivered Him up in appearance; the Jews seized Him in appearance[3], and the apostles...[4]. Even His blood was poured out in appearance; the Evangelists preached the Gospel in appearance; Christ came from Heaven in appearance, and He (176) ascended in appearance. The salvation of mankind was also in appearance, and not in truth. Why then does Christ say, "I am the truth?"[5]

EUTR.   Marinus is emphatic: in word Christ says, I am the truth, but in fact He does nothing true!

b 2   MARINUS.   I maintain from the Scriptures that He came with a heavenly body.

AD.   So there is fleshy essence and substance in Heaven?[6] You must show from the Scriptures that there is in Heaven an essence that has flesh and blood, and bones, and then proceed to give the proofs.

---

[1] The Christology of Marcion was essentially Docetic. In harmony with his view that the Creator God was of inferior worth, Marcion could not believe that Christ ever clothed Himself with anything earthly or material, so there could be no question of His taking flesh formed by the God of Creation. Therefore, when Jesus Christ came on earth He did so in a body that was only apparent, a 'phantasma' (φάντασμα) similar to what the angels wear (cf. Lietzmann, *History of the Early Church, op. cit.*, vol. 1, p. 258). But a Docetic Christology was held also by the Gnostics fairly generally, for suffering and death are but qualities of matter, matter being evil in their view. With this issue Eutropius as arbitrator is made to open the Fifth part of the Dialogue according to Rufinus' translation.

[2] See Matt. 27:2.

[3] The Greek of this clause is δοκήσει καὶ Ἰουδαῖοι κατέσχον αὐτόν. Rufinus, however, has *et Iudaei putabantur clamare*. It is difficult to determine what word lies behind *clamare* (to shout out) and whether the Greek or the Latin has the correct reading.

[4] The Greek has a lacuna here. Rufinus fills it by "defended Him". Bakhuyzen suggests that "stood by Him" and that (παρῆσαν αὐτῷ) stood in the original text.

[5] Jn. 14:6.

[6] Note the use of οὐσία and ὑπόστασις as practically synonyms. See pt. 4, n. 18, *supra*, and n. 13 *infra*.

MAR.   I will give proof respecting the body. The Apostle says, "there are heavenly bodies and there are earthly bodies"[7].

AD.   The Apostle calls heaven, sun, or moon a body. He says this: "There are heavenly bodies and there are earthly bodies. One is the glory of the sun, another the glory of the moon, and another the glory of the stars. Star differs from star in glory.   c So also is the resurrection of the dead"[8]. So show whether flesh and blood, and bones have substance in Heaven.

MAR.   Body and flesh are the same.

EUTR.   The Apostle undoubtedly declares heaven, sun, and moon to be bodies[9].

AD.   They[10] are not the same. We cannot call Heaven 'flesh', but we call it a 'body'. So first show that flesh and blood, and bones, have essence in Heaven, and then offer the proofs.

EUTR.   Adamantius asserts that Christ assumed earthly flesh — that is, from us, but Marinus is emphatic that He took heavenly flesh. d It must be shown, then, whether there is fleshly substance[11] in Heaven, and then we must turn to prove whether He assumed flesh from the earthly or from the heavenly substance.

AD.   [Let the Word Himself teach him who will not be taught by this.][12] As it is clear that fleshly substance[13] (178) exists, I too will produce evidence from the Scriptures that the heavenly Word assumed flesh, blood and bones. From the Gospel first: [It is fully related how He was bound; beaten with whips, and fastened to a cross, nailed hand and foot; also how His side was pierced by a soldier with a spear so that blood flowed

[7] 1 Cor. 15:40.
[8] 1 Cor. 15:40-42.
[9] Rufinus has instead of this, "In what way does the Apostle speak of sun and moon as celestial bodies?" This is a good instance of the freedom taken by the Latin translator in rendering from the original: he is prepared to go so far as to alter the sense. Bakhuyzen rightly points out that, as Rufinus has it, Eutropius wants to have the preceding argument more fully explained, but as the Greek text runs, he is convinced, apparently, that Marinus is correct. This tendency to 'improve' the text has to be constantly watched in Rufinus who very often paraphrases rather than translates.
[10] "They" presumably refers to the "body and flesh" mentioned by Marinus, not to the statement of Eutropius that intervenes.
[11] οὐσία σαρκός (lit. "substance of flesh").
[12] The enclosed passage is from Rufinus. We cannot be sure of its authenticity.
[13] The Greek τῆς ὑποστάσεως τῆς σαρκικῆς, apparently varying from the notion underlying the similar expression just previously [though indicating that the author is not used to making a distinction between *ousia* and *hypostasis*? Ed.].

out.][14] After the resurrection from the dead, when Thomas did not believe, he said, "Put your finger into the marks of the nails and your hand into my side, and be no longer unbelieving but believing. A spirit does not have flesh and bones, as you see Me to have"[15].

EUTR.   Christ plainly showed that He had flesh and bones. e So it must first be shown that there is substance[16] in Heaven possessing flesh and bones, and then you both will discover which is the sounder argument.

MAR.   I have proved that His body was a heavenly one.

EUTR.   In that case, it is proved that He assumed the flesh and bones of stars — which is impossible!

AD.   Paul will most surely stop you by showing the distinction between body and flesh: "You also were once thus,   852a enemies of God, and strangers from the promise of the Covenants; but now He has exchanged (you) in the body of His flesh"[17]. He has thus plainly shown that Christ assumed both body and flesh.

[EUTR.   Let him show whether there is a substance in Heaven having flesh, blood and bones.][18]

MAR.   Christ had a heavenly body, and we prove that it was heavenly.

AD.   From what kind of substance? From angelic substance? or that of Ruling Power? or of Lordship?[19] Please tell us from what source Christ assumed a body.

---

[14] The words in brackets are found only in the Latin. While there is no guarantee of their genuineness, their insertion at this point is appropriate since they lead up quite naturally to the account of the post-resurrection appearances. [Cf. Jn. 19:34 for the Biblical allusion, yet with water being also mentioned. Ed.].

[15] Jn. 20:27; Lk. 24:39 (with slight variations from the main recensions).

[16] οὐσία. This and subsequent references to substance immediately below remain with this usage.

[17] Ephes. 2:12, 16; Col. 1:21-22 (with variations from the main recensions, the most important of these being ἀντικατήλλαξεν (exchange) for ἀποκατήλλαξεν (reconcile). There seems to be no other MS evidence for the reading in 'Adamantius', and Rufinus has *reconciliate estis*.

[18] The enclosed words are found only in the Greek. They seem to be an intrusion, for without them, the following statement of Marinus fits very neatly on to that of Adamantius preceding. But of course Rufinus may have omitted the words in the interests of style.

[19] For ruling powers: τῆς ἐξουσίας. For lordship: κυριότητος. For the latter we are reminded of the same expression in Col. 1:16; Ephes. 1:21, where as here the reference seems

EUTR.   Your party[20] has not proved that there is a substance, and yet you claim that he assumed heavenly flesh. So you must believe that he assumed a body from non-existent elements.

4   MAR.   We say that Christ assumed a body in appearance. Just as the angels appeared to Abraham,   b and ate and drank with him, thus also he appeared.

AD[21].   Why then did He come to teach us the truth so that we could be saved through Him? Or did He, by your theory, speak falsely when He promised us salvation? If indeed Christ calls us to life through falsehood, the false promise was not true; but if he was a teacher of truth it is clear tht He was speaking (180) the truth from the first. Let Marinus and his friends therefore decide which of the two statements they intend to call false: c that of themselves, or that of Christ. Since they deny the birth of Christ according to the flesh and the plan of salvation through Him, how is it that they listen to Him when He calls Himself Son of Man? If He was revealed in a form that only 'seemed' to be man, what need was there to call Himself Son of Man? He should have said simply "The Man must suffer many things"[22].   d If He wanted to teach men the truth, why did he call Himself, not man, but Son of Man, falsely claiming to be what He was not? Rather would He simply and truly say of Himself that which He really was. He would not make Himself more esteemed by being thought a man, instead of God, nor would they believe on Him more if they considered Him to be a man, rather than God[23]. Moreover, if He came into the world because He wanted the truth to be known as the teachers of Docetism[24]

to be to grades of angelic powers which were believed to form the hierarchy of heaven. The hosts of the angels of God were sometimes divided into nine ranks: seraphim, cherubim, thrones, dominions, powers, empires, principalities, archangels, angels — all arranged in that descending order of importance. Cf. also Rom. 8:38-39.

[20] That is, Marinus and his friends.

[21] The following passage, as Bakhuyzen suggests, should be compared with Methodius (Bonwetsch edn., p. 269).

[22] Cf. Mk. 8:31; Lk. 9:22.

[23] The Greek of this sentence is not perfectly clear. Bakhuyzen thinks it may be defective. Perhaps the thought is, "Christ makes it plain that He did really come as a man. Why did he claim this if it were not the truth? He had nothing to gain by being thought a man rather than God. People would not esteem and believe in Him more readily if He were a man, and not God!"

[24] Docetism — the form of belief.which maintained that the humanity and sufferings of our Lord were only apparent, not real — arose early. It may be that we have indications of such teaching in the Johannine letters (e.g., 1 Jn. 4:2-3; 2 Jn. 7) and in Colossians the error combatted may have included this idea [cf. C.F.D. Moule, The Epistle of Paul the Apostle to Colossians and to Philemon: an introduction and commentary, Cambridge, 1957. Ed.]. The

understand it, he ought not to have been transformed so as to appear to be what he was not, but rather to have been unknown. Again, He ought not to have kept secret what he really was, calling Himself man instead of God. And we should say this if He called Himself simply man, but when He asserts that He is Son of Man, how can my opponents e cunningly contrive to put forward the lie that it was because He was seen in human (182) form He was actually thought to be Son of Man?[25] And why do I speak only of form? For men are seen not only in form but also in substance, since they are human by nature. Adam and Eve were not 'sons of men', nor were they so 853a called. If the term 'son' were indicative of the substance of human beings, Adam and Eve, being human beings, ought to have been called 'sons of men'. The holy angels, too, ought to have used the name 'son of man' in this way, since they have very often appeared in the form and likeness of human beings.

EUTR.   The word "son" does not show the substance of human beings, but their birth from human beings.

5   MAR.   *I* believe that just as the angels appeared to Abraham, and ate and drank and conversed with him, so Christ appeared to humans.

AD.   They were types[26] before the coming of Christ, but when the Truth had come, the types ceased, according to the Apostle; "The Law is a shadow of the good things to come"[27] b [not the exact image of the things.][28] So if Christ Himself came as the angels did — as a shadow and prophetically — we ought, by your view, to look now for another who is truly Son of Man; One who truly dies, is buried and rises from the dead; One who will give true salvation to humanity.

MAR.   If the angels were types of Christ, how is it that they ate and drank with Abraham? Did they really eat, or not?

Gnostics were particularly attracted by the Docetic teaching, as indeed was Marcion, for it fitted in with the view of both that Christ, the Divine Logos, could not possibly have had any real contact with the created world of matter, which was the work of the Demiurge. Docetism was strongly opposed by Ignatius and other anti-Gnostic writers, while the name itself (Δοκηταί) seems to have been first used by Serpion, Bishop of Antioch (190-203). According to the Docetists, Christ avoided death, e.g., through changing place with Judas or Simon of Cyrene just prior to the Crucifixion.

[25] This was exactly what the Docetic teachers held, that the term 'Son of Man' (υἱὸς τοῦ ἀνθρώπου) means, not that our Lord had a genuinely human birth, but that He had a human form.

[26] τύποι ('type' here referring to the persons or things used by God in OT times to indicate persons or things in the future).

[27] Heb. 10:1.

[28] The bracketed phrase is from Rufinus' quotation of the Scriptural passage.

AD.   The angels, since they prefigured[29] the Truth — that is, the Saviour Christ — really ate, although the food gave their bodies no additional growth.   c Just as fire consumes and destroys everything put before it, so it was with the angels who were with Abraham. The Apostle says this: "These things happened to them as types; and they were written for our instruction, upon whom the end of the world has come"[30].

EUTR.   It certainly seems to me that the Apostle uses a shadow and type of future Truth, of which the angels were also figures. Therefore the metaphor of the angels as a type will agree with the apostolic letter most appropriately and well. If Christ appeared in the same manner as the angels, presenting (184) a likeness and figure of the Truth,   d another Christ must be sought whose likeness and figure both the angels and Christ present. It is also futile for Christ to say, "I am ... the Truth"[31].

6   AD.   I want to discuss with greater clarity the matter of the 'likeness', the 'figure' and the 'truth'. The figure of the angels was intangible and untouchable, but the Truth (that is, Christ) was seized and suffered; He had flesh, blood and bones, and was raised from the dead. Again, the angels did not confess themselves to be human beings, as Christ did when He said, "Who touched Me? For I perceived that power went out from Me"[32]. Thomas also was convinced when he touched the scars of the wounds.   e Did Christ then want to deceive His hearers — particularly His true disciples — or by teaching them the truth, did He want them to know that He was untouchable, and had thus assumed flesh, blood and bones? But if (as the Docetists claim) He was without flesh and blood, when He gave the bread and the cup, and commanded His disciples to commemorate Him through them, of whose flesh [or body][33] or blood were they the likeness? The Apostle is also among those commanded, for he testifies to these things and says that the bread and the cup of blessing are the communion[34] of the flesh and blood.   f But if the   854a Lord

---

[29] πρότυποι γενόμενοι. Πρότυπος being 'pre-image'.

[30] 1 Cor. 10:11, reading τύποι συνέβαινον (with [A]D G al Ir^arm Coptic and TR) for τυπικῶς συνέβαινεν of the main recensions. Marcion has ἀτύπως, "without a type". See also sect. 832c/II, 18 where this same Scripture is quoted, and refer to pt. 2, nss. 85-87.

[31] Jn. 14:6.

[32] Lk. 8:45-46, reading ᾐσθήθην for ἔγνων, and ἐξελθοῦσαν for ἐξεληλυθυῖαν, of main readings.

[33] "or body" is not found in Rufinus, and is open to question.

[34] κοινωνίαν αἵματός τε εἶναι καὶ σαρκός. See 1 Cor. 10:16. κοινωνία which may be rendered either, "a means for attaining a close relationship with the blood (body) of Christ," or, "participation in the blood (body) of Christ".

had all that a perfect man has[35] — a rational soul, and flesh and blood —
yet (as the Docetists think) in appearance, and not in reality, Paul did not
proclaim the truth either[36], and (by my opponents' theory) we strive in
vain after the truth: for the Lord did not want to make it known either
through Himself or the Apostle. In addition to opposing ... we want to
know what He does not want us to know[37]. But if Christ is true, being
absolute truth, He who has suffered, then Paul also, who was sent by
Him, will be true when he says, "Or do you seek a proof that Christ is
speaking in me?"[38] We ought to heed the writings of the Apostle as we do
the words of (186) Christ.   **b** Through him we learn that Christ had
both body and blood; that He truly died for our sakes, and set us free
indeed by His own death and blood. It is impossible to believe that
Christ, who came down from Heaven, suffered these things if He did not
assume flesh. That the Apostle does not preach 'death' and 'blood' in a
veiled[39] sense, but quite openly, I will show by reading. This is the way he

---

[35] The Greek text is, ὅσα ἄνθρωπος τέλειος ἔχων, which does not make a complete sentence. Bakhuyzen conjectures that perhaps the author actually wrote ὅσα ἄνθρωπος τέλειος
ἔχει, ἔχων. The suggestion has been accepted for the English translation.

[36] Bakhuyzen thinks that the text here may perhaps be emended to read, "neither through
Him nor though Paul was the truth proclaimed".

[37] The Greek text here is unintelligible. Bakhuyzen suggests that we should read, "In
addition to this, we oppose Him if we desire this..." But lack of better MSS must leave the
matter in doubt. Rufinus has, "and more — we are found to be acting against the will of God
when we desire to know what He did not want even His own disciples to know".

[38] 2 Cor. 13:3.

[39] παρακεκαλυμμένως: disguised, cloaked, covered. Here we may have a reference to
the allegorical method of exegesis so dear to the Alexandrian Fathers. By this means, several different hidden significations may be conveyed by a single passage of Scripture. Alle-
gory, of course, is in itself legitimate enough, and is found in the Bible (e.g., Isa. 5:1-6;
Ps. 80:8-16). Allegorism was used by Philo and the Rabbinical schools of Palestine, and
by Paul (as in Gal. 4:21-31 on the two covenants). The method is also found in Barnabas,
Clement of Rome, Irenaeus, and Tertullian. But it was left to the Alexandrian School to
carry it to an excess. The Alexandrian Fathers found an allegorical meaning in almost
every passage of Scripture, even to the extent, on occasion, of denying that the words had
a literal sense at all. Clement of Alexandria interpreted Scripture from four points of view:
the literal, mystical, moral and prophetical. Origen looked at the Bible from three angles:
the literal, moral and spiritual, corresponding to threefold division of man into body, soul
and spirit. Of these three, Origen put special emphasis on the last, the spiritual. The
Fathers of the Latin Church, particularly Ambrose and Augustine, hold, in the main, a
middle position, accepting both a literal as well as an allegorical sense in a large number
of OT passages. In the Dialogue of 'Adamantius', there is little evidence of allegorism,
which is in harmony with the view that the work was composed in or near Syria, the
home of the Antiochian School, the members of which used the allegorical method spar-
ingly. Cf. Kelly, *Early Christian Doctrines, op. cit.*, pp. 69-78 [cf. also R.L. Wilken, *Judaism
and the Early Christian Mind: a study of Cyril of Alexandria's exegesis and theology*, Yale,
1971. Ed.].

speaks: "I make known to you the Gospel which I preached to you, which also you received, and in which you stand. By it you are also saved if you hold the word fast with which I preached to you — unless you have believed in vain. c For I passed on to you first and foremost that Christ died for our sins; that He was buried, and that He rose again the third day"[40]. If then anyone has not "believed in vain," but holds what the Apostle delivered, makes known the Gospel by which we are saved, and holds this...[41].

EUTR. The Apostle shows this most accurately when he says, "Christ died for our sins; He was buried, and on the third day arose". On this view, what is said will be false if Christ did not have flesh, but was only a spirit having an appearance of a human being. d A spirit could not be delivered up, since it is intangible; nor die, since it does not belong to mortal nature. And a spirit cannot be buried! What more must we say? Spirit does not naturally have blood. Moreover, if the Scriptures announce the salvation of mankind through the death and blood of Christ, yet the Docetists deny that He has flesh and blood, then He did not really die, not was He buried and rose again[42] — for He did not have blood! Instead, these things are said to have happened to Him, not in reality, but in appearance. Consequently, we have not been saved in reality, but only in appearance, just as the world could not be saved when those others came in appearance. e (I speak of the angels in the time of Abraham, and of any other case that may have been recorded). Thus we have been (188) deceiving concerning our faith, in that we have obtained hope and salvation only in appearance.

AD. Give me your attention a little longer, and you will hear stronger proofs from the Apostle. He says, "If Christ has not been raised from the dead, then our preaching is senseless and our faith is also senseless"[43]. So if (as the Docetists claim) He suffered in appearance, and not in reality, He did not truly die. It is evident then that He was not truly raised from the dead, and in actual fact, the preaching will be in vain, and like-

---

[40] 1 Cor. 15:1-4 (abbreviated).

[41] The Greek text is here defective, and Rufinus is no help, owing to his freedom of rendering. Bakhuyzen thinks that the author may have written, "If anyone, then, has not believed in vain, but holds what the Apostle delivered, and makes known the Gospel by which we are saved he holds this fast".

[42] The words "and rose again" are not in the Greek text, but would appear to have fallen out, since the following words do not make sense without them.

[43] 1 Cor. 15:14 (with slight variations from main recensions).

wise our faith. Then he adds, "And if Christ is preached risen from the dead,[44] He is the first-fruits of those who have fallen asleep, for since through a man came death, through a man came also resurrection of the dead. For as in Adam all die, so also in Christ all will be made alive. As the first-fruits[45], Christ".

7   EUTR.   You believe the Apostle, Marinus?

855a   MAR.   I certainly do believe him; however, note how the same Apostle states, "He who descended is He also who ascended"[46]. And in the Gospel it says, "No one has ascended into heaven, except He who descended from heaven — the Son of Man[47] [who is in heaven]"[48]. You see, it distinctly states that He came from Heaven.

AD.   These proofs may strengthen our teaching.

MAR.   How?

AD.   Rather does the Gospel show clearly that, unless the Word had come down from heaven, the human being would not have gone up into heaven.   **b** It declares, "No one has ascended into heaven, except He who descended from heaven". The "has ascended" is indicative of a past time. It did not say that no one will ascend, but "no one has ascended". It therefore clearly showed that before Christ no one had ascended. This is as the Apostle says, "the firstborn"[49]; and again, "the first-fruits of those who have fallen asleep"[50]. Yet further he says, "the first-fruits, Christ; then those who belong to Christ"[51]. So before the Word of God descended and took upon Himself humanity from the womb, no human had gone up, but after Christ ascended, then also those who are His. The Apostle spoke thus, "As the first-fruits, Christ; then those who belong to Christ". By the statement, "He who descended is He also who ascended", the Apostle wishes to show that the Word is impassible[52] and unchangeable.   **c** In actual (190) fact,

---

[44] 1 Cor. 15:12. The Greek text omits 'risen' (ἐγήγερται); it has been supplied from Rufinus.

[45] 1 Cor. 15:20-23 (with slight variations from the main recensions).

[46] Ephes. 4:10.

[47] Jn. 3:13.

[48] The enclosed words added from Rufinus.

[49] Col. 1:18; πρωτότοκος, this word referring to Christ as the first-born of God's new humanity, which is ultimately to be glorified as Christ is. Cf. Rom. 8:29.

[50] 1 Cor. 15:20

[51] 1 Cor. 15:23

[52] Cf. *supra*, pt. 4, n. 83.

He who descended is the very One who ascended, since He did not change
from what He was, that is, God.

8   EUTR.   These words agree with the views of Adamantius. However, I want both sides to explain the matter.

   AD.   The Word of God came down and assumed humanity from
the undefiled virgin Mary in the womb, and Christ was born without sexual union with man. He who was conceived of Mary by the Holy Spirit
endured all human sufferings so that He might save man.

   MAR.   When the man was suffering, was the Word present at the
same time, or not?

   EUTR.   First put forward your explanation.

d   AD.   Permit me first to answer Marinus' question, then let him
put forward his explanation. The Word of God was present with the man,
but He suffered no injury, just as adamant[53] remains sound when it is
struck by iron, and on the contrary, causes injury to the very thing meant
to injure it. Again, asbestos[54], when it is consigned to the fire, remains
unbroken and unspoiled, without any damage. Nor is the fire, when cut by
a sword, divided, for the dense flame runs back on itself and remains indi-
visible. If, then, material substances exert their strength against other substances and cannot be consumed, much more surely did the Word of God,
e being of an impassible and unchangeable nature, remain impassible, and
absorbed[55] the sufferings. With your permission, I read in the Gospel that
Christ was born of Mary.

---

   [53] Ἀδάμας, 'the invincible'. The term was used of the hardest iron or steel. Pliny has the
word referring to white sapphire, and it was later applied to the diamond. Ἀδάμας was
once thought to be a rock or mineral consisting of fabulous but contradictory properties.
The English term 'adamant', though derived from the Greek word, is now often merely a
poetic or rhetorical name for impregnable hardness. The Church Fathers applied ἀδάμας
to Christ, because of its great strength (so Cyril of Alexandria, d. 444). Sometimes they
used it of strong souls (so Eusebius of Caesarea, d. 339; Chrysostom, d. 407); or again, of
a hard nature (so Basil of Caesarea, d. 379) [cf. Lampe, *Patristic Greek Lexicon, op. cit.*, s.v.
Ed.].
   [54] ἀμίαντος ('undefiled', 'pure') here referring to a variety of asbestos of a mineral character that split up in to fibres. Ἀμίαντος is also used by the Protevangelium of James (second
century AD), and by Athanasius (d. 373).
   [55] This word ἀναλίσκω, here means 'destroy', conveying the idea of taking up, or absorb-
ing the suffering, and so destroying it. Rufinus has *suscipiens passiones*. Gregory of Nazianzus
(d. *ca.* 390) uses the term of the soul reunited with the body after death.

9 MAR. We, too, admit that He was born through Mary, but not from Mary[56]. Just as water passes through a pipe, adding nothing on the way, so also the Word passed through Mary but was not born from Mary.

AD. Request that the Gospel be read.

EUTR. Let it be read.

AD. I read how the angel said to Mary, "The Holy Spirit will come upon you, and the power of the Most High will overshadow you. Therefore also the Holy child born of you will be (192) called the Son of the Most High"[57].

f EUTR. Perhaps you will say, Marinus, the voice of the angel came 'in appearance,' but what would more truly express the matter than the statement of the angel: "Therefore also the holy child **856a** born of you?" It does not say, 'which will be born through you' but 'of you'. Would it not most certainly be senseless to admit that the Word came through Mary (as through a channel), and yet deny that He received anything from her? If you and your friends, Marinus, deny His birth from a virgin out of a sense of shame (assuming that it is right to ascribe the feeling of 'shame' to the Godhead), you still admit the act of passing through the natural channel of a virgin — to which shame is attached — and yet deny something that is more honourable and more fully part of the Divine plan: for if the Word did not consider it shameful to pass through Mary, no more was He ashamed to receive humanity from her. Furthermore, why was it necessary for Christ to pass through Mary if He was not to receive something from her?[58]

---

[56] διὰ Μαρίας, ἀλλ' οὐκ ἐκ Μαρίας. This concept is definitely attributed to Gnostic teaching by Irenaeus (in *Adv. Haeres.*, 3, 11, 3). The whole reasoning of the paragraph shows the straits to which those who denied the real Incarnation of Christ were reduced in their desire to prevent the divine Word from having contact with matter. Whatever difficulties may be felt in the doctrine of the Virgin Birth, the dogma of Marinus enunciated here surely stretches faith to breaking point, and it is small wonder that the Church opposed it.

[57] Lk. 1:35. "of thee" (ἐκ σοῦ) is not found in the main recensions, but is attested by θ, fam.1, 13 a c e f¹ vg(11); Valentinus, Marcion, Tertullian, *et al.* Also, in place of "Son of the Most High" the main recensions have "Son of God".

[58] It is difficult to bring out the meaning of the Greek text adequately in the passage: "If you and your friends, Marinus ... something from her?" In an effort to do justice to the original, the English translation follows to some extent the rendering of Rufinus. This runs in full, "When, therefore, as you people say, birth from a virgin is denied because of the disgrace — if, in fact, any disgrace is to be ascribed to the Divine nature in His circumstances — that which actually does belong to disgrace (his passing through the natural channel of a virgin) you acknowledge, and yet that which is clearly noble and necessary for our common salvation you decline. If the Word of God was not ashamed to pass through the material of the flesh,

10   AD.   If He had not assumed humanity from Mary, how would the words spoken by the Apostle be substantiated?   **b** How will He be "the firstborn from the dead" and "the firstfruits of those who have fallen asleep"? Let Marinus and his friends explain it. If they claim that Christ appeared only in an outward form, like the angels He cannot be the first-born, nor the firstfruits.

MAR.   How is that?

EUTR.   Did the angels appear before Christ, or Christ before the angels?

MAR.   The angels appeared to Abraham, a long time before Christ[59].

EUTR.   If the angels and Christ both were revealed in appearance, Christ cannot be 'firstborn', since the angels were seen first, by your own admission, and needs must that   **c** those who were first were 'firstborn'!

11   AD[60].   In what sense will Christ be the firstfuits of them that sleep when the son of the Shunammite[61] arose from the dead a long time before Him, and when the widow of Sarephta's son[62] and Lazarus likewise preceded Him[63]. If then, Christ did not really die, yet these events took place, not in appearance, but in actual fact (just as John the Evangelist says: "The Law was given through Moses; grace and truth came through Jesus Christ")[64], (194) let Marinus explain how Christ is "the first-fruits of them that sleep".

MAR.   Give us your explanation.

---

how was it that He resisted assuming something from it? Why did He have to pass through, if He did not seek to receive something therefrom?"

[59] Cf. Gen. 18:2-4.

[60] The reasoning of Adamantius in the following paragraph is reminiscent of the argument of Methodius in his *Dialogue on the Resurrection*, (cf. Bonwetsch edn., pp. 255, 257; Migne, *Patrol. Graec.*, vol.18, col. 319: "But if anyone, unable to accept this [the preceding statement], should answer, 'How is it then, if no one arose before Christ went down into Hades, that some are already recorded as having arisen before Him — among whom are the son of the widow of Sarephta, the son of the Shunammitess, and Lazarus?' we must reply, But these arose only to die again…"

[61] Cf 4 Kgs. 4:12, 36 (LXX). The spelling of the name of the mother of the boy varies in the MSS of the Bible and our dialogue.

[62] 3 Kgs. 17:9-10, 23 (LXX); Lk. 4:26.

[63] Jn. 11:43-44.

[64] Jn. 1:17

AD.   I maintain that Christ really is both "firstborn from the dead" and the "firstfruits of them that sleep".   **d** For as Adam, the first-born, died, so Christ was the first to rise. As evidence, I will cite the very words of the Apostle: "As in Adam all die, so also in Christ all will be made alive; as the first-fruits, Christ, then those who belong to Christ"[65]. Whom else should we find teaching us so clearly both things: that Christ died, and that He was a man — that which died? If Christ, who was raised from the dead, is "the first-fruits of them that sleep", **e** in order that the resurrection from the dead might be through man, and this resurrection be understood to happen in the same manner as death came through man, these persons are two men, the one, Adam, through whom came death; the other, Christ, through whom came the resurrection. [It does certainly say, "The first man was of the earth, earthly: the second man was from heaven"[66]. But just as he who is called 'earthly' could not have been called 'man' unless he had been 'breathed into' from heaven (for, "God breathed into his face the breath of life; and man became a living soul")[67], so also He who is said to be 'from heaven' could not be called 'man' unless human flesh were united with the heavenly Word. This was in order that, just as at that time he who was of earth assumed the image of the divine nature, so also now, at this time, He who was from heaven might assume the image of human nature, and thus, as our image had been restored in Him, so now at last His image might be revived in us.][68] One of two things must, then, have happened: either the Word who came down from Heaven, or man (whose humanity He assumed) died[69]. It must logically follow — and my opponents will acknowledge it — that He who descended from Heaven was God[70], and that it was for the purpose of setting us free He assumed mortal flesh. Through this flesh we were set free, and He thus became the first-fruits of the resurrection,   **f** because this was the first to be raised from the dead. Having acknowledged in this way that Christ is truly God according to the

[65] 1 Cor. 15:22-23.

[66] 1 Cor. 15:47.

[67] Gen. 2:7 (LXX).

[68] Enclosed passage found only in Rufinus. The Latin translation of the whole of this speech of Adamantius is very paraphrastic; we cannot, therefore, be certain that the words bracketed are authentic, although their thought is not inconsistent with what has preceded.

[69] "...man (whose humanity He assumed) died." The Greek of this is, ὁ ἐξ οὐρανοῦ καταβὰς λόγος ἀπέθανεν, ἢ ὃν ἀνέλαβεν ἄνθρωπον, κτλ. This is an instance of "inverse attraction", where the antecedent is attracted into its relative clause. The usage is classical (see W.W. Goodwin, *A Greek Grammar*, London, 1894 edn., p.221, sect. 1037) and also found in the NT (e.g., 1 Cor. 10:16).

[70] Bakhuyzen changes an ἤ of the text to καί (on what seem to be sufficient grounds) to make this reading possible.

spirit, and truly man according to the flesh[71] we shall hold the Faith, not "in appearance", but as it is, true and steadfast. It is this indeed that the Apostle 'delivered': (196) that Christ died according to the flesh, was buried, rose from the dead, and is the first-fruits of the resurrection of them that sleep[72].

12   MAR.   You said that many arose before Christ. How then can He be the first-fruits?

AD.   Those who arose before Christ died again[73], but "Christ, having risen, dies no more; death no longer has dominion over Him. For, in regard to His death, He died to sin, once for all, but in regard to His life, He lives to God"[74].   857a Over what, then, did death have dominion? The statement "no longer has dominion" shows that it did have dominion formerly.

EUTR.   It is evident that if death did not have dominion over the flesh which the Word assumed, we shall have to say that death had dominion over the Word — that is, if the Word did not really assume flesh. However, I do not consider it reverent to say that death had dominion over the Word of God!

AD.   Now hear what the Apostle has to say about Christ's death, showing that He did really die, and did not merely appear to do so; hear also what he says regarding Christ's blood, showing that it was truly poured out for our salvation. These are his words: "But God shows His love towards us, **b** because while we were still sinners, Christ died for us. Much more, since we have been justified by His blood, shall we be saved from wrath"[75]. Here again: "For although He was crucified in weakness, He yet lives by the power of God"[76]. And this also: "Do you not know that all of you who were baptized into Christ Jesus, were baptized into His death?"[77] If He did not die, who can doubt that there is no bap-

---

[71] κατὰ πνεῦμα and κατὰ σάρκα. These phrases from Rom. 1:3-4 are rendered by the NEB rather suggestively as "on the level of the spirit," and "on the human level". [Note the anticipation of the Christological definition of the Council of Chalcedon, AD 451. Ed.].

[72] See 1 Cor. 15:3-4, 20. This, of course, was an essential part of the early Kerygma and of the Creeds.

[73] οἱ πρὸ χριστοῦ ἀναστάντες πάλιν αὖθις ἀπέθανον. Compare this with Methodius' οὗτοι εἰς τὸ καὶ αὖθις ἀποθανεῖν ἀπέστησαν. The sentence nicely illustrates the use made of Methodius although, rather than long extracts, shorter sentences and phrases are used, and these are closely fitted into the literary structure of the Dialogue. This becomes more noticeable when the topic of the General Resurrection comes under consideration later in the Dialogue.

[74] Rom. 6:9-10.

[75] Rom. 5:8-9.

[76] 2 Cor. 13:4

[77] Rom. 6:3.

tism? The Apostle goes on: "He hath graciously blessed us in His beloved Son in whom we have redemption through His blood"[78]. Further: "For you suffered the same things from you own countrymen, as they also did from the Jews   c who killed both the Lord Jesus and the prophets"[79]. [He did not say, "and the angels who showed themselves only in appearance", to whom you Marinus, and your colleagues likened Him, but, "and the prophets" — people who had genuine flesh, and not (in harmony with your party's theory) a mere human appearance! They died, one by having his flesh cut asunder; another by being stoned, while the rest were put to death by the sword.][80] In addition to this, I will produce the Saviour's own statements, the words which announce His sufferings beforehand. This is how He speaks: "The Son of (198) Man must suffer many things. He must be rejected by the elders, high priests and scribes, and be crucified and after three days rise again"[81]. Once more, after the Resurrection, when He was trying to convince certain ones, He said,   d "O foolish men and slow of heart to believe all that I have spoken to you[82], that Christ had to suffer these things[83], [and so to enter into His glory".][84] Still further, the Evangelist speaks of a genuine (not an apparent) death when he introduces his account of it: "And Jesus, crying with a loud voice, said, Father, into Thy hands I will commit[85] my spirit, and He expired; and behold a man named Joseph begged the body and wrapped it in linen and laid it in a new tomb"[86]. Let my opponents have the courage to say who this was. It was certainly no spirit that "gave up the ghost", since that is eternal and incorruptible. On the contrary, there was, in fact someone who had the spirit, someone who did actually give

[78] Ephes. 1:6-7. Adamantius adds υἱῷ αὐτοῦ (His Son) with D G vg[s][d] sy[h] sa, Marcion, and Origen.

[79] 1 Thess. 2:14-15.

[80] Cf. Heb. 11:37. The passage enclosed is absent from Rufinus, and its authenticity not beyond doubt.

[81] Mk. 8:31; Lk. 9:22.

[82] ἐλάλησα. Probably this is the reading of Marcion. The main recensions have ἐλάλησαν οἱ προφῆται. Cf. discussion in Introduction, sect. D. The main recensions have ἀποκτανθῆναι, "be killed", instead of Adamantius σταυρωθῆναι.

[83] "That Christ had to suffer these things", etc. again follows Marcion, who is here joined by MS D. The main recensions have, "Ought not Christ to have suffered these things and so to enter into His glory?" Rufinus also translates this as a question.

[84] Lk. 24:25-26. The section of the quotation bracketed is found in Rufinus, but not in the Greek text, possibly for the sake of completing Jesus' statement.

[85] Adamantius has παραθήσομαι, following the LXX of Ps. 31:6, while most versions read παρατίθεμαι, as does Rufinus in translation.

[86] Lk. 23:46, 50-53. In verse 53, instead of "new tomb", the main recensions have, "a tomb hewn in the rock."

up the ghost: it was He who, when breathing out His last, committed His spirit to the Father;   e He whom Joseph wrapped in fine linen. It is certain that he did not wrap up and bury a ghost, but rather One who had been nailed to a tree! As a matter of fact, this is what the Lord said to the disciples after His resurrection, when they thought He was an apparition: "Why are you troubled, and why do questionings arise in your hearts? See my hands and feet that it is I Myself, for a spirit does not have flesh and bones, as you see that I have"[87]. But why do I spend so much time on proofs, and prolong words? It was sufficient that He confessed Himself to be Son of Man.

f 13   MAR.   Of what man is He the son?

AD.   Of the seed of David, according to the flesh, just as the Gospel states.

MAR.   In the Gospel it is recorded that when the Jews said that Christ was son of David, Christ Himself gave judgement against them; if you will allow me, I will read it.

EUTR.   Read it, please.

MAR.   Jesus says, "What do you think of Christ? Whose son is He? They say to Him: David's. Jesus says to them: How then does David in spirit call Him Lord, saying, 'The Lord said to my Lord, "Sit on My right hand"'? If David   **858a** then in spirit calls Him Lord, how is He his son?"[88] Observe that He gives judgement against those who said that he was son of David by denying it Himself.

AD.   The "how" is not a denial but an inquiry. In (200) fact, this word occurs in the Scriptures, not once, but often, to express not denial but an inquiry. For instance: "How can one chase a thousand?"[89] Again, ["How has the faithful city Sion become a prostitute?"][90] And, "How has Lucifer fallen from heaven, who used to rise in the morning?"[91] Christ did not say 'how' to deny but to make an inquiry.

---

[87] Lk. 24:38-39.

[88] Matt. 22:42-45. The second "in spirit" is omitted by the main recensions, but is added by D θ, etc.

[89] Deut. 32:30 (LXX).

[90] Isa. 1:21 (LXX). This passage is omitted in the Latin translation — probably inadvertently.

[91] Isa. 14:12 (LXX).

MAR.   David acknowledges Him to be Lord[92], not Son.

b   AD.   David does not acknowledge Him to be Lord according to the flesh, but according to the spirit, which means that the Word of God is Lord, not only of David, but also of "all rule, authority and dominion, and every name called upon, not only in this age, but also in that which is to come"[93]. He knew, since he had foreknowledge[94], that the Jews were sceptical of what was "according to the spirit"[95]. So He asked, "If David then, in spirit[96] calls Him Lord, how is He his son?"[97] Christ did not say, "If David, then, in the flesh calls Him Lord," but "in spirit", so acknowledging Him to be Lord in the spirit, but son according to the flesh.   **c** I will demonstrate more clearly from the Gospel how Christ Himself agrees that this is the saving and steadfast faith. With your permission, I read.

14   EUTR.   Read, please.

AD.   Because Megethius[98], who holds Marcion's teaching, is present, I will read from their Gospel: "Now it happened as He drew near to Jericho, that a certain blind man sat by the way-side, begging. When he heard the crowd passing by he asked what this meant, and he was told that Jesus was passing by. He called out, 'Jesus, son of David, have mercy on me!'

---

[92] κύριον. In Greek usuage, κύριος has a wide range of meaning, from the courtesy title "sir" to the designation of God. In the Psalm here referred to by Marinus (110:1) (LXX, 109:1), the Fathers understood the first κύριος as applying to God, and the second as speaking of Christ. The use of the title for Jesus as it is found in the Gospels — especially frequently in Luke — raises him at once above the merely human level (Jn. 20:28); see this emphasis becoming stronger still in the Acts and the Epistles, and reaching its peak in Pauline confessions, (Rom. 10:9; 1 Cor. 12:3; Phil. 2:11).

[93] Eph. 1:21.

[94] προγνώστης ὤν. This word is not found in the NT, but occurs in 2 Clement 9:9, Justin Martyr, and Theophilus of Antioch. Its kindred form, πρόγνωσις, appears in Acts 2:23 and 1 Pet. 1:2, while the verb προγινώσκω is used five times in the NT. In none of these cases is the reference to Christ. The prescience of the Incarnate Christ, therefore, does not seem to be explicitly taught in the Bible, but it may be implied in such passages as Jn. 2:25; 16:30; 21:17, and Col. 2:3. The statement of Adamantius, however, merely expresses the logical outcome of the Christological thinking of the early Church: if Christ shares the nature of God, then He must possess the qualities of that nature: and omniscience is one of those qualities. It was left to other writers to discuss whether omniscience was one of the attributes of which the Christ divested Himself when He became incarnate, or not (cf. Phil. 2:5-11, and the modern kenotic theories).

[95] τὸ κατὰ πνεῦμα. Rufinus parapharases, "His divine nature".

[96] ἐν πνεύματι is rendered "through (or "by") the spirit", with some modern versions.

[97] Matt. 22:45.

[98] οἱ περὶ Μεγέθιον. This could by rendered, "Megethius and his party", but with less likelihood. Rufinus translates simply "Megethius".

Jesus, stopping, commanded him to be brought. And when he had come near, he asked him   d 'What do you want Me to do to you?' He said, 'Lord, that I may receive my sight!' Answering, Jesus said, 'Receive your sight: your faith has saved you'. And immediately he received his sight"[99].

EUTR.   It appears to me that it was because he had the right faith that the blind man justly received his sight. He was obviously far removed from the faith held by Megethius and Valens, or by Droserius and Marinus. In his case, because he had (202) the appropriate faith, he received his sight; in theirs, because they are impelled by ignorance, they are blind in mind, in face of the fact that Christ so clearly commends the blind man's faith when He says, "Receive thy sight; your faith has saved you". The believing blind man confessed His advent both according to the flesh and according to the spirit, accepting it that in both respects God was in man. e In fact, he perceived the man first, and then immediately recognized the Lord. Acknowledging the man, he says; "Son of David, have mercy on me", and confessing God, "Lord[100], that I may receive my sight!" Thus, judged by the view of Marinus, if He is not son of David, Christ contradicts Himself, partly in commanding a blind man, who had fully believed that He was, to receive his sight; partly through denying that He was son of David in His question to the Jews. Quite certainly, by your theory, Marinus, Christ is contrary to and acts against Himself! This dilemma comes to those who have dealings with unstable heresy[101].   f Whenever they attempt to use illogical and fictitious arguments, such absurdities must meet them. We should, then, follow that belief[102] by means of which the blind man had his eyes restored safe and sound[103], the belief by which

---

[99] Lk. 18:35-38; 40-43. [Note here the explicit quoting from Marcion's Bible. Ed.].

[100] κύριε. This would seem better translated here, and in similar passages, "Sir", as a term of address offered to persons respected, but not necessarily regarded as having powers above the human level. Eutropius, however, understands it to convey the sense of divinity.

[101] τῇ ἀσυστάτῳ αἱρέσει. The word αἵρεσις is found in early Christian literature with three main significations: 1) a way of thought (i.e., the Christian faith); 2) a system of thought, a school, or sect. (i.e., Jewish, pagan or Christian); 3) heresy, false teaching claiming to be Christian. This use is found, e.g. in Ignatius (Eph. 6:2); Clement of Alexandria (*Stromateis*, 1:19); Origen (*Contra Celsum*, 2:3); the Clementine Homily (2:17); Cyril of Jerusalem (*Catech.*, 4:4), and Athanasius (*Hist. Arian. ad monachos*, 45). Such Fathers considered that it was the work of the Devil or demons, or the result of over-curious speculation (Gregory of Nyssa, *Homil. Cant.*, 11). In the Dialogue of Adamantius, Eutropius is clearly using αἵρεσις in the third sense.

[102] δόγμα is opinion, fixed belief, creed, precept.

[103] σώας, from σῶς, whole, entire, healthy. Of persons, σῶς means alive and well (cf. Latin *salvus*). The word is classical, but rare in the LXX, and not found at all in the NT or earliest Christian literature.

Christ also testified that his faith was well founded.   **859a** It seems to be only right, therefore, to reject and repudiate the faith held by Marinus, since it is far from the truth, and in no respect compatible with the Divine nature. As he accepts fables, fantasies and a phantom appearance, he will also hold in his teaching that salvation consists in fable, fantasy and phantom appearance. So I think that Marinus should desist from this contentious argument, and calmly busy himself with[104] the third proposition — that is, the discussion of the Resurrection.

b 15   MAR[105].   If you wish to discuss[106] this in the interests of truth, I am ready to give it careful consideration.

EUTR.   This is no ordinary audience we have here: let *them* say whether I have overstepped the bounds of impartiality[107]. If you have been vanquished because you are dominated by the pereconceived idea enslaving you, do not blame me!

MAR.   If you want the inquiry to be into the whole truth, reject philosophical speculations, and be guided only by the Scriptures.

AD.   Let us be guided by the Scriptures!

EUTR.   Both sides are clearly in agreement on that point.

16   MAR.   I think that you and your party do not have a proper understanding[108] of the question.

c   AD.   As the argument proceeds, it will refute him who has the wrong grasp of the subject.

MAR.   Let Adamantius, please, explain what kind of (204) body rises: this one with which we are clothed, and in which we are bound, or another, a spiritual one.

---

[104] ἐγκαταγινόμενον: "be occupied with, be possessed by".

[105] With the following words, the fifth and last section of the Dialogue begins in the editions of de la Rue and Migne. The Latin of Rufinus does not make any division here, however, for in his case the fifth book has already begun (=850f).

[106] "Discuss" translates διαλέγεσθαι, which is a conjectural emendation of the Greek text by Bakhuyzen. The Greek MSS have γενέσθαι, but this hardly makes sense as it stands. Rufinus has, "If you want to decide in accordance with truth..."

[107] Or (with Rufinus), "whether I have passed judgement contrary to justice" (ἐξέβην τοῦ δικαίου is the Greek; *contra justitiam judicavi* is the Latin).

[108] In the Greek text ἐπιβάλλετε. Bakhuyzen suggests the Middle voice, and this has been accepted for the translation.

AD.   I believe that the body with which we are clothed rises.

MAR.   Immediately a clear refutation of this presents itself to overturn Adamantius' false view of the matter; the human body does not remain the same from childhood to old age, but exists as a   **860a** substance in a state of flux[109]. So what body do you say rises — that of youth, maturity or old age?[110]

AD.   Although wall-painters paint pictures of shipbuilders, pilots and sailors, they do not know how to build or steer ships[111]; in the same way, Marinus puts an argument forward, but he has no experience and proof of the argument itself.

EUTR.   I should like to know more clearly how it is that the body is "not the same from childhood to old age."

MAR.   Because the body consists of a substance in a state of flux, it gradually passes away, and becomes another body by means of food. It is, for instance, consumed by diseases[112].

b   AD[113].   Even if most of its parts do pass away and perish, other parts are added afresh.

---

[109] ῥευστῆς οὐσίας. The expression itself is found in Plutarch (1st and 2nd cent. AD), while Aristotle (4th and 5th cent. BCE) and Porphyry (3rd cent. AD) use ῥευστή of ἡ ὕλη, matter. The word is reminiscent of the philosophy of Heraclitus of Ephesus (ca. 535-475 BCE). In his work "On Nature" it is stated that everything is in a condition of eternal flux. The only permanent thing is the fact of change. "Being" is actually a constant process of "becoming". In our Dialogue, the remark of Marinus, "that the body does not remain the same from childhood to old age, but exists as a substance in a state of flux", expresses the same principle as Heraclitus' words, "You cannot step twice into the same rivers, for fresh waters are ever flowing in upon you".

[110] From sects. 859c/V, 16–863c/V, 22 (inclusive) there are numerous references, either direct or indirect, to the work of Methodius: *De Resurrectione*. The present passage, e.g., "body … or old age?" echoes the words of Aglaophon: "for while the substance itself is flowing throughout, undiscernible and changeable, like the current of a river, coming and going, so that it never (even for the smallest moment) is to be held as the same — which body will arise? The youth's, the old man's or the child's?" (using here Bakhuyzen's translation of the Slavonic version of Methodius in the Bonwetsch's edn., pp. 78-79). Further, on his page 82, Methodius allows Proclus to speak about the body's being in a "state of flux" much in the way Marinus expresses himself. According to Epiphanius (ca. 315-403), in his *Panarion* (ed. K.W. Dindorf, *Opera*, Leipzig, 1859, vol. 2, sect. 605, p. 540) this is literally the teaching of Origen.

[111] Compare with this, Methodius: "just as painters attempt to represent, by means of imitation, shipbuilders, ships, and pilots, although they do not know how to build ships and be pilots" (Bonwetsch edn., p. 106. Cf. also Epiphanius, *Panan.*, p. 609).

[112] For the similarity of this reply of Marinus to a passage of Methodius; see Bonwetsch edn. pp. 81-82.

[113] The following speech is attributed to Marinus in the Greek MSS, but, as Bakhuyzen points out, it is not likely that Marinus would conclude with words that largely negate what he had said previously. Further, Rufinus gives the speech to Adamantius.

MAR[114]. What body then do you claim rises: the one (206) wasted by diseases, the childhood body, or that of the old man?

AD[115]. Although you promised to convince the audience mainly from Scripture, Marinus, you have made reference to medical science, and have forgotten the terms of the discussion. However, I myself, although I have not practised medicine, will not hesitate to drive your wrong notions from you. If the body consists of a substance in a state of flux, one body taking the place of another[116], when parts of the body (i.e., an ear, finger or nose) are amputated, they ought to be replaced by means of food. The scars[117], too, made by the wounds, ought not to remain up to old age if (as you say) the bodies gradually pass away.   c In actual fact, bodies do not gradually pass away in disease, and others take their place. When the mind receives no response to its signals[118], the body will close itself[119] just as wet wool shrinks; but when its requirements meet with a response, the body extends and enlarges itself. When the body has recovered from sickness, it is not thus ... very easily[120] the parts that took so long to grow are restored.

[EUTR. If the body were in a state of flux, one (208) body taking the place of another, it[121] would be impossible to discover the actual body[122], for it would be immaterial[123].

[114] For the following words, compare Methodius (Bonwetsch edn., p. 82).

[115] Jahn, in his edition of Methodius (1865), conjectures that the whole passage "Although Marinus promised ... men are more powerful than God" has been entirely taken from Methodius. Comparison with Bonwetsch's critical edition, however, does not bear this out.

[116] "When parts of the body... by means of food". Cf. Methodius: (Bonwetsch, p. 218, Slavonic translation). "Thus the amputated members of the body, whether a hand, of a finger, or something else, ought to be replaced from the food absorbed".

[117] "The scars, too,... and others take their place". Cf. Methodius (Bonwetsch, pp. 219, 220, and p. 93).

[118] ὅταν ἡ ψυχὴ μὴ δέξηται τὰ αὐτῆς ὀρεκτά. Lit., "when the soul does not obtain its desires".

[119] The Greek of the MSS in this section is very corrupt, and the Latin of Rufinus equally so. After reviewing all the evidence from MSS, editions and Rufinus, Bakhuyzen concludes that the author of the Dialogue originally said, "The body will close itself just as wet wool shrinks". It is clear from a comparison with Methodius that our author is considerably indebted to him for the substance of the passage (see Bonwetsch, Slavonic translation, p. 220).

[120] There is clearly a lacuna in the Greek text, for Rufinus here has, "Nor does it [i.e., the body] require so much time for restoration as it consumes in growing from childhood to manhood, but that which has been enfeebled by diminution to weakness is repaired in a short time".

[121] For the following words, the printed editions of the text have, "Therefore it is impossible to find the body without substance". This makes no sense. The MSS themselves vary in wording. Jahn, in his edition of Methodius, reconstructs, "... it would also be impossible to discover what the unsubstantial body is." This is possible, but the English translation is based on the emendation of Bakhuyzen.

[122] ὃ ἦν εὑρεῖν τὸ σῶμα. Lit., "to find the body which exists (existed)".

[123] ἀνυπόστατον. Without substance; immaterial.

MAR.   How is that?

EUTR.   Take an example from life: suppose someone should want
to model a figure of a man in a wax, and   **d** at first fashions it on a small
scale[124]. Afterwards, when he spreads fresh wax and attempts to shape the
image so as to give it height and size, he cannot[125]; the figure must remain
unfinished, because the original material of the wax is disappearing and
other material is taking its place! The sculptor is not to complete his
work!][126] But the human, retaining the childhood body, continues to grow.
Consequently, the scars of wounds and the amputation of limbs survive to
old age,   **e** and it is pointless to say that the body is in a state of flux.

17   MAR.   If the body that endures from childhood to old age rises,
would Adamantius please explain what blood it is that rises with the human
being — that which flows out in blood-lettings[127], or that which is the
result of haemorrhages? Some people expel blood every (210) year by
blood-letting. Will Adamantius, then, please tell me what blood it is that
rises with Man[128].

AD.   [To understand the mystery of the Resurrection requires
another lengthy discussion in the light of the Scriptural evidence. Still,
because you have fallen headlong from its truth, I should answer what you
have asserted.][129] Those who practise blood-letting do not expel the most
vital and real blood, but the impure and foreign — that which comes from
the animal juices[130]. As this is neither vital nor real, it bursts out in haem-

[124] βραχείᾳ ὑποστάσει ἀποτυπωσάμενος, "having fashioned it with a little material".
[125] The Greek of the passage is far from clear. Bakhuyzen suspects that there has been dislocation of words, or alternatively, that some words have dropped out.
[126] The enclosed lines are not found in Rufinus. Yet they must be genuine, since they are
taken from Methodius (Bonwetsch, Slavonic trans.), p. 217, cf. p. 86).
[127] φλεβοτομία. Bloodletting, or the art of blood letting; i.e., venesection, the cutting of a
vein for the purpose of withdrawing blood. The practice was known in ancient times, and is
mentioned by Hippocrates, Aristides, Arrianus, Herodotus, Archigenes, Caelius Aurelianus
and others, from the fifth century BC to the fifth century AD.   The belief was held that the
morbid "humours" causing disease might be eliminated in this way. Phlebotomy was thus
practised in all types of sickness, and even on healthy persons, with a view to preventing the
accumulation of fluids injurious to the body. In the Middle Ages, along with "cupping" and
"leeching", phlebotomy was used by physicians as their main remedial method.
[128] For the substance of this speech of Marinus, see Methodius, Bonwetsch, p. 82
(Slavonic trans.) and p. 89. The section of Methodius to which the words refer carries the
title, "Epitome of Origen's works". The text of 'Adamantius' at this point has suffered somewhat through injury, as a comparison with Rufinus will show.
[129] Words bracketed are not found in the Greek MSS, but are in the Latin. They are possibly added by Rufinus as a kind of introduction to what follows.
[130] ἐκ τῶν χυμῶν. Χυμός as "animal juices" or "humours" is mentioned by Hippocrates,
Aristotle, Galen, Porphyry and others, from the fifth century BC to the third century AD.

orrhages. For this reason, the members of the medical profession, knowing that the foreign substance from the animal juices   **861a** (although it is not the most vital blood) becomes red like the blood, keep watch when they let blood, to observe when all the impure (the so-called "black"), blood is expelled. Immediately the reddish and more vital blood appears, they staunch the flow, lest through the loss of the vital blood, the patient should die[131].

EUTR.   It is a proposal born of ignorance to assume that impure fluids and foreign substances from food consist of genuine and most vital elements. When food[132] is taken into the body and converted into fluid, part becomes blood, part phlegm[133], and part saliva. So I ask you both to cease discussing the elements that are alien to the blood, and to give attention to those that more truly belong to it.

18   MAR[134].   The human is composed of earth, water, fire and air[135]; **b** when, therefore, one dies and goes into dissolution, each of the blended substances[136] returns to its original state. For instance, the part that came

The *Shorter Oxford Dictionary* defines a "humour" as "specifically, one of the four chief fluids (cardinal humours) of the body (blood, phlegm, choler, and melancholy or black choler) by the relative proportions of which a person's physical and mental qualities and disposition were formerly held to be determined". Thus in mediaeval times, the combination of the four cardinal humours of the body constituted the temperament, which was therefore said to be sanguine, choleric, phlegmatic, or melancholic, according to the relative proportion of each fluid in the whole combination.

[131] The passage, "Those who practise blood-letting ... the patient should die," is from Methodius (Bonwetsch, Slavonic trans. p. 219).

[132] ἡ τροφή, κτλ. With regard to the belief of the ancients in the triple purification and separating of foods, Athenagoras, the Christian Apologist (d. *ca*. 177 AD), states, "...in the nourishment of every animal there is a threefold cleansing and separation" (*De Resurr.*, 5). Just previously, Athenagoras had spoken of the first change through digestion as taking place in the stomach; the second change through digestion in the liver. A final change takes place after this through digestion into something else.

[133] φλέγμα (Latin: *pituita*). One of the humours in the body (see *supra* n. 130). Mentioned by Herodotus the historian, and Hippocrates (both of the fifth century BC).

[134] The speech of Marinus following is taken from that of Proclus in Methodius (Bonwetsch, pp. 84-86) and of Memianus, also in Methodius (Bonwetsch, p. 244).

[135] This was the teaching of Empedocles, philosopher and physician of Agrigentum in Sicily, b. *ca*. 490 BCE. Against Heraclitus, who maintained that change lies at the very heart of the world-substance, Empedocles said that "what is" does not actually come into being, nor cease to exist, nor change in any way. That which it is, it always is, in spite of the endless combinations in which it is involved. The implication is, of course, that there are several kinds of elemental bodies. For Empedocles, these are just four: earth, air, fire and water, and they are quite distinct from one another, each unchangeable within its own class or kind. The different proportions in which these four elemental bodies combine explains the many differences in things as we know them. Of the four, fire constitutes the essence of life, while the other elements are the basis of matter.

[136] ἑκάστη οὐσία.

from fire goes back to it; that from water to water; that from air to air, and
that from earth to earth. How then can humans, who are composed of
parts mingled together, rise in the resurrection? It would be like someone
pouring water into the open sea[137], and then stoutly maintaining that he
will recover it again — an impossibility! Hence one human must arise in
place of another.

AD.   By your theory, humans are shown to be much more powerful than God,   c and the Saviour's statement is pointless which says,
"Things that are impossible for humans are possible for God"[138].

MAR.   In what way are humans more powerful than God?

AD.   Indeed, by using skill and knowledge, human beings separate
wine that has been mixed with water, and silver[139] from brass. They also
know how to separate most things of this (212) kind[140]. It is quite certain,
then, that God, the Craftsman unsurpassed in power, and the Creator of all
things, to Whom fire, air, water and earth are subject as they serve Him in
fear, each holding to its own part, would give to everyone their own body
in the Resurrection. Fire, subjected to God, and obeying His command[141]
did not injure the Three Brothers when they were cast into a furnace of fire,
d but returned them to its Master safe and sound[142]. Water received Jonah
into its depth for three days and nights, and then restored him quite
sound[143]. Air carried Elijah up to Heaven[144], and earth restored Lazarus on
the fourth day[145]. And it is a fact that when fresh water flows into the sea,
and mixes and rolls along with it, it gushes forth again through the clouds
as fresh water, having been separated from the salt water in the process.
This is what the Prophet refers to when he says, "He who summons the
water of the sea, and pours it out upon the face of the earth"[146].

[137] Compare Jerome, *Epist.*, 38, to Pammachius; Methodius (Bonwetsch, p. 284).
[138] Lk. 18:27.
[139] ἀργύριον. Literally, "a piece of silver". Bakhuyzen suggests ἄργυρον as the correct reading here, but the language of our Dialogue is late Greek, and ἄργυρον is much less frequently
found than ἀργύριον. Refer also to 1 Cor. 3:12. Rufinus has *argentum*.
[140] For the passage "Indeed by using skill ... most things of this kind," cf. Methodius
(Bonwetsch edn., p. 245, Slavonic trans. — which is must shorter, and also p. 216).
[141] νεύματι. Νεῦμα is a nod or sign. It is derived from νεύω, to beckon in token of command, or to nod in the general sense.
[142] Dan. 3:21-27.
[143] Jonah 2.
[144] 4 Kgs. 2:11 (LXX).
[145] Jn. 11:39-44.
[146] Amos 5:8. The section "And it is a fact ... upon the face of the earth" is from Methodius (Bonwetsch edn., Slavonic trans., p. 246, 250).

e 19   EUTR.   Although Marinus promised to prove his case from Scripture, he has turned to the investigation of natural causes and phenomena, and to medical matters; from this he has reached the conclusion that mortals are more powerful than God!

MAR.   I can easily prove my thesis from Scripture, if Adamantius is amenable to reason.

EUTR.   Adamantius is not the cause of the digression, but your own obstinate opinion.

AD.   Let him think what he likes. With truth on my side, I am ready to meet him on all issues.

MAR.   Well, what Scriptures do you accept? I will prove from them that the flesh does not rise.

AD.   I accept all the canonical[147] ones.

f   MAR.   Very well; I read a denial of the resurrection of the flesh in the Old Testament[148], where God declares, "My Spirit shall most certainly not remain among these men, because they are flesh and blood"[149].

862a   AD[150].   Then, if He said, "My Spirit shall most certainly not remain among these men", it is clear that it remains (214) among others; "among these men" refers to a particular group and the denial does not include all.

20   MAR.   I will convince you from Scripture that neither prophets nor apostles made mention of flesh or blood, but only of soul. It was this that they besought God to save. Take David first: "Because Thou has delivered my soul from death"[151]. Again in the same writer: "My soul thirsted after the living God"[152]. Once more. "My soul has trusted in Thee,

---

[147] ταῖς ἐνδιαθέτοις. Ἐνδιάθετος is literally, "internal, immanent, ingrained, deep-seated," then "covenanted," and so of Holy Scripture, "canonical". In this sense it is used by Basil of Caesarea (d. 379), Epiphanius (d. 403), Palladius (d. before 431), and John of Damascus (d. 749). Rufinus has *quas habet ecclesia* (recognized by the Church).

[148] πρώτη διαθήκη. Διαθήκη is first "testament, will," then "covenant". From this it came to mean "written covenant, Scriptures of the Old or New Testament", and finally "record".

[149] Gen. 6:3 (LXX). Marinus, however, adds καὶ αἷμα and omits εἰς τὸν αἰῶνα.

[150] The reasoning that follows is also found in Methodius (Bonwetsch edn., Slavonic trans., p. 229).

[151] Ps. 55:14 (LXX), 56:14 (Hebrew).

[152] Ps. 41:3 (LXX), 42:3 (Hebrew).

[and in the shadow of Thy wings I will hope]"[153]. [This too: "Return, O my soul, to your rest"][154]. And this: "Thou wilt not leave my soul in the Underworld"[155]. You can see that they prayed only that God might save the soul, not flesh and blood!

b   AD.   Will Marinus please explain whether the soul is mortal or immortal?

MAR.   Obviously it is immortal.

AD.   Why then does it say, "Deliver not up to wild-beasts the soul that praises Thee"[156]. Can beasts harm a soul if it is immortal?

EUTR.   Beasts do not harm soul, but body. When it says, "Do not deliver up to wild beasts a soul that praises Thee", it clearly means the whole human.

---

[153] Ps. 56:2 (LXX), 57:2 (Hebrew). The bracketed portion is not in Rufinus, but it is part of the original Biblical passage, and Rufinus may have omitted it as not being particularly relevant to Marinus' argument.

[154] Ps. 114:7 (LXX), 116:7 (Hebrew). This is in Rufinus only. Bakhuyzen considers it probably genuine.

[155] Ps. 15:10 (LXX), 16:10 (Hebrew). "Underworld" renders the Hebrew *Sheol* and the Greek *Hades*. According to L. Koehler ("Problems in the Study of the Language of the Old Testament", in *Journal of Semitic Studies*, I/1, [1956] pp. 9, 19), *Sheol* is not a foreign loan-word, but pure Hebrew. It refers to something desolate or devastated, fittingly expressed by the German "Unland" ("No-land"). To quote Koehler, "It means the world (below our world) where are found shadowiness, decay, remoteness from God (Isa. 38:18; Ps. 6:6): nothingness." It is therefore not inappropriately rendered the "underworld" in English, and ᾅδης in Greek (originally the name of the god of the Underworld). A brief survey of the concept of the latter in Patristic thought is worth providing here: 1. *Intermediate state and dwelling place of souls of pre-Christian people*, either all souls (Athanasius, *adv. Arian.*, 3); or only souls of the wicked (Clement of Alexandria, *Strom.*, 6,6; Origen, *Homil.*, 18,2 *in Jerem.* — a view attacked by Eustathius of Antioch, *De Engast. contr. Origen.*, 17); 2. *Intermediate place for all souls* until final judgement (cf. Irenaeus, *Advers. Haer.*, 5, 31,2; Hippolytus *Advers. Graec.*, 2); regarded not as a local habitation, but as a spiritual state (Gregory of Nyssa, *De Anim. et Resurr.*); the Virgin Mary exempt from it (John of Damascus, *Homil.*, 8,12); 3. *The equivalent of Gehenna*, γέεννα, hell: a place of punishment for the wicked, where the impenitent remain after the preaching of Christ (Clement, *Strom.*, 6,6; Origen, *Comment. in Johan.*, 13,37), including varying degrees of punishment and applied also to this world which, according to Origen, is a place of punishment for fallen spirits (Origen, *De Princip.*, 4,3,10). Basil of Caesarea admits degrees of punishment (*Regul. Brev. Tract.*, 267); without rest (Clement *Homil.*, 11,10); with no hope of repentance and God's love (Gregory Nazianzus, *Orat.*, 16,7; Chrysostom, *Homil.* 18,6 *in Rom.*); or a place involving separation from God as the result of grave sin (pseudo-Basil, *Comment. in Isa.*). Different classes of human beings are to be found there (Dorotheus Abbas, *Doctr. Divers.*, 10,5); and it is dark and without joy (Chrysostom, *De coemet. et Cruce*, 2). Cf. also *supra*, pt. 2, n. 37.

[156] Psa. 73:19 (LXX). The Hebrew text reads, "Do not give Israel, your dove, to the hawk".

AD.   Perhaps Scripture may convince you still more clearly that by "soul" it means Man consisting of body and soul. Thus: "The sons and daughters that Jacob had were three souls"[157]. It also says,   c "And Jacob went down into Egypt with seventy souls"[158].

EUTR.   Judging by what Marinus believes, the sons of Jacob went down to Egypt without bodies! But it is proved that Scripture means the whole human by the "soul", and we cannot doubt this.

21   MAR.   I offer the Apostle as a truer witness than the prophets to the fact that the body is the fetter of the soul and the cause of all evils[159]. He speaks of it in this way: "Unhappy man that I am, who will deliver me from this body of (216) death?"[160]

AD.   In what respect is the body the fetter of the soul?

MAR[161].   It says that when the soul had sinned and transgressed the command of God, "God made garments of skins[162] and clothed

---

[157] Gen. 46:14. This is a reference to the passage, rather than a strict quotation.

[158] Gen. 46:27. Again a reference or loose quotation. Over against the "seventy" of Adamantius, the LXX has "seventy-five". The Hebrew agrees with Adamantius.

[159] τῶν κακῶν, plural. This may also be rendered "evil". Rufinus has *malorum*.

[160] Rom. 7:24. I.e., "from the body condemned to this death."

[161] This speech of Marinus, along with the previous reference to the body as "the fetter of the soul", is largely an abridgement of Methodius (cf. Bonwetsch, Slavonic trans. pp. 73-76, 110). Aglaophon there says, "if as you claim there is a resurrection of this whole body, and a transformation into immortality, explain why God at the outset created humans without the clothes (or rag-cloak) of the body, as Scripture itself teaches? For the clothes of skin which He made for Adam and Eve after their transgression are clearly the bodies with which we have been clothed after we transgressed the command: clothed with such a fetter for reasons of penitence... And the prophet Jeremiah says in Lamentations, 'Chains did He name them, bound of the earth...'" "Therefore he also admits that it (that is, the flesh) is the death and ruin of the soul ... saying, 'I am a wretched man! Who will deliver me from the body of death!' So the body is a kind of torture (chamber) and a prison because of the transgression,... whereby we received a more painful punishment of disobedience".

[162] See Methodius (Bonwetsch, pp. 108-109, 111, 122, 134). In commenting on the coats of skin, Origen, of course, does not interpret them literally. He mentions two other views: 1) they represent the body of flesh with which God clothed Adam and Eve. However, as they already possessed this prior to the Fall he feels that the better interpretation of the coats is that they are meant to represent the liability to die which our first parents incurred by their disobedience (see Feltoe, *Letters and other Remains of Dionysius of Alexandria* [Camb. Patr. Texts], *op. cit.*, p. 229, n. 9). Apparently, Origen had referred to the body as "given to the soul as a fetter after the Fall, and that previously it lived without a body; but that this body which we wear is the cause of our sins; wherefore also he called it a fetter, as it can hinder the soul from good works" (*apud* Methodius, *De Resurr.*, *apud* Photius, *Bibliot.*, 1, Ant.-Nic. Lib. edn. p. 153). Again, if Methodius is to be believed, Origen says "that by the coats of skin is signified death. For he says of Adam, that when the Almighty God saw that by

them"[163]. **d** This means the body[164]. Jeremiah the prophet also speaks of us as "captives bound of earth"[165], because God has bound the soul in the body on account of its sin. You are, therefore, saying that the body, the cause of all evil, rises so that the soul may also be tortured[166] by chains![167]

AD[168].   You stated, Marinus, that the soul was bound is the body because it had sinned. Now a little later, you assert that the body is the

---

treachery he, an immortal being, had become evil, just as his deceiver the devil was, He prepared the coats of skin on this account; that when he was thus, as it were, clothed in mortality, all that was evil in him might die in the dissolution of the body"; *ibid.*, 8 (pp. 154-155). It is interesting to compare with this the view of Gregory of Nyssa: "For since, He [Moses] says, the first men became implicated in things forbidden and were stripped naked of blessedness, the Lord clothed His first creatures in suits of skins. I do not think he uses the word 'skins' in its literal sense... But since every skin taken from an animal is a dead thing, I am sure the skins mean the attribute of death... He who heals our wickedness subsequently provided him with the capacity to die, but not to die permanently. For a suit is an external covering for us. The body is given the opportunity to use it for a while, but it is not an essential part of its nature" (*Logos Katech.*, 8). By this statement, Gregory appears to align himself with the second view attributed to Origen: that the coats of skin represent the liability to die.

[163] Gen. 3:21 (LXX).

[164] "This means the body" (τουτέστι τὸ σῶμα). Such teaching is of course as stoutly denied by Methodius as by Adamantius: "Now the question has already been raised, and answered [cf. Anastasius Sinaita in *Doctr. Patr. de Verb. Incarn.*, 25] by Epiphanius, *Haer.*, 64, who contends that the 'coats of skins' are not bodies". But in a passage given by Pitra (*Anal. Sol.*, iii, 597: Cod. Vatic. 2022), and printed by Feltoe (*Letters and Other Remains of Dionysius, op. cit.*, pp. 228f.), we have the interpretation of the "curtains of Solomon" (δέρρεις Σολομῶν) of Cant. Sol. 1:4: "I think that the 'curtains of Solomon' means the coats of skin stitched and stretched out over the former pure body; with which our peaceful and peace-loving Lord clothed Man — this explains the term 'Solomon' [שָׁלוֹם soundness, welfare, peace] — and clothed with which the human being through disobedience was cast out of Paradise". Whether this was written by Dionysius of Alexandria (d. *ca.* 264) or not, it reveals something of the typically allegorical interpretation of Scripture favoured by the Alexandrian school, and so probably represents the view of Origen himself.

[165] Lam. 3:34 (LXX), γῆς δεσμίους, literally "bound, or captives of earth". Most of the modern versions translate the Hebrew אֲסִירֵי אָרֶץ by "prisoners".

[166] ἐξετάζηται. Ἐξετάζω: "scrutinize, be under scrutiny: examine, approve; question"; although the passive, "be counted among," hence, "be found", suggests a softer alternative translation "always be found in chains".

[167] Rufinus translates the sentence, "Because then the body is the cause of all evils, you say this rises in order that the soul may always be held in chains". The Slavonic rendering of Methodius in the parallel passage runs, "... in order that we may also be eternally bound in corruptibility in the kingdom of light" (Bonwetsch edn., p. 77).

[168] For the following speech, see Methodius (Bonwetsch, p. 109): "For having granted that souls did sin incorporeally, since the command was cheated, and after stating that because of their lawlessness, God afterwards gave them garments of skins in order that they might suffer punishment by bearing them like dead bodies to the burial, now, forgetting the previous statement — your first premise — you say that the soul cannot sin of itself, for it was not actually born for this, but that the body has become in part the cause of all kinds of evil to it,... for the body was given to it as an avenging chain ... when it had transgressed the command". (Similarly, *Slavonic trans.*, pp. 75, 108, 117, 167, 176).

cause of all evil, although the soul had sinned before ever it was bound in the body. If then the soul can sin apart from the body, why is the body the cause, when it (218) is the soul that sins?[169]

EUTR.   If you say that the soul had sinned before it was bound, it is pointless to claim that the body is the cause of evil.   e If it sinned prior to the body, the soul will again sin, once it has been released from the body, for it had sinned previously. Therefore the body is not the guilty party, but the soul.

AD.   If the body was attached as the fetter of the soul, but the fetter is meant to check the sinner, and to keep him from wrong-doing, the body is not a fetter of the soul but its helper.

MAR.   How is that?

EUTR.   The fetter does not assist the prisoner to sin,   863a but confines and restrains him from it, but the body is an aid to the soul in committing murders and adulteries[170]. It is plain, then, that God has given the body to the soul, not as a fetter, but as an assistant[171].

22   MAR.   Will Adamantius please state whether he accepts the Apostle?

AD.   I fully accept Paul, who possessed Christ and the Spirit[172].

MAR.   Well then, if you accept him, listen when he declares, "Flesh and blood cannot inherit the Kingdom of God; neither can the perishable inherit immortality"[173]. What could be more apparent than this,

---

[169] Rufinus has: "If then the soul can sin apart from the body, the body will not be the cause of the soul's sinning".

[170] The reasoning here seems to be somewhat inconsistent and strained, especially in the light of the statement of Adamantius above! However, as the heathen adjudicator makes the remarks, this may be intentional on the part of the author.

[171] The preceding passage, "If the body was attached ... as an assistant", is largely moulded on the reasoning of Methodius (Bonwetsch, pp. 114-120). There are minor borrowings that do not require mention, but to be noted is this passage from p. 118 of Methodius (Bonw.): "So, then, I said, Aglaophon, that the body is not the fetter, either by your view or another's, but that it is an assistant to the soul for each — either for the good or the evil" (cf. also Bonwetsch edn., pp. 108, 168, 176).

[172] τῷ χριστοφόρῳ καὶ πνευματικῷ Παύλῳ. Ignatius (d. ca. 110) in 1 Eph. 9:2 uses the term χριστοφόρος with the article in the sense, "the Christ-bearer"; while later on Athanasius (d. 373) has, ὁ χριστοφόρος ἀνήρ, ὁ μακάριος Παῦλος, "O Christ-bearing man, blessed Paul!" (Orat. contr. gent. 5). Rufinus, at this place in our Dialogue, renders, "in whom Christ speaks and in whom the Holy Spirit dwells".

[173] 1 Cor. 15:50.

what more clear? This proof which I avow, coming from a source that my opponents accept, cannot be disputed, for it is clear and genuine[174].

AD. Those who do not grasp the spiritual[175] sense (220) of the words spoken by the Apostle fix on the mere words and err from the truth. **b** The Apostle calls disgraceful and worthless acts "flesh and blood". He terms those who think fleshly thoughts "fleshly," and those who practise spiritual deeds "spiritual"[176]. Come now: let me show you where the Apostle himself clearly states that those who do not live according to faith are "fleshly" and deluded because they perform fleshly deeds. This is what he says, "That the requirements of the law might be fulfilled in us who walk not according to the flesh, but according to the spirit. For those who walk according to the flesh are intent on the things of the flesh; but those who walk according to the spirit are intent on the things of the spirit. **c** For the way of thinking of the flesh is enmity towards God, but the way of thinking of the spirit is life and peace. But *you* are not in the flesh, but in the spirit"[177]. Does Marinus really believe that those to whom this was written are without bodies? Again Paul says, "I gave you milk to drink, not solid food, for you were not yet able to take it; and you are still fleshly. For where there is among you strife and dissension[178], are you not fleshly? [For whenever someone says: 'Indeed I belong to Paul'; and another: 'I belong to Apollo'; are you not ordinary men?"][179] Once more, "for when you were in the flesh, the sinful passions, which came through the flesh, were at work among you[180]... **d** But now you are not in the flesh, but in the spirit"[181].

[174] This sentence is very corrupt in the Greek, and the English translation merely follows a conjecture of Wettstein, supported by Migne. It is not accepted, however, by the critical editor, Bakhuyzen, who despairs over the correct ascertainment of meaning. Rufinus renders, "Can any proofs be added to these? It is impudence to resist such very plain meanings".

[175] "the spiritual sense": νοητῶς. Rufinus: *spiritualiter*. In the LXX of Prov. 23:1 νοητῶς has the sense, "carefully".

[176] For the words "The apostle calls ... 'spiritual'", see Methodius (Bonwetsch, Slavonic trans.): "Just as 'flesh' is understood in a double sense, so from 'flesh' [we understand] 'from fleshly deeds'" (p. 227); "Therefore the Apostle said, 'Flesh and blood cannot receive the Kingdom of God,' referring, not to this flesh, but to the desires of the flesh"(p. 229).

[177] Rom. 8:4-6, 9.

[178] The main recensions have ζῆλος καὶ ἔρις. Adamantius follows P⁴⁶ D G Irenaeus, Origen (Lat.), Cyprian, and others in reading ἔρις καὶ διχοστασία (but Adamantius has the singular of the last word, whereas the other authorities listed have the plural).

[179] 1 Cor. 3:2-4. The bracketed portion of the quotation is not found in Rufinus, but was almost certainly written by our author. Rufinus may have omitted it because he felt that it was not strictly required by the argument.

[180] Rom. 7:5. For "among you", the main recensions have "in our members", and for "by the flesh", they have "by the law".

[181] Rom. 8:9.

However, they had not divested themselves of the flesh![182] All this proves that Paul uses the term "flesh" for the way of life both fleshly and evil. In the same manner he calls this way of life "human". Who is there (222) that does not realize that though they were saying among themselves, one, that he belonged to Paul, and another to Apollos, they were not a whit less sons of humans with regard to substance[183]; and that those to whom the Apostle writes, "when you were in the flesh," were even then not without flesh, as far as substance is concerned? What Paul called "flesh" is the fleshly and corrupt way of life which he naturally banishes from our expectation because it cannot inherit the Kingdom of God[184]. Once it is granted that the flesh of the body cannot attain to this expectation (as my opponents believe),   864a what need is there of baptism and washing?[185] The Apostle speaks in this way: "But you were sanctified"[186]. Will Marinus and his friends please state what it is that is washed and sanctified? However, since Megethius[187] happens to be listening, I must quote from his apostolicon[188], suiting my argument to both sides. Well then, in writing to the Galatians, Paul said, "And the life I now live in the flesh, I live by faith in the Son of God who loved me"[189]. Again: "Of the others, let no one make trouble for me without cause,   b for I carry the marks of Jesus on my body"[190]. Now

---

[182] The Biblical passages Rom. 8:4-9 and 7:5 are used by Methodius for the same purposes as that for which Adamantius quotes them. Methodius continues: "If the Apostle was not deprecating here the life according to the flesh, but the flesh, had he already departed and was not out of this life, along with those to whom he was writing, or was he still in the flesh? It cannot be claimed that he wrote these words when he was not in the flesh, for it is clear that not only he himself but those also to whom he was writing were in the flesh" (Bonwetsch edn., pp. 179-80).

[183] "substance" here (and again *infra*) is the translation of οὐσία.

[184] The first words of this sentence in the Greek do not properly connect with the preceding. Rufinus: "But he called 'flesh' the life devoted to the flesh..."

[185] λουτροῦ. In Eph. 5:26 and Titus 3:5 (the only places in the earliest Christian literature where the word occurs) the reference is to the ceremonial washing of Christian baptism.

[186] 1 Cor. 6:11.

[187] Although defeated in his debate with Adamantius earlier, Megethius joins in the following ones from time to time (at sects. 824d/II, 6; 825d/II, 7; 836e-f/III, 7), and it is interesting to note that the orthodox speaker still desires to catch his ear, even though he is not now directly involved (see again, 858c/V, 14). This, along with the fact that Megethius occupied the stage before any of the other opponents of orthodoxy, suggests that our author regarded the Marcionite teaching as the most formidable, and the doctrine most requiring his skilful refutation.

[188] The present debate is with Marinus, a follower of Bardesanes. What Adamantius says here seems to imply that the Scriptural canon accepted by Marinus (and therefore, presumably, by Bardesanes) was a wider one than that of Marcion.

[189] Gal. 2:20.

[190] Gal. 6:17. In place, however, of τοῦ λοιποῦ of the main recensions, Adamantius has τῶν δ᾽ ἄλλων εἰκῇ of the Marcionite Apostolicon. (See Harnack's reconstruction of Marcion's Bible in his *Marcion, op. cit.*, Beilage III, pp. 65-124; Beilage IV, pp. 165-221). For εἰκῇ in this verse, our Dialogue is the sole authority. Cf. also the Introd. to the Dialogue, sect. D.

then, let us see what these statements mean: "The life I live in the flesh I live by faith…" This obviously means that the life of faith is in the flesh; the body bears the marks of Christ through which we have our salvation. How then can it be that, that which bears the marks of salvation, and has the life of faith is not (by my opponents' theory) saved? Either it is no advantage to have the life of faith and the marks of Jesus, or (if salvation depends on this) flesh is really saved. And Paul admits this; writing to the Corinthians he said, "Know you not that your bodies are bodily parts of Christ? c Shall I then take the bodily parts of Christ and make them parts of a prostitute? Heaven forbid!"[191] If the bodies are bodily parts of Christ, either the parts of Christ perish or the flesh is saved.

23   MAR. Paul says "body", not "flesh".

AD. [This is really of no consequence, so far as humans are concerned, but since you think otherwise,][192] it is proved in what follows: He continues, "For do you not know that he who joins himself to a prostitute becomes one in body with her? 'The two', it says, 'shall become one flesh'"[193]. [You see how, when he speaks of the human, he considers flesh and body to be (224) one?][194] [Yet again the Apostle says, "For a man indeed ought not to cover his head, because he is the image and glory of God"[195]. d If that which is covered is the visible body, it is the flesh, and that again is the glory and image of God. It can therefore be saved, for if it does not admit of salvation, it cannot be the image and glory of God. But the flesh really is, as it stands written, the image and glory. Obviously then, just as the flesh admits of this, so also it is capable of being saved.][196] But so that I may establish the case more firmly, will you please request that the text of the Apostle be read to Marinus?

EUTR. Let it be read.

[191] 1 Cor. 6:15.
[192] The enclosed sentence is from Rufinus, and absent from Greek text. It may be genuine, but could, on the other hand, be an attempt on the part of the Latin translator to give the following words a smoother connection with the preceding ones.
[193] 1 Cor. 6:16, cf. Gen. 2:24.
[194] Enclosed passage is from Rufinus only. It is probably authentic, for without some such statement, the quotation from 1 Cor. 6:16 is not altogether clear in its relevance to the argument.
[195] 1 Cor. 11:7.
[196] The passage enclosed is not found in Rufinus, but suits the context, and is probably therefore to be accepted. Bakhuyzen draws attention to the fact that our author quotes the books of the Bible in the exact order of their appearance in the Marcionite Canon: Gal.2:6; 1 Cor. 6:15; 1 Cor. 6:16; 1 Cor. 15, and so on. Furthermore, the quotation in the bracketed section — 1 Cor. 11:7 — is brought in exactly between 1 Cor. 6 and 1 Cor. 15, and is most appropriate in that position.

AD.   I am reading in the first letter to the Corinthians, where he says, this, "What do those who are baptized for the dead mean[197], if the dead are not raised at all? why are they baptized for them? Why also do we face danger every hour, dying[198] daily? I assure you, brethren, by the pride that I have in you, in Christ Jesus our Lord.   e If (in human terms) I fought with beasts at Ephesus, what is my gain? If the dead are not raised, 'let us eat and drink, for tomorrow we shall die'[199]. Do not make any mistake: 'Bad company destroys good character'[200]. Be sober, as you ought, and sin no longer. For some have no knowledge of God. I say it to your shame. But some one will say, 'How are the dead raised? With what sort of body do they come?' Foolish question! What you sow does not sprout into life[201] except it die first[202]. And what you sow is not the body that will come to be,   865a but bare seed, as of wheat, or of some of the other grains. But God gives it a body as He had planned; each of the seeds receives[203] its own particular body. Not all flesh is the same; there is one kind for the human[204], another for animals[205], and another for fishes. There are also heavenly bodies and earthly bodies, but the glory of the heavenly bodies is one (226) kind, and the glory of the earthly is another kind. There is one glory of the sun; another glory of the moon, and another glory of the

[197] "Baptized for the dead". There are many different interpretations of this passage. "Dead" could mean "dead in sin", or "on behalf of the dead". Again, the reference could be to martyrdom regarded as the equivalent of baptism for the unbaptized. It has even been suggested that the text is irreparably corrupt. Perhaps it is best, however, to explain the verse as referring to vicarious baptism on behalf of dead relatives or friends by Christians. This particular practice was found among the Montanists and the disciples of Cerinthus, and it continued among the Marcionites to the fifth century (see Eznik of Armenia [fifth cent.], *Confut. Sect.*, cf. B. Altaner, *Patrology, op. cit.*, p. 306).

[198] ἀποθνησκόντες. Adamantius follows the Marcionite Bible here. The main recensions have ἀποθνησκω.

[199] A quotation from Isa. 22:13, representing there the cry of the despairing people of Jerusalem. It is the cry in part of the Rich Fool in the parable of Jesus (Lk. 12:19). We are also reminded of the conduct of the desperate Athenians during the plague at Athens as recounted by Thucydides (*Hist.*, 2, 7, 53): "So they resolved to spend quickly and enjoy themselves, regarding their lives and riches as alike things of a day."

[200] The quotation is from the poet Menander *ca.* 230 BCE (in iambic trimeter from the *Thais*) that probably became a popular saying. Menander may have meant that people go down the social scale by association with their inferiors. Paul has given the saying a moral connotation.

[201] ζωοποιεῖται, "come to life". In the same verse, "Foolish question!" translates ἄφρον. The main recensions have ἄφρων.

[202] Adamantius follows Marcion, the manuscripts D G and Origen *et al.* in reading πρῶτον before ἀποθάνῃ. The main recensions omit.

[203] This word is omitted by the main recensions, which read, "and to every seed its proper body".

[204] ἀνθρώπου, with Marcion. The main recensions have ἀνθρώπων.

[205] Adamantius omits "another (flesh) or birds" of the main recensions.

stars, for star differs from star in glory. It is thus also with the resurrection of the dead"[206]. And a little further down Paul says, "Behold, I impart to you a mystery.   **b** We shall not indeed all sleep[207], but we shall all be changed in a moment, in the twinkling of an eye, at the sound of the last trumpet; for the trumpet will sound, and the dead will be raised imperishable; and *we* shall be changed. For this that is perishable must put on the imperishable; and this that is mortal must put on immortality"[208].

24   MAR.   He does not say that this body arises, but another, as is seen from the statement, "But God gives it a body as He had planned"[209].

AD.   When wheat is buried in the earth, it rises again as wheat, and when a human is consigned to the ground, he arises as human, and not as something else, according to the Apostle's word: "And   **c** He gives to each seed its own particular body"[210].

EUTR.   So clearly and forthrightly have these things been stated by the Apostle that no explanation is needed. The soul cannot be buried in the ground for it is immortal — and has been acknowledged as such[211]. But the flesh can be sown like wheat. We observe that the body is sown as wheat. Paul says, "that which you sow does not sprout into life, except it die first"[212]. It is quite clear then that what is sown and cast into the ground is the flesh.

MAR.   But you note that he says, "You sow, not the body that will come to be, but bare seed, as of wheat"[213].

d   AD.   Wheat is sown bare, and rises by the will of God; it puts forth the blade and becomes "clothed". It flourishes, but does not change

---

[206] 1 Cor. 15:29-42. Major deviations from the main recension have already been noted.

[207] The main recensions have, "We shall not all sleep, but we shall all be changed..." with which the critical text of our Dialogue is in agreement. Bakhuyzen, however, points out that in all the Greek manuscripts of 'Adamantius' the reading is, "we shall not all be changed", with the exception that in the MSS A and H the "not" before "all" has been erased. Thus we cannot be sure what the author of the Dialogue actually wrote. Rufinus has, "We shall all rise, but we shall not all be changed". Here he agrees with the Vulgate and the Old Latin texts.

[208] 1 Cor. 15:51-53.

[209] 1 Cor. 15:38a.

[210] 1 Cor. 15:38b.

[211] The doctrine of the immortality of the soul is first found in Greek literature in Pindar, *Frag.* and then Herodotus, *Hist.*, 2.123. Plato provides a number of references, e.g., *Phaedr.*, 246a, *Repub.*, 608d. Origen accepted the doctrine (*Discourse with Heraclides*, cf. Quasten *Patrology, op. cit.*, vol. 2, p. 64).

[212] 1 Cor. 15:36.

[213] 1 Cor. 15:37.

into anything different from what is was by nature. So it is with Man[214]: Consigned to the ground, he rises again by the will of God, and is "clothed" with immortality just as the Apostle says, "This that is mortal must put on immortality, and this that is perishable must put on the imperishable"[215]. (228)

e 25   MAR.   [The Apostle states most clearly][216], "it is sown as a physical body, it is raised as a spiritual body; it is sown in corruption, it is raised in incorruptibility"[217].

AD.   [This is what we said in our previous answer, (229) that the body consigned to the ground does not rise again bare nor unadorned, but had cast off all the weakness of corruption. The grain of wheat, that the Apostle uses as an illustration, is cast into the ground and emerges as new grain. It is no longer spoken of as the grain from which it arose, but is called a blade, a stalk or an ear. So it is with the human body. With all the weakness of the flesh left behind, it rises just as the Apostle states. With corruption thrown off, it becomes incorruptible; with its weakness left behind, it is said to rise in strength; with its mortality abandoned, it becomes immortal; and with its dishonour left behind, it will rise in glory. It is a body such as this, cleansed of all imperfections, that the Apostle called "spiritual". However, he did say "body", and whether he called it immortal, or glorious or spiritual, he did not thereby abandon the term "body". So he says, "It is sown as a physical body: it will rise as a spiritual body"[218]. In the same way he might say, "It is sown a grain of wheat; it rises a green stalk and an ear". What reasonable person would claim that because a green blade came up from the dry grain originally sown, therefore it was different from the healthy seed that had been sown? We may therefore conclude that

[214] "So it is with Man: consigned to the ground," etc. Compare with this a passage from Methodius (Bonwetsch edn., p. 269, ch. 11-13).

[215] 1 Cor. 15:53. Our author transposes the terms.

[216] The enclosed sentence is taken from Rufinus; it is absent from the Greek, but probably authentic.

[217] 1 Cor. 15: 42, 44. In the Greek text just prior to this quotation by Marinus, there is a passage that Bakhuyzen (following Zahn) considers an interpolation:-
"Mar.   In our Apostolicon, he does not so speak.
Ad.   But how is that?
Mar.   He does not say, 'God giveth it a body as He will,' but '*God giveth it a spirit as He will*'".
Reasons for supposing the words to be interpolated are: 1. They offer an argument that is not afterwards answered by Adamantius: 2. Rufinus appears to know nothing of them, since he does not translate them. The passage is best regarded as a marginal note, which finally found its way into the text (although the *dialogue* form for such a note seems peculiar).

[218] 1 Cor. 15:44 (Latin text).

the Apostle, in using these terms, refers at one and the same time to substance and quality: when he speaks of *body*, he means a substance, but
when he says *physical*, or *spiritual*, he refers to qualities. If he asserts, then,
that the physical quality of the body must be changed into a spiritual quality, he does not therefore injure the essential nature[219] of the substance.
What he says is that it goes forward into something better. In the same way,
one could not claim that the essential nature[220] of the wheat is either
changed or perished when a green blade or an ear rises from a fresh seed.
Consequently, even though what rises again is called "spiritual", it cannot
be maintained that it is anything other than the body, for it comes up from
the seed of this body. The same substance[221] endures; only the quality will
be transformed — into something better and more glorious][222]. In your
view, Marinus, "God gives it a spiritual body". Well, then, if what is given
by God is spiritual, what is that which receives it?   (228)

MAR.   That which receives it is the soul.   (230)

AD.   Then the soul is buried! [This is what the apostle says: "And
what you sow is not the body that will come to be, but bare seed, as for
instance, of wheat; but God gives it a body as He had planned"][223].

EUTR.   After describing the soul as immortal Marinus is now
forced to try to persuade us, not only that it is mortal, but also that it is
buried in the ground. Yet is is quite clear that what is buried is a body.

f 26   [224][MAR.   There is no need for proofs, for it was (231) settled at
the beginning. Let us yield everything to the attestation of the Scripture!
Try to blot out these words from the Apostle: "Flesh and blood will not
inherit the Kingdom of God"![225] Nothing is clearer than that! It cannot
rise again, because it is pronounced foreign to the Kingdom of God.

AD.   We explained this earlier, but if that is not sufficient, we will
answer again.

[219] *substantiae veritatem.*

[220] *substantia.*

[221] *eadem substantia.*

[222] The whole of the enclosed passage is taken from Rufinus. There is nothing to corre-
spond in the Greek, but the reasoning seems to fit into the development of the argument,
and Bakhuyzen thinks it is probably authentic.

[223] 1 Cor. 15:37-38. The words in brackets are found only in Rufinus, but are accepted
by the editor as probably genuine.

[224] From this point to the end of 866d [= most of V, 27] the rendering is that of the Latin
of Rufinus. Bakhuyzen accepts it as probably having formed a true part of the original text of
the Dialogue. The subject matter and style justify his decision.

[225] 1 Cor. 15:50. Marinus has "will not" for the "cannot" of the Biblical text.

MAR.   Was the Apostle, in this passage, discussing qualities and imperfections — as you interpret it? Did he therefore mean by "the flesh" fleshly-minded people? His subject was the Resurrection! Following his statement, "Flesh and blood will not inherit the Kingdom of God", he continues, "Behold, I impart to you a mystery. We shall all indeed rise; but we shall not all be changed"[226]. It is very clear from this that Paul called "flesh" the very same nature that will not gain the Kingdom of God.

AD.   How is that? Actually, the Apostle's thought is not contrary to our faith. He denies, as you say, that flesh will possess the Kingdom of God. However, he mentions body. Let us see what the authority of Scripture teaches about this difference. Do you admit that this flesh, before it was fashioned, had been mud of earth?

MAR.   Scripture says so.

AD.   At any rate, even then, when it was mud of earth, it was in fact called a body, inasmuch as it was earth. Nevertheless, it was not called flesh, because "flesh" is, for example, a kind of name peculiar to it in this life. It is peculiar to flesh to be hungry; to thirst; to experience desire; to feel cold; to receive injuries and troubles; and to deteriorate through sickness and weakness. In the beginning, God took mud of earth, and changed it into flesh. Henceforth, it is more appropriate to call it "flesh" than "earth", because what was invisible in that earth has been changed. So it is in regard to the future: when God has rebuilt the nature of this flesh into a spiritual body, it will no longer be called "flesh", because it will have discarded that which is peculiar to flesh: it will neither hunger nor thirst; it will not feel cold, nor will it suffer pain; neither will it be tormented by desire nor deteriorate through a diversity of diseases. Turning again to the flesh as it is constituted at present, it may be noted that however much it is "flesh" with regard to quality, it is also called "earth" by the determination of God, because its origins are from earth. In the same way, the future body is called (233) "flesh" by a spiritual law, because its origin is from flesh. It becomes certain from this that the Apostle spoke not of the nature of the flesh, but of its qualities or condition when he said, "Flesh and blood will not inherit the Kingdom of God". Consequently, whatever the future body

---

[226] 1 Cor. 15:51. Again, as in 865a/V, 23, Rufinus renders in harmony with the Latin text (see supra n. 207). In writing to Minervius and Alexander, Jerome says, "I remind you of what is written in the Latin codices: 'We all indeed shall rise again, but we shall not all be changed.' This is not found in the Greek codices"; *Epist.*, 119. Vallars edn.). Here he is not quite correct, for codex D has "we shall rise," along with Marcion, and also "but we shall not all be changed."

is to be, it is this flesh which will rise, and there will not be another in place of it. The Apostle speaks thus: "For this that is perishable will put on the imperishable"[227]. This, at any rate, sounds just like the voice of the Apostle, propounding and explaining the matter. Nor is there any biased judgment in this, inasmuch as my own flesh and blood are indicated by the term "body" — sometimes called "body", sometimes "flesh". Of these, one term belongs to it in this life, while the other is appropriate to it in the future life. Likewise the soul is also called "spirit", but one and the same thing is meant. Nevertheless, the term "soul" is considered as more suitable when it is among humans, and "spirit" as more fitting when it shall be among the angels...[228]. However, "flesh", more suitable in the present life, is called "body" in the future one, especially when its progress towards immortality and glory results in its being named not merely a "body", but a "spiritual body". Nevertheless, it would be flesh (and not something else) that has then progressed, by the will of God, towards this goal.

EUTR. Adamantius has clearly explained that, while the nature or substance of the flesh remains, in the Resurrection the condition is changed; and I see that the body has a nature capable of changing its condition frequently by the will of God. For instance, according to what you two were reading from Genesis, God first formed the body from earth. This shows that, though the substance remained, the quality or condition was changed. Actually, God Himself discloses that man continues in the body when he says to him, "Earth you are, and unto earth shall you go"[229]. Again we observe that when humans die, the quality or condition of the body is once more changed from flesh. It becomes, in fact, earth or dust. However, the substance[230] remains undiminished and unharmed. Why should it seem incredible or impossible if, when the whole substance remains unimpaired, its condition (which is indeed, frequently changed by God's will) should be altered again into a better and more glorious body by the will and power of

---

[227] 1 Cor. 15:53.

[228] There is a lacuna in the Latin text at this point. Bakhuyzen suggests that some such words as "Thus also flesh is called 'body', and by both appellations one and the same thing is designated," were in the original.

[229] Gen. 3:19 (LXX). With regard to his Biblical quotations, it is not always easy to determine whether Rufinus is using the Latin versions known to him (e.g., the Old Latin or the Vulgate, the NT of the latter being finished *ca.* 390), or is simply translating the Biblical text of his Greek original. In the case of 1 Cor. 15:51, it appears to be a Latin version: but in the present instance (Gen. 3:19) the wording of the passage follows the LXX closely, and deviates from the Vulgate, suggesting that Rufinus was here translating from his Greek MSS.

[230] *ratio substantialis*, this expression being equivalent to *substantia*, and being translated so in the Dialogue. Similarly in the two other cases below, where the English word "substance" represents the same Latin phrase.

God (as it has been written), and yet the essential substance be believed not to have perished? So it actually was when man became flesh from the earth, and (235) afterwards earth again from flesh. The substance did not perish!]²³¹

27   AD.   Perhaps these arguments do not seem to be (234) sufficient proof of the Resurrection. Let us carry the investigation a little further, then. Listen to the Apostle where he speaks more decisively: "You are an epistle   866a of Christ, cared for by us, and written: not with ink but with the Spirit of the living God; not on tablets of stone but on tablets of the human heart"²³². If now the flesh does not rise (as my opponents foolishly imagine) the epistle of Christ, written in fleshly hearts by the Spirit of the living God, does no good. But the epistle of Christ has not been written by the Spirit of the living God in vain: it was meant to give life to those for whom it was written. The Apostle himself teaches this in the passage immediately following: "for if what is transitory came with splendour, how much more splendid is that which endures and is not transitory!"²³³ If the epistle of Christ has been written in the fleshly hearts,   b it is evident that they also remain — the hearts in which is written remains and has not been done away. Again Paul states, "yet we hold this treasure in earthen vessels, so that the extraordinary power may be God's and not ours"²³⁴. Now then, let the advocates of error choose the way in which they are prepared to understand this assertion. To what do they think the phrase "this treasure" refers? To the inner man, to harmonize with their theory? If the inner man is made of earth, soul will, by their view, be an earthen vessel. But the flesh is the earthen vessel, and is, as they say, the outer vessel. So then, the treasure was in the flesh.   c Therefore one of two things must be true: either that which contains this treasure perishes, or, incontrovertibly, the flesh that has the treasure is saved. Here is the Apostle again: "For we who live are being constantly handed over to death, so that the life of Christ may also be revealed in our mortal flesh"²³⁵. His statement that the life of Jesus is

²³¹ At this point the English trans. takes up the Greek text again from where it was left at sect. 865f/V, 26.

²³² 2 Cor. 3:3.

²³³ 2 Cor. 3:11. The last clause ("and is not done away") is absent from the main recensions, but is found in Marcion.

²³⁴ 2 Cor. 4:7, where the main recensions have the classically correct μή, but Adamantius οὐχ (see the Introd., n. 38).

²³⁵ 2 Cor. 4:11. Rufinus and the main recensions have "Jesus" for "Christ". In the following comment on this verse, even Adamantius uses the name "Jesus" in repeating the words, which would suggest that he was accustomed to read "Jesus" rather than "Christ" in this NT passage. It may therefore be that Rufinus actually read "Jesus" in the Greek copy before him.

manifested in the flesh requires no explanation! Again Paul: "When what is mortal is absorbed by immortality"[236]. What else can be understood here than that the mortal goes forward into life? then this: "I myself with my mind serve the law of God;   d but with my flesh, the law of sin. There is now therefore no doom for those who are in Christ Jesus, for the Spirit's life-giving law in Christ Jesus has set us free from the law of sin and death"[237]. If the mind serves the law of God, but the flesh (236) the law of sin, and the law of the spirit of life, in Christ Jesus, has delivered us from the law of sin and death, it is obvious that it has delivered that which served the law of sin from sin. Yet it was not the mind that served the law of sin, but the flesh. Consequently, the flesh has been delivered from death. Now let Marinus please explain how that which was delivered from death by the law of the spirit of life in Christ is saved[238],   e for I myself am increasingly ashamed to be arguing against the ignorance[239] of these opponents of mine!

28   EUTR.   To sum up: ignorance is the cause of all the wicked teachings in which Megethius; Droserius and Marcus; Valens and Marinus have grown up together and blossomed. They have turned from the straightforward and true doctrine[240].   **[866]e/871b** They have hunted down the words of Scripture, and ensnared them to serve their own mischievous and preconceived ideas. They walk along thorny paths to ruin, and have (240) forsaken the way that leads to Heaven.   **c**[241] Of this way   **d** Adamantius proves to be the champion. He has led us along a smooth and even path, and has shown us the true Faith. From this Faith falsehood has been

---

[236] See 1 Cor. 15:54, and 2 Cor. 5:4 (a loose quotation).

[237] Rom. 7:25; 8:1-2. The "us" is supported by Rufinus, Marcion, Methodius, and a few other authorities; "me" by A D Latin, etc.; "thee" by X B G and the main recensions.

[238] That is to say, "Let Marinus now explain how 'that which was delivered from death… is saved' on *his* theory — for he does not believe in the salvation of the flesh!"

[239] ἀπαιδευσίαν. Rufinus: *imperitia vel imprudentia* ("inexperience or ignorance"; "want of competent cultivation").

[240] At this point in the Greek MSS and the editions of the Greek text, the "misplaced pages" are found, which the critical editor, Bakhuyzen, restores to what he believes is their rightful position on pp. 96-110 of his own critical edition (pp. 98 to 107 of this English trans.). For further details, see pt. 2, n. 88.

[241] At this place, Bakhuyzen deletes a number of lines which have so suffered at the hands of copyists as to make the argument unintelligible. He then proceeds to emend so that his resultant text corresponds to the Latin of Rufinus. In his explanation (pp. 236, 238), he shows that the interpolated words are an attempt to knit the pages of the Greek MSS together, after the section indicated at n. 240 above had strayed from its rightful place. They were probably originally written in the margin, but were later incorporated by a copyist with the concluding speech of Eutropius in the text.

expelled, and every speculative idea[242] driven out. It sets forth the one and only God[243]; not a false God, alien, strange and poverty-stricken, who shares his neighbour's house and desires His possessions[244]. This is what the heretics, who do not worship the true God, teach, but the true Faith sets forth Him who is the Creator of what He owns, and to whom all things are subject[245]. Neither matter nor anything else exists coeval with Him, but in His goodness He has put together that which is from that which is not[246]. His Word assumed humanity in accordance with a just Plan, and did make a genuine appearance[247]. e He was not ashamed to assume for our salvation that which He had created! f He has also promised that He will raise Man (242) holy, to share with his body[248] in immortality, and to enjoy His

---

[242] πᾶσα φαντασία. Rufinus: *omnis fucus adulterini dogmatis* ("every deceit of false doctrine").

[243] Here and in two other places below, the Greek MSS have passages which are not in the Latin of Rufinus. All three bear sufficient marks of their spuriousness, while the first two speak of the Trinity, and appear to be post-Nicaean interpolations.

[244] A glance at the Gnostic Demiurge, who is an inferior being, neither wholly good, nor wholly bad. Thus, as it was put by the Valentinian Gnostic Ptolemy (*ca.* AD 160), *Epist. ad. Flor.*, 1: "For if the Law has not been given by the perfect God Himself, as we have taught, and certainly not by the devil, a thing which it is not right to say, someone other than these two must have given the Law. He is the *Demiurge* and creator of this whole universe and what is in it, and he is different in essence from these two, standing in the midst between them, he should rightly bear the name of 'the Intermediary'... And this god will be lower than the perfect God and less than *His* justice, for indeed he is also begotten and not unbegotten ... but he will be greater and more powerful than the adversary, and will have a different essence and nature from the other two". Refer also to our Dialogue at sects. 805a/I, 2; 824e/II, 6.

[245] τὰ πάντα ὑποτέτακται. Cf. 1 Cor. 15:28; Phil. 3:21.

[246] ἐξ οὐκ ὄντων τὰ ὄντα ... συνεστήσατο. Compare Hermas (2nd cent. AD), Shep. vis. 1, 1, 6: κτίσας ἐκ τοῦ μὴ ὄντος τὰ ὄντα.

[247] Lit.: "whose Word (λόγος), having assumed humanity according to a just Plan, was really (ἀληθῶς) shown forth".

[248] The emphasis placed, in our Dialogue, upon the resuscitation of the body at the Resurrection, culminates in the remark of the adjudicator here that humans will be raised *with their bodies*, and that the body is to share in immortality. Like Methodius, from whose writings he has so generously borrowed, 'Adamantius' believes that the resurrected body is the earthly one that has survived death, but in a "spiritual" or transfigured form (see Dialogue sects. 859c/V, 16; 865a-b/V, 23-24; 866a-e/V, 27). This is known as the "traditional" view, maintained by the majority of the early Church Fathers (see, e.g., Clement, *Homil.*, 9; Justin Martyr, *Apol.*, I, 19; Athenagoras, *Apol.*, 36; Irenaeus, *Adv. Haeres.*, 33; Tertullian, *De penit.*, 3; cf. *De Resurr.*, I; Chrysostom, *De Resurr.*, 7.

The view of Origen differs in some important respects from the "traditional" view. Reference has already been made to them in the Introduction, sect. B, 1, b, iii. As Origen himself says (*Contr. Cels.*, 4, 57): "Accepting the belief in the resurrection of the dead, we claim that there will be changes in the qualities of the body". His teaching on this point has been summarised by Methodius thus: "Origen therefore thinks that the same flesh will not be restored to the soul, but that the form of each, according to the appearance by which the flesh is now distinguished, shall arise stamped upon another spiritual body; so that everyone will again appear the same in form; and that this is the resurrection which is promised. For, he says, the

bounteous gift[249]. It is He who has been rightfully appointed to bring all men to judgment, by virtue of their possessing free will. Nothing is prone to resist Him, but every power is submissive. The whole world and the company of bishops rightfully serve Him, and their College as well. 872 Kings[250] and all rulers listen to the bishops and associate with them. With them they cast their vote for the truth, and try to expel and exclude falshood. It is only by truth itself that the Catholic[251] Church lives a righteous, godly and holy life, and those who have turned away from her and gone astray turn out to be far from the truth. In theory they profess to know truth, but in actual fact they are far distant from it. I therefore consider it right that Marinus[252] should not reject my judgment and counsel,

material body being fluid, and in no wise remaining in itself, but wearing out and being replaced around the appearance by which its shape is distinguished, and by which the figure is contained, it is necessary that the resurrection should be only that of the form" (*apud* Photius, *Bibliot.*, 12 [*Ant.-Nic. Lib.* edn.], p. 168). Cf. also Kelly, *Early Christian Doctrines*, *op. cit.*, pp. 270ff.

The classic Biblical passage frequently appealed to by the Fathers is 1 Cor. 15, where the Apostle Paul shows that there is a difference as well as a continuity between the body of earth and that of heaven. The actual physical particles of Man's earthly body will not be resurrected, but the person will be given a "spiritual body" at the heavenly level different from his/her earthly one, although continuous with it. This body will be the expression of his/her entire personality, and it will be fashioned to resemble the glorified body of Christ. (Note esp. verses 35-53; Phil. 3:21).

[249] ἀφθόνου δωρεᾶς ἀπολαύσοντα. Or, "have the benefit of the ungrudging gift".

[250] βασιλεῖς καὶ πάντες ἄρχοντες. Rufinus: "God ... to obey whom the kings of the earth, the leaders of the people and every human race (*genus*) gather together." This may well represent the original reading more accurately than the Greek MSS. One might naturally ask whether the writer had in mind some hoped-for future state of affairs, because, even if we suppose the date of the composition here to be in the reign of Constantine, the first Christian emperor, the statement of the Greek text is still something of an exaggeration. The exaggeration, however, is parallleled in the Latin of Rufinus, which translates the Greek text of the *earlier* period.

On the other hand, if the Greek text here be genuine, it (as well as the Latin of Rufinus) could refer to the last years of the Second Long Peace (AD 260-303). Christianity had grown rapidly in this period, spreading by 300 AD to all parts of the Empire. It had many adherents in the army, and had gone up considerably in the social scale, even claiming in its ranks many government officials, although still a *religio illicita* (see Lietzmann, *History of the Early Church, op. cit.*, vol. 3, p. 58). The toleration policy of Gallienus (260-268) had been largely continued, and persecution was practically non-existent throughout the period. With perhaps pardonable exaggeration, the "whole world" might be said to serve the Christian God, and "kings and all rulers" to "associate with bishops" in the years immediately preceding the last great persecution of Diocletian. This would tend to support the date suggested for the composition of the Dialogue — about AD 290-300 (see Introd. sect. B, 2).

[251] ἡ καθόλου ἐκκλησία: Literally: "the Church Universal," or "the whole Church". Rufinus: *ecclesia catholica*. (Καθόλου here is strictly adverbial: in Ecclesiastical Latin, "catholica" means "catholic" or "orthodox".

[252] τοὺς περὶ Μαρίνον. This could mean, "Marinus and his companions"; in later Greek, however, it may stand for Marinus himself..

but depart from irregular, unbalanced and misleading teaching. He should disown what is disgraceful, and return to the true and rightful Faith. He will thus be saved along with us, and be initiated[253] into the divine knowledge[254].

[253] μύσται. The word μύστης stands for "one initiated", cf. Phil. 4:12; but Rufinus has *doctrinae participes* ("sharers" or "partners" in the teaching).

[254] In all the Greek MSS, the following *prologue* is placed at the head of the Dialogue:

"A debate of Adamantius, (who is also Origen) concerning the true faith in God, with the heretics Megethius, Marcus, Droserius, Valens and Marinus. Each presented his own heresy, but all clearly came together at one accord with malicious intent to dispute with Adamantius concerning the orthodox faith. They all chose the pagan philosopher Eutropius as the adjudicator of each one's arguments. In the course of the debate, while the orthodox faith was being put to the test, Eutropius was persuaded by the truth, and became a Christian, together with many pagans and heretics — for there was a crowded audience. The victory went to the Catholic Church, and the arrogance of the heretics was scattered like chaff before the wind."

In the Paris Codex F there are *two* prologues. Of these, the larger one is put first, and its first lines (up to the words "the faith of Christ") appear in red ink. It runs as follows:

"A discourse of Adamantius (who is also Origen) concerning the true faith in God. By means of this many heretics who had maintained various heresies came to hold the faith of Christ correctly. While Origen in Alexandria was attending to his customary duties, and meditating upon holy things, sometimes many pagan philosophers, and sometimes many heretics, would resort to him to engage in conversation. Since discussion frequently took place, and he persuaded many pagans to abhor idolatry, he prepared to win for himself a crowning testimony (μαρτυρίου στέφανον ἀναδήσασθαι παρεσκεύασεν). Among these was Ambrosius, who became an enthusiast for Origen. After he had been instructed in the teaching by him, he withdrew from the heresy of Valentinus and Marcion. About this time, certain of the heretics heard of this and came with malicious intent to engage in discussion with Adamantius. Choosing as an adjudicator a certain pagan philosopher named Eutropius, they opened the debate. Victory finally went to the Catholic Church. Many pagans and heretics believed, along with the adjudicator Eutropius, and accepted the Faith (ἐπίστευσαν).

The Discourse is not concerned with casual matters. It is a learned and elegant work. You will find in it many arguments drawn from the natural world, and also the views of the learned pagans. Even more, there will be arguments drawn from the sacred and holy Scripture. The reader will learn how he ought to understand and interpret many Scriptural terms, and many other propositions, by means of the arguments brought forward. The darts of the heretics were cast in no feeble manner against the learned [Origen?] and he in turn, like invincible adamant by nature, courageously defended the true Faith, blunting and shivering to atoms with the truth all the darts cast upon him. On the one side, the heretics are Megethius, Marcus, Droserius, Valens and Marinus. Each presents his own heresy. The main points brought forward in the discourse are:

"That there are Three Principles — the good God, the Demiurge, and the Evil One, and that each of them has others under his authority'..." A table of contents immediately follows.

Bakhuyzen (p. xxiv) gives three reasons why neither of the prologues may be accepted as genuine: 1. the prologue takes place more than one form; 2. Origen is named as the author of the Dialogue; 3. Rufinus does not mention or offer either form of the prologue.

In the codices A B D E F H and the Latin translator Humphrey (but not in codex C, nor in the Latin translators Rufinus, Picus, and Perionius) the following *epilogue* is placed at the conclusion of the Dialogue of Adamantius:

"O divine and most learned [Origen?], adorned with knowledge, you have admirably shown that the five champions of doctrines which deny the true God were really inspired against God. Therefore all we faithful believers honour and crown you by comparing you to David: David laid the tyrant Goliath low, and Adamantius has laid the doctrine that opposes God low. 'They have removed reproach from the sons of Israel'" (cf. 1 Kgs. 17:26 (LXX)[Alexandrine text, and vs.36]).

We may agree with Bakhuyzen (p. xxv) that this epilogue comes from an admiring reader of the Dialogue of Adamantius.

SELECT BIBLIOGRAPHY

Altaner, B., *Patrology* (trans. H.C. Graef), Freiburg, 1960.

Auvray, P., Polain, P. and Blaise, A., *The Sacred Languages* (trans. S.J. Tester), London, 1960

Bardenhewer, O., *Patrology*, Freiburg,1908.

Bardenhewer, O., *Geschichte der altkirklichen Literatur*, Freiburg in Breslau, 1914, vol. 2.

Bareille, G., "Adamantius," in A. Vacant, E. Mangenot and É. Amann (eds.), *Dictionnaire de théologie Catholique*, Paris, 1930, vol. 1, s.v.

Blackman, E. C., *Marcion and his Influence*, London, 1948.

Brandhuber, P., "Die sekundären Lesarten bei 1 Kor. 15, 51. Ihre Verbreitung und ihre Entstehung," *Biblica* 18 (1937): 303-33.

Broek, R. van den, "The Present State of Gnostic Studies", *Vigiliae Christianae* 37 (1983): 41-71.

Buchheit, V., *Studien zu Methodios von Olympus* (Texte und Untersuchungen zur Geschichte der altchristichen Literatur 69), Berlin, 1958.

Cayré, G., *Manual of Patrology* (translated by H. Howitt), Paris, 1935, vol. 1.

Charles, R. H., *Religious Development between the Old and the New Testament*, Oxford, 1914.

Cross, F. L. (ed.), *The Oxford Dictionary of the Christian Church*, Oxford, 1957.

Cross, F. L., *The Early Christian Fathers*, London, 1960.

Deakle, D.W., "The Fathers against Marcionism: a study of methods and motives in developing patristic anti-Marcionite polemic" (Doctoral dissert., Saint Louis University), Ann Arbor [microf.], 1991.

Foakes-Jackson, F. J., *History of the Christian Church to A.D. 461*, Hall & Son, Cambridge, 1914.

Funkenstein, A., *Heilsplan und natürliche Entwicklung*, Munich, 1965.

Haase, F. *Zur Bardesanischen Gnosis* (Texte und Untersuchungen zur Geschichte der altchristlichen Literatur 34/4), Leipzig, 1910.

Harnack, Adolf von, *Marcion: das Evangelium vom fremden Gott*, Leipzig, 1921.

Hertz, J. H., *The Pentateuch and Haftorahs*, London, 1952.

Jonas, H., *The Gnostic Religion*, Boston, 1963.

Kelly, J. N. D., *Early Christian Doctrines*, London, 1960 edn.

Koehler, L., "Problems in the Study of the Language of the Old Testament," *Journal of Semitic Studies* 1/1 (1956): 1-21.

Knox, J., *Marcion and The New Testament: an essay on the early history of the Canon*, Chicago, 1942 (new edn., New York, 1980).

Latourette, K. S., *A History of Christianity*, London, 1954.

Lietzmann, H. *History of the Early Church* (trans. B.L. Woolf), London, 1953, 4 vols.

Meer, F. van der, and Mohrmann, C., *Atlas of the Early Christian World* (trans. M.F. Hedlund and H.H. Rowley), London and Edinburgh, 1958.

Moffatt, J., *The First Five Centuries of the Church*, London, 1938.

Murphy, F.-X., *Rufinus of Aquileia (345-411): his life and works*, Washington, D.C., 1945.

Norden, E., *Agnostos Theos; Untersuchungen zur Formen-Geschichte religiöser Rede*, Leipzig and Berlin, 1913.

Oulton, J.E.L and Chadwick, H., "Introduction," to *Alexandrian Christianity* (Library of Christian Classics, vol.2), London, 1954, pp. 15ff.

Outler, A.C., "Introduction"," to *Augustine, Confessions and Enchiridion* (Library of Christian Classics vol. 7), London, 1955, pp. 13ff.

Parker, T.M., *Christianity and the State in the Light of History*, London, 1955.

Prestige, G. L., *God in Patristic Thought*, London, 1959.

Quasten, J., *Patrology*, Utrecht-Antwerp and Westminster, 1962-3, vols 2-3.

Robinson, J.A., "Introduction," to *The Philocalia of Origen*, Cambridge, 1893, pp. iff.

Stommel, E., "Adamantios" in M. Buchberger (ed.), *Lexicon für Theologie und Kirche*, Freiburg, 1957, vol. 1, s.v.

Smith, W. and Wace, H. (eds.), *Dictionary of Christian Biography*, London, 1877-1888, 4 vols.

Taylor, V., *The Text of the New Testament*, London, 1961.

Tixeront, J., *History of Dogmas* (trans. H.L.B.), St. Louis and Freiburg, 1921.

Turner, H. E. W., *The Pattern of Christian Truth*, London, 1954.

Unnik, W.C. van, *Evangelien aus den Nisland*, n.p., 1959.

Walker, W., *A History of the Christian Church*, Edinburgh,1959 edn.

Wand, J. W. C., *A History of the Early Church to A.D. 500*, London, 1949 edn.

Watkin, E. I., *The Church in Council*, London, 1960.

Wikenhauser, A., *New Testament Introduction* (trans. J. Cunningham), London, 1958.

Wilken, R.L., *Judaism and the Early Christian Mind; A study of Cyril of Alexandria's exegesis and theology*, Yale, N.H., 1971.

Whitman, A.R., *The History of the Christian Church to the Separation of East and West*, London, 1957 edn.

Zahn, T., "Die Dialoge des 'Adamantius' mit den Gnostikern" *Zeitschrift für Kirchengeschichte* 9 (1887): 193-239.

Zahn, T., *Geschichte der Neutestamentlichen Kanons*, Erlangen, 1888-92, vol. 2.

INDICES

Apostolic Fathers and Related Materials

Early Gnostic

SUBJECTS

PRINTED ON PERMANENT PAPER • IMPRIME SUR PAPIER PERMANENT • GEDRUKT OP DUURZAAM PAPIER - ISO 9706

ORIENTALISTE, KLEIN DALENSTRAAT 42, B-3020 HERENT